Sustainable Energy Solutions with Artificial Intelligence, Blockchain Technology, and Internet of Things

The text provides sustainable energy solutions using smart technologies such as artificial intelligence, blockchain technology, and the Internet of Things. It further presents several case studies on applications of the Internet of Things, artificial intelligence, and blockchain technology in the field of sustainable energy.

- Focuses on the integration of smart technology including artificial intelligence and sustainable energy.
- Covers recent advancements in energy management techniques used in residential and commercial energy systems.
- Highlights the use of artificial intelligence, machine learning, and their applications in sustainable energy.
- Discusses important topics such as green energy, grid modernization, smart security in the power grid, and fault diagnosis.
- Presents case studies on the applications of the Internet of Things, blockchain, and artificial intelligence in sustainable energy.

The text showcases the latest advancements, and the importance of technologies including artificial intelligence, blockchain, and the Internet of Things in achieving sustainable energy systems. It further discusses the role of machine learning, applied deep learning, and edge computing in renewable energy. The text covers key concepts such as intelligent battery management systems, energy trading, green energy, grid modernization, electric vehicles, and charging station optimization. It will serve as an ideal reference text for senior undergraduate, graduate students, and academic researchers in fields including electrical engineering, electronics and communication engineering, computer engineering, and environmental engineering.

Smart Technologies for Engineers and Scientists

Series Editor: Mangey Ram

Applications of Mathematical Modeling, Machine Learning, and Intelligent Computing for Industrial Development
Madhu Jain, Dinesh K. Sharma, Rakhee Kulshrestha, and H.S. Hota

Sustainable Energy Solutions with Artificial Intelligence, Blockchain Technology, and Internet of Things
Edited by Arpit Jain, Abhinav Sharma, Vibhu Jately, and Brian Azzopardi

Sustainable Energy Solutions with Artificial Intelligence, Blockchain Technology, and Internet of Things

Edited by
Arpit Jain
Abhinav Sharma
Vibhu Jately
Brian Azzopardi

CRC Press
Taylor & Francis Group
Boca Raton London New York

CRC Press is an imprint of the
Taylor & Francis Group, an **informa** business

First edition published 2023
by CRC Press
2385 NW Executive Center Drive, Suite 320, Boca Raton, FL 33431

and by CRC Press
4 Park Square, Milton Park, Abingdon, Oxon, OX14 4RN

CRC Press is an imprint of Taylor & Francis Group, LLC

© 2024 selection and editorial matter Arpit Jain, Abhinav Sharma, Vibhu Jately and Brian Azzopardi; individual chapters, the contributors

Library of Congress Cataloging-in-Publication Data
Names: Jain, Arpit, editor. | Sharma, Abhinav, editor. | Jately, Vibhu, editor. | Azzopardi, Brian, editor.
Title: Sustainable energy solutions with artificial intelligence, blockchain technology, and internet of things / edited by Arpit Jain, Abhinav Sharma, Vibhu Jately and Brian Azzopardi.
Description: First edition. | Boca Raton : CRC Press, 2024. | Includes bibliographical references and index.
Identifiers: LCCN 2023010595 (print) | LCCN 2023010596 (ebook) | ISBN 9781032392752 (hardback) | ISBN 9781032411804 (paperback) | ISBN 9781003356639 (ebook)
Subjects: LCSH: Renewable energy sources--Technological innovations. | Power resources--Technological innovations. | Artificial intelligence. | Blockchains (Databases) | Internet of things.
Classification: LCC TJ808 .S8567 2024 (print) | LCC TJ808 (ebook) | DDC 621.0420285/63--dc23/eng/20230629
LC record available at https://lccn.loc.gov/2023010595
LC ebook record available at https://lccn.loc.gov/2023010596

ISBN: 978-1-032-39275-2 (hbk)
ISBN: 978-1-032-41180-4 (pbk)
ISBN: 978-1-003-35663-9 (ebk)

DOI: 10.1201/9781003356639

Typeset in Sabon
by MPS Limited, Dehradun

Contents

Preface

Renewable energy is one of the world's strongest growing industries; more than 100 countries have developed sustainable energy policies. Renewable energy resources are projected to be one of the major economic engines of the coming decades. Denmark, for example, aims for 100 percent renewable energy by 2050. When we discuss renewable energy, we should take many issues into consideration. Implementation of sustainable energy sources helps in fighting climate change and will be crucial for the economic development of countries. The global transition to renewable energy will need artificial intelligence (AI) technology to manage decentralized grids. This book focuses on the applications of AI, blockchain technology, and Internet of Things (IoT) for sustainable energy solutions. The layout of the book is as follows:

Chapter 1 provides a comprehensive review of technologies in renewable and sustainable energy and the role of AI in disrupting and innovating the older generation production methods and resulting in higher efficiency production techniques. This chapter provides information on the use of AI tools to optimize and transform the generation of hydrogen from various sources, and the latest trends in harnessing geothermal energy.

Chapter 2 provides a summary of recent advancements in the applications of AI and machine learning algorithms for predicting power generation and monitoring the condition of wind and solar energy systems.

Chapter 3 focuses on how the applications of state-of-the-art AI techniques in various renewable resources like solar, wind, hydroelectric, geothermal, and biomass help in the accurate prediction of power generation.

Chapter 4 discusses a practical and important use case for smart home energy management with the help of AI algorithms. The authors implemented AI techniques to monitor load using appliance load monitoring and non-intrusive load monitoring methods. The chapter also evaluates the performance of various deep-learning algorithms on a common household dataset.

Chapter 5 provides a detailed analysis and design of a Home Energy Management System. The proposed algorithm is applied for energy optimization and results are compared on the basis of various factors including power consumption and the cost of electricity bill. Furthermore, the chapter investigates the algorithms using multiple case studies for different possible scenarios to compare its robustness and efficacy.

Chapter 6 presents a detailed study of the application of metaheuristic algorithms in estimating solar cell parameters. The performance of various state-of-the-art algorithms is compared and acts as a guide for researchers and practitioners who are looking to implement these algorithms into further research or production.

Chapter 7 reviewed various optimization techniques to efficiently control the speed of brushless DC motor. Due to its high-power density, the use of optimization techniques to control brushless DC motors can help in increasing the efficiency in various applications such as solar-PV irrigation systems and electric vehicles.

Chapter 8 investigates techniques for increasing the energy efficiency of mobile devices in energy harvesting systems with device-to-device offloading capabilities. In this chapter, the authors proposed state-of-the-art computation offloading algorithms that help in the efficient operation of edge devices.

Chapter 9 summarizes the book by providing details of how blockchain can be used in sustainable energy solutions. This chapter will act as a conclusive guide for the researchers and practitioners who are looking to develop blockchain solutions in energy. The authors have provided a comprehensive review of blockchain technology followed by a detailed analysis of advancements in the consensus EI (Energy Internet) system. The authors have also discussed current technology challenges and future prospects of practical applications of blockchain in the energy sector.

AI techniques have the potential to reduce energy wastage, lower energy costs, and facilitate and accelerate the use of clean renewable energy sources in power grids. AI can also improve the planning, operation, and control of power systems. Thus, these technologies are closely tied to the ability to provide clean and cheap energy that is essential to development. IoT has revolutionized the field and provided detailed insights that can enable smart devices such as Amazon Alexa, Google Home, and Google Nest to interact with their thermostats and other control systems to monitor their energy consumption. The digital transformation of home energy management and consumer appliances will allow automatic meters to use AI to optimize energy consumption and storage. Furthermore, blockchain can lay out the foundation to secure energy trading and provide a secure way of supply chain management in the vulnerable world of energy distribution. We believe this book will help readers brainstorm through the applications of AI, IoT, and blockchain in the domain of sustainable energy and will empower researchers to propose novel techniques in the field of sustainable energy.

Acknowledgments

The Editor acknowledges CRC Press - Taylor & Francis Group for this opportunity and professional support. My special thanks to Gagandeep Singh, Publisher Engineering, CRC Press; Gauravjeet Singh Reen, Senior Editor Engineering; and Isha Ahuja, Editorial Assistant Engineering for the excellent support provided us to complete this book.

Thanks to the chapter authors and reviewers for their availability for this work.

Arpit Jain, QpiAI India Pvt. Ltd., India
Abhinav Sharma, University of Petroleum and Energy Studies, India
Vibhu Jately, University of Petroleum and Energy Studies, India
Brian Azzopardi, Malta College of Arts, Science and Technology (MCAST), Malta

Editors' Biography

Dr. Arpit Jain currently working as Technical Project manager at QpiAI India Pvt. Ltd., India. He is a multidisciplinary engineer having experience in Machine Learning, Data Science, Control System, and Fuzzy Logic systems with an excellent vision towards industry-focused education and state-of-the-art consulting solutions. He is a seasoned academician having 12+ years of diverse experience in academics, edtech, and IT consulting domains. He has worked as an assistant professor for 10 years at University of Petroleum & Energy Studies (UPES), India, a part of Global University System (GUS), Netherlands. His research profile includes Indin patents, research articles in SCI/Scopus indexed Journals, and edited books with IEEE, Emerald, RIVER, CRC, and many other reputed publishing houses. He received his B.Eng. degree from SVITS, Indore in 2007, M.Eng. degree from Thapar University, Patiala in 2009, and Ph.D. degree from UPES, India in 2018.

Dr. Abhinav Sharma is presently working as an assistant professor (Selection Grade) in the Department of Electrical & Electronics Engineering at the University of Petroleum & Energy Studies (UPES). He received his B.Tech. degree from H. N. B. Garhwal University, Srinagar, India in 2009, and the M.Tech. and Ph.D. degrees from Govind Ballabh Pant University of Agriculture and Technology, Pantnagar, India in 2011 and 2016, respectively. He has rich teaching and diversified research experience. His research interests include Signal Processing and Communication, Smart Antennas, Artificial Intelligence, and Machine Learning. He has published research articles in SCI/Scopus indexed Journals and in national and international conferences.

Dr. Vibhu Jately received his Ph.D. degree from G. B. Pant University, Pantnagar, India. Following that, he worked as an assistant professor under the United Nations Development Program within the Department of Electrical and Computer Engineering at Wollo University, Ethiopia. After that, he worked as a post-doctoral research fellow for two years at MCAST Energy Research Group, Malta, where he was a task leader of European H2020 projects. Currently, he is working as an assistant professor (Selection Grade) within the Department of Electrical & Electronics Engineering at the University of Petroleum & Energy Studies, Dehradun, India. He has over 8 years of teaching and research experience. His research interest includes power electronics applications in renewable energy systems and he has worked in formulating MPPT algorithms, control strategies in grid integration of PVs, microgrids, and optimization algorithms in PV applications. He is an active researcher and has published several research articles in top-quality peer-reviewed journals and international conferences.

Dr. Brian Azzopardi received a B.Eng. (Hons.) degree from the University of Malta (UM) and a Ph.D. degree from the University of Manchester in 2011. He also received teaching and pedological qualifications from MCAST (2008) and PGCHE from Oxford Brookes University (2012). He is a Senior Lecturer II at Malta College of Arts, Science and Technology. He is a consultant at University of Malta. He is currently working with Malta College of Arts, Science and Technology (MCAST), visiting senior lecturer at UM, and a consultant. Since 2011, he held senior academic and research positions in United Kingdom and Lithuania, and has served the industry, government agencies, and ministries and research since 1998. He is a senior member of IEEE and a member of the IET, EI, RSC, and Chamber of Engineers. In 2008, he received the Eur. Ing. title followed by the CEng and the EI Chartered Energy Engineer titles in 2012. He is an editor and co-author of two books, 100+ research papers in peer-reviewed impact-listed journals and conferences, and an invited speaker.

Contributors

Nafees Ahamad, DIT University, Dehradun, India

Narendra Akiti, Jubilant Pharmova Limited, Nanjangud, Karnataka, India

S. Arunkumar, Thiagarajar College of Engineering, Tamil Nadu, India

Chiranjit Biswas, Tripura University, Agartala, India

Abanishwar Chakraborti, NIT Agartala, Agartala, India

Abhay Chhetri, University of Petroleum and Energy Studies, Dehradun, India

Sonali Deshpande, MITSOE, MITADT University, Pune, India

Praveen Kumar Ghodke, National Institute of Technology Calicut, Kozhikode, Kerala, India

Govind Rai Goyal, University of Engineering & Management, Jaipur, India

Vibhu Jately, University of Petroleum & Energy Studies, Dehradun, Uttarakhand, India

Nilima Kulkarni, MITSOE, MITADT University, Pune, India

A. Subarna Kiruthiga, Thiagarajar College of Engineering, Tamil Nadu, India

Sri Phani Krishna Karri, National Institute of Technology, Andhra Pradesh, India

J. Felicia Lilian, Thiagarajar College of Engineering, Tamil Nadu, India

Wei Hong Lim, Faculty of Engineering, Technology and Built Environment, UCSI University, Kuala Lumpur, Malaysia

Surajit Mondal, University of Petroleum & Energy Studies, Dehradun, Uttarakhand, India

Swanirbhar Majumder, Tripura University, Agartala, India,

Amit Kumar Mondal, Manipal Academy of Higher Education, Dubai, United Arab Emirates

Sumit Pundir, Graphic Era Deemed University, Dehradun, Uttarakhand, India

Akanksha Rai, University of Petroleum & Energy Studies, Dehradun, Uttarakhand, India

P Swapna Reddy, National Institute of Technology Calicut, Kozhikode, Kerala, India

Kamesh Reddi, CSIR-Indian Institute of Chemical Technology [IICT], Tarnaka, Hyderabad, India

Abhinav Sharma, University of Petroleum & Energy Studies, Dehradun, Uttarakhand, India

Abhishek Sharma, Graphic Era Deemed University, Dehradun, Uttarakhand, India

Mayank Saklani, University of Petroleum and Energy Studies, Dehradun, India

R. Thirisha, Thiagarajar College of Engineering, Tamil Nadu, India

Vikas Thapa, University of Petroleum & Energy Studies, Dehradun, Uttarakhand, India

Shelly Vadhera, Department of Electrical Engineering, National Institute of Technology, Kurukshetra, India

L.N. Sastry Varanasi, National Institute of Technology, Andhra Pradesh, India

Chapter 1

Recent Developments of Artificial Intelligence for Renewable Energy

Accelerated Material and Process Design

P Swapna Reddy, Praveen Kumar Ghodke, Kamesh Reddi, and Narendra Akiti

CONTENTS

1.1 INTRODUCTION

The goal of the computer science and engineering discipline of artificial intelligence (AI) is to develop intelligent or smart computers, systems, and gadgets that mimic the intelligence of the brain and take quick decisions [1]. It can also be described as a system's capacity to correctly comprehend other available data, adapt and learn from that knowledge, and put new learnings into practice in order to complete specific tasks and goals rather than flexible adaptability. Through the key policies of developed countries, support for AI, renewable energy, and sustainability is currently rising. In addition to the energy industry, AI has several applications in the fields of

DOI: 10.1201/9781003356639-1

food, agriculture, education, health and safety, business, and the arts, among others. According to earlier studies [2,3], the utilization of renewable energy systems (RESs) to make up for energy shortfall has been proven. In contrast to fossil fuels, renewable energy provides hygiene to homes with a small carbon footprint. More significantly, numerous studies have demonstrated that the usage of RESs lowers atmospheric greenhouse gases (GHGs) [4,5]. The application of RES has also advanced and changed. However, there are chances to solve the current emerging difficulties and opportunities in renewable energy through the utilization of intelligent systems, especially the usage of AI.

1.2 ROLE OF AI IN RENEWABLE ENERGY

AI is perfect for powering renewable energy facilities since it offers various features like predictive analytics, automated process monitoring and optimization, and feedback loops [6]. Natural conditions are perhaps the biggest obstacle to renewable energy due to its unpredictable and unreliable nature. Without sufficient tide power, a tidal power plant cannot operate, a simple cloud cover can result in daily financial losses for a solar field, and unexpectedly light winds would not generate any electricity at a wind farm [7]. Since AI's predictive analytics can be used to produce exact weather predictions, offer significant benefits in planning operations. Technically, it is still "forecasting" the weather, tools and techniques used by AI-based systems are far superior and accurate compared to online or TV weather reports.

The AI uses much previous information on energy operations, weather conditions (humidity, wind direction, speed, and cloud cover), machine readings, throughput metrics, cycle anomalies, and other information. In order to get insights into how previous environmental circumstances affected energy production and comprehend how they directly affected the assets, it gathers and organizes all the data that has been gathered from numerous sources and is saved in various file kinds and formats. Based on this extensive frame of reference, the AI monitors current environmental and machine data using satellite images and the Industrial Internet of Things (IIoT) [8]. In order to make well-informed planning and management decisions, it compares the present situation to the past and forecasts how operations will change.

In the present situation, technology tools like web-based energy forecasting programs use ML algorithms in conjunction with data mining operations. Based on the atmosphere in a particular area, they create weather models. These cutting-edge forecasting tools give complete visibility into industrial activities, which leads to better control and planning [9]. Another significant AI application for growing resources and commercial viability of renewable energy sources is energy grid optimization. The grid can be connected to a network of sensors to collect real-time environmental data and asset performance metrics. It will allow the collection of vast amounts of operational data that can yield important insights into load predictions, functional conditions, failure events, maintenance needs, etc. The operations can be kept at consistently high efficiency by enhancing energy usage and reducing energy consumption. Additionally, it gives suppliers adaptable means to control supply in response to changing market conditions.

Applications supported by tech behemoths like Google are focused on lowering emissions and energy usage for industrial equipment. After deployment, these apps achieve 40% server cooling by using a web of sensors to track variables like temperature and power consumption per asset. Now fully automated systems are available to accurately track operational conditions around the clock with AI-enabled industrial asset monitoring [10]. Because they can detect issues like leaks and machine strain and take appropriate action, such systems improve the safety of assets. The system might set off a trip switch to protect the asset from additional harm, send messages to the appropriate individuals, or set off an alert. Reducing accidents not only makes sure that asset health is maintained wisely but also enhances staff safety.

With the emergence of smart industries, AI is driving us towards the next iteration of Industry 4.0 by enabling large-scale automation of process-driven tasks and intelligent workflows. AI is becoming more capable of doing human-level tasks like observation and recommendation. The renewable energy industry will be able to target a broader market and grow operations more profitably if AI technology is widely used.

1.3 ADVANCEMENTS OF AI TOWARDS SUSTAINABLE ENERGY

By integrating smarter systems like Internet of Things (IoT) and AI, RESs are getting more advanced. This makes them robust and responsive. All RESs, including solar photovoltaic systems, wind, solar, hydro, ocean, and geothermal systems, are now using AI technologies [11]. The energy sector can benefit from AI technology by utilizing the expanding opportunities that result from the use of the IoT and the incorporation of renewable energy sources [12]. Big data management, extremely powerful computing, information technology, and enhanced ML and DL algorithms are all components of AI technologies. The renewable energy sector will highly benefit from AI's digital technologies, together with highly secure system operations, improved monitoring of power infrastructure, and innovative market designs [13].

1.3.1 Improved Machine Learning Models

Energy systems (ESs) will be benefited from the widespread usage of ML models with the usage of modeling and prediction techniques. An ES is a collection of arranged components intended for the production, management, and alteration of energy [14,15]. The development of ES must make difficult decisions to satisfy both demand and contradicting goals while considering factors like environmental impact, efficiency, financial crisis, etc. [16]. Smart sensors are progressively employed in both the production and consumption of energy [17,18] Due to their accuracy, efficacy, and speed, machine learning (ML) models in RES are gaining importance for modeling of production, consumption, and market analysis [19,20]. Artificial neural network (ANN), multilayer perceptron (MLP), extreme learning machine (ELM), support vector machines (SVMs), wavelet neural network (WNN), adaptive neuro-fuzzy inference system (ANFIS), decision trees, deep learning (DL), ensembles, and sophisticated hybrid ML models are some of the common ML models utilized in RES.

SVMs are ML algorithms for structural risk minimization that are based on statistical learning theory. SVMs perform better than alternative approaches in pattern classification, recognition, and regression analysis. Due to its capacity for generalization, SVM has a wide variety of applications in the area of load predicting. Local minima also have no negative effects on SVM. A brand-new method for optimizing the oxygen-to-steam ratio during coal gasification was introduced by Arabloo et al. [21]. Support vector machine classification of power quality disturbances was studied by Arikan et al. [22]. A soft sensor (a field-support vector regression) was created by Ma et al. [23] to increase the estimation accuracy of solar irradiance levels using photovoltaic electrical parameters. This newly developed soft sensor can be inserted into a thermometer, a current sensor, or a solar module.

WNNs combine the advantages of wavelet theory and neural networks. The feedforward neural network used in this technique has one hidden layer. Also, WNNs can determine to predict expected output using the input by training the network using the available data [24]. WNN is superior to other neural networks in a number of ways. A forecast methodology for renewable energy sources was created by Doucoure et al. [25] to encourage the usage of remote and grid-connected power systems for RES. Gu et al. (2018) [26] investigated the prediction of heat load by different models, including the ELM, WNN, SVM, and genetic algorithm-based back propagation neural network. He et al. [27] developed a hybrid anticipating model to lessen the impact of noise within the unstructured data series in order to produce attributes from the actual data.

Further, Aguado et al. [28] proposed a technique for railway electric ES that takes into account regenerative braking capabilities, hybrid electric energy storage systems, and solar and wind energy sources as renewable energy sources. Using a scenario tree methodology, the uncertainties surrounding renewable energy sources were considered. Costa et al. [29] developed an approach based on a decision tree used to predict potential interruptions in combined natural gas and electric power networks. An innovative two-stage method to assess the hazard of a shutdown in an electrical power system was presented by Kamali et al. [30]. A unique tool for using decision trees was developed by Moutis et al. [31] for scheduling storage systems in microgrids and managing energy resources to maintain energy balance for strategic communal microgrids.

Another advancement is hybrid ML models which utilize the combined form of ML-AI techniques. In order to improve the accuracy of the hybrid ML models one needs to use data processing and optimization tools together for improved prediction capabilities. A hybrid short-term load-predicting model that was optimized via switching delayed particle swarm optimization was presented by Deng et al. [32]. In order to forecast electric load, Peng et al. [33] developed a technique that combines "support vector regression" and the "particle swarm optimization algorithm". A hybrid wind speed anticipating model based on the "fruit fly optimization algorithm" and "ensemble empirical mode decomposition" was introduced by Qu et al. [34].

The development of ML models is necessary for the evolution of RESs. It should be noted that energy extraction from wind, solar, and other renewable energy resources is now more acceptable due to the recent increase in the popularity of RES due to worries about climate change and sustainability. The fundamental characteristics of all RES are their reliance on the environment and significant obstacles to management and planning. However, if energy demand and wind and solar energy oscillations are not effectively handled, they can have a detrimental effect on the grid and its users. ML models are becoming crucial in these ESs as a result.

1.3.2 DL Models

DL uses stacked multi-layer information processing modules to simulate the hierarchical characterization of data prediction patterns. DL has become increasingly popular as processing power and data sizes have grown. Deep neural networks were used by Chemali et al. [35] to offer an ML approach in Li-ion batteries for "state of charge (SOC) estimation". In this study, a novel method for calculating battery SOC that makes use of deep neural networks was described. A DL model for time series forecasting on the Graphics Processing Unit was presented by Coelho et al. [36]. The given technique was used in a hybrid metaheuristic model to solve the predicting issue for mini/microgrids. A non-intrusive load monitoring system using a cutting-edge DL method was presented by Kim et al. [37]. This study put forth a long short-term memory recurrent neural network (RNN) model and enhanced DL for energy disaggregation. A new technique for forecasting solar electricity using deep convolutional neural network (DCNN) and wavelet-transform was introduced by Wang et al. [38]. The nonlinear features present at each frequency were extracted using the DCNN.

RNNs, a kind of ANN in which connections between nodes produce a directed graph, are the ancestors of deep RNNs [39]. RNNs are suitable for forecasting renewable energy because, unlike feedforward neural networks, they can use the intrinsic states of the brain to develop a continuous sequence of inputs [40]. Further DCNN, "stacked extreme learning machines", and "generative adversarial networks" are a few of the other DL structures that are suggested for feature extraction and not for projecting renewable energy. The fact that the network topologies in the DL-based forecasting framework are not all the same is another problem. Therefore, several "heuristic optimization techniques" have been developed to discover the global minima and to exceptionally determine the network architecture. Particle swarm optimization (PSO) and genetic algorithms (GA) have been utilized often for this purpose up to now. The following two significant issues, however, also face DL-based forecasting models.

- Theoretical issues with DL are mostly seen in two areas, namely statistics and computation power. We need to comprehend the complexity of the prediction samples when it comes to forecasting renewable energy sources. Further, it is required to give the number of training samples to train the DL network and also the processing power required to predict the output. Additionally, since DL models are typically "nonconvex functions" and training deep networks and optimizing their parameters is theoretically challenging.
- DL's core goal is to increase the accuracy of predictions by directly and spontaneously learning more useful features. Through feature learning at each successive layer, DL facilitates learning from continuous data from renewable energy sources. An important problem is what way to create a hierarchical model with strong feature learning. Another issue that needs to be resolved is choosing the best DL-based prediction model for a particular predicting dataset.

1.3.3 Optimization Techniques

The need for energy has significantly expanded due to the generality of agricultural, industrial, and residential activities, especially in emerging nations. Renewable energy has many benefits, but there are also significant drawbacks. For example, because the majority of renewable energy supplies depend on the environment, their utilization necessitates sophisticated design, planning, and control optimization techniques. Lagrangian relaxation, linear programming, Nelder-Mead simplex, quadratic programming, etc. are examples of conventional optimization techniques. On the other hand, it should be emphasized that, up until now, the majority of computer optimization techniques have concentrated on resolving issues with a single objective optimization problem. Further, Multi-objective algorithms have been presented by certain authors due to the wide applications for the simultaneous optimization of multiple and competing objectives. Aggregate weight functions and Pareto-based optimization techniques are the two primary categories into which these multi-objective approaches are frequently subdivided. In aggregating functions, all optimization goals are combined into a single mathematical function, and relative weights are used to modify each goal's relative importance [41]. The weights of the objectives to optimize might be quite difficult to change, especially when they have various scales, despite the simplicity of the approach. A significant constraint arises from the fact that this approach only produces one solution, requiring the decision-maker to choose one solution from a range of choices. Using the Pareto-based multi-objective optimization [42] builds links between the non-dominated solutions which finally result in the so-called Pareto optimum set, which typically includes a number of options. Finding the Pareto set, or a typical solution of it, is the goal of multi-objective optimization because each objective is equally essential.

The best solution among the various RES is extremely important from the design point of view as well as future ESs due to the key investment expenses linked with developing a RE structure. Planning for community-scale RES is a crucial issue that entails defending the distribution of energy resources and services, developing local regulations regarding energy use, economic growth, and analyzing the relationships among them. Interval linear programming (ILP), chance-constrained programming, and mixed integer-linear programming (MILP) techniques have been used by some authors to solve this complex problem and produce solutions that can produce the desired energy resource/service allocation and capacity-expansion plans with a minimum amount of system cost, a maximum amount of system reliability, and a maximum amount of energy security [43]. Due to the presence of several uncertainties, novel optimization strategies are crucial for short-term energy planning [44]. A simulator of a RES with wind, solar, energy storage, and stand-by plants that can compute energy flows and optimize the scheduling of the stand-by plant or grid connection was presented by Mitchell et al. [45]. Energy planning issues are complicated issues with many different decision-makers and criteria. Reviews of multicriteria decision-making techniques for renewable energy issues can be found in the literature ([46,47]).

1.4 DIGITAL TRANSFORMATION OF RENEWABLE ENERGY INDUSTRY

One of the most important elements of sustainable socioeconomic growth is energy. Making energy policies and transitioning to sustainable energy use are difficult tasks for national and international governments. Putting together and evaluating cases in various places while taking into account elements like geographic location, technological advancements, economic situations, and cultural influences is a crucial task in developing and implementing changes to sustainable ESs.

1.4.1 Hydrogen Production from Biomass

1.4.1.1 Background and Motivation

There is a sharp increase in energy consumption due to the great rate of economic development and growing of the world population. About 87% of global energy consumption is currently dominated by the fossil fuels-related energy market [48]. Because of this, there is environmental concern over the reduction of fossil resources and indicative GHG emissions and thus, it is prior important for alleviating the problem by considering and utilizing renewable and clean energy [49]. In view of the mentioned scenario, there has been a continuous effort in understanding renewable and clean possibilities for sustainable resources [50]. Out of these, the best and most plentifully available renewable resource is biomass. At present, it contributes to about 12% of the world's energy supply, while it accounts for 40–50% energy supply in developing countries [51]. Thus, research in this area is attracting huge importance due to its "waste-to-energy" application. For example, 150 GT of vegetable bio-matter generated worldwide every year can give about 1.08×10^{10} GJ energy [52]. However, the major disadvantage lies in the fact of utilizing low efficiency in biomass conversion to useful products. In some countries, biomass is commonly used for heating and cooking wherein the thermal efficiency ranges between 10% to 30%. And thus, it is clear that utilizing biomass for aqueous and gaseous fuels, electricity, and more specifically for hydrogen production is possibly the best and most sustainable way of biomass utilization.

The production of energy from biomass is classified into two general classes and those are biological and thermochemical processes. Under biological processes, direct biophotolysis, photo-fermentation, biological water–gas shift reaction, indirect biophotolysis, and dark fermentation are the five main processes. Whereas, combustion, pyrolysis, gasification, and liquefaction are the four main thermochemical processes. [50]. Among the two mentioned processes, thermochemical methods provide a promising approach, as it reduces the disposal of residues and emits lower noxious substances [53] and amid the thermochemical methodologies, gasification is considered the best and widely used waste-to-energy (WtE) technique [54]. This technique involves subjecting the waste residues to increasing temperatures, due to which the biomass residue would disassociate into their elements in a suitable gasifying environment like steam, air, CO_2, or a combination of them, giving rise to a final gas composed of H_2, CO, CO_2 and short-branched hydrocarbons which may be later used for the production of chemicals, power, hydrogen, and liquid fuels [55].

The moisture content of biomass plays a major role in the production of combustible gases, i.e., when the moisture content is higher than 35%, it is expected to gasify biomass with supercritical water conditions. Biomass is speedily decomposed into small molecules or gases in a few minutes with high efficiency under the severe conditions established by pressurizing it above its critical pressure (22 MPa) and heating water to a temperature above its critical temperature (647 K) [56].

Diversified biomass resources can be considered to convert to energy. These resources can be classified into four general categories [50]: (i) Agricultural waste and residues: crop waste and animal waste, (ii) Energy crops: herbaceous energy crops, agricultural crops, woody energy crops, industrial crops, and aquatic crops, (iii) Industrial and municipal wastes: sewage sludge and industrial waste, municipal solid waste (MSW), and (iv) Forestry waste and residues: mill wood waste, shrub residues, and trees and logging residues.

1.4.1.2 Catalytic Conversion of Biomass to Hydrogen through Gasification

Taking into account the catalyst in the biomass conversion can benefit both "steam gasification (SG)" and "supercritical water gasification (SWCG)" in terms of decreased reaction temperature, improved carbon gasification rate, and better hydrogen selectivity ([57,58]).

It is observed that there is a high chance of tar formation during the SG process when compared with SWCG and fast pyrolysis [59]. Here, tar is a complex mixture of phenols, alcohols, and aromatic and aldehyde compounds. Because of tar formation, there exist several problems such as pipeline blockage which increases maintenance and operation costs [60]. However, tar consists of components that can be converted into energy and thus, can significantly improve the gasification efficiency. This improvement is achieved by introducing a catalyst for tar cracking and reforming any condensable fractions. The commonly practiced and utilized catalysts are alkaline earth metallic, mineral-based, and "metal-based (e.g., Ni, Ce, La) catalysts". The catalyst is directly added to the raw materials or introduced in a secondary reactor to crack the tar formation in the reactor [61]. A summary of different catalytic gasification processes along with operating conditions and hydrogen percentages are reported in Table 1.1.

1.4.1.2.1 Alkaline Earth Metallic Catalysts

Alkali metals are traditionally and most commonly used catalysts for biomass gasification. A few of the alkali metals used are KOH, K_2CO_3, $KHCO_3$, NaOH, and $Ca(OH)_2$. With the use of these metals, the volatility of gaseous phase increases and also improves the steam reforming reactions.

Table 1.1 Survey on biomass gasification for hydrogen production

Feedstock	Reactor type	Catalyst used	Operating Temperature (°C)	Hydrogen production (vol%)	Reference
Sawdust	Not known	Na_2CO_3	700	48.31	[62]
			800	55.4	
			900	59.8	
Sawdust	Circulating fluidized bed	Non-Catalytic	810	10.5	[63]
Wood	Fixed bed	Non-Catalytic	550	7.7	[64]
Sawdust	Fluidized bed	Ni	830	62.1	[65]
Sawdust	Fluidized bed	K_2CO_3	964	11.27	[66]
		CaO	1008	13.32	
		Na_2CO_3	1012	14.77	
Pine sawdust	Fluidized bed	Not known	700–800	26–42	[67]
Almond shell	Fluidized bed	La-Ni-Fe	800	62.8	[68]
		Perovskite	900	63.7	
Switchgrass	Moving bed	Cu-Zn-Al	700	48.31	[69]

1.4.1.2.2 Metal and Metallic Oxides Catalysts

It is found that in addition to alkali metals, metals and metal oxides can even catalyze biomass conversion to hydrogen production. These catalysts have shown potential for efficient conversion with high selectivity, availability, and recyclability [70,71]. The most widely used metal is Nickel-based catalysts which have achieved good carbon conversions in addition to this, it can also promote rapid pyrolysis of hydrocarbons for steam reforming and water-as-shift reactions. Thus, exhibiting high catalytic activity [72] and good practical application.

1.4.1.2.3 Natural Mineral Catalysts

Dolomite ($MgCO_3 \cdot CaCO_3$) and olivine ($2MgO \cdot SiO_2$) are a few of the natural minerals which also exhibit catalytic effects on biomass gasification to hydrogen production [73]. It is found that the composition of hydrogen increases and carbon monoxide decreases when these natural minerals were used in the gasification process.

1.4.1.2.4 Hybrid Catalysts

Hybrid catalysts have shown great potential for biomass gasification to hydrogen production.

Researchers investigated the effect of ZrO_2 catalysts along with 20 % nickel and 1% calcium or sodium or magnesium or potassium (as oxides) on the final content of gaseous products [61]. It is found that these hybrid catalysts consisting of alkali and alkaline earth metals have a significant effect on cellulose conversion to hydrogen at high temperatures. The introduction of alkali and alkaline metals on the surface of nickel catalysts along with the addition of calcium has increased the hydrogen production significantly. It further resulted in the reduction of coke deposition on the Ni catalysts, thus making the presence of Ni catalyst even more prominent.

1.4.1.3 Current Challenges in Biomass Conversion to Hydrogen

i. To study and research the gasification behavior, mathematical models such as stoichiometric models, non-stoichiometric models, and kinetic models, or ML models such as SVM, DT, ANN, or a combination of the above models (such as hybrid models).

ii. It is observed that most of the developed models which are reported in the literature are under time-independent "static models" scenario. This makes these models only applicable for general evaluation and cannot be used to study or investigate the dynamic behavior of the gasification process. Therefore, it is now necessary to focus the studies/research work on understanding the dynamic changes in the biomass gasification process. There are a few dynamic models which fall under time-dependent models such as (a) "Nonlinear auto-regressive with exogenous inputs neural network (NARXNN)", to model dynamic state behavior of a gasification process for hydrogen production rate prediction and (b) "Kalman filter (KF)", which is a pure time-domain filter with good performance and a very powerful tool for controlling noisy systems.

iii. In case of ML methods, the study should be carried out by performing regression techniques, i.e., support vector regression, decision tree regression, polynomial regression, and multilayer perceptron to predict CO, CO_2, CH_4, H_2, and HHV outputs of the biomass gasification process.

iv. In case of SCWG, to address the challenges, modeling approaches through ML must help in determining appropriate catalysts and optimal conditions to enhance the SCWG with hydrogen production using different biomass resources.

1.4.1.4 Intervention of AI/ML in H2 Production from Biomass

In the below table, we have listed the summary of ML studies carried out for non-catalytic gasification processes for hydrogen production using varied gasifying agents such as air, steam, air-steam and supercritical water gasification, and gasifying reactors which are fixed bed (downdraft and updraft) and fluidized bed reactors (circulating and bubbling fluidized bed). As ML studies are data-driven, the data samples are collected either by conducting experiments or through simulation results of chemical engineering software, i.e., ASPEN PLUS taking into account the real flow process of gasification. The input parameters include ultimate and proximate analysis along with operating parameters such as steam-to-biomass ratio, gasifying temperature, pressure (in case of supercritical gasification), etc. While there are numerous ML algorithms, the most widely used technique is ANN due its ability to predict the output parameters taking into account the non-linear nature of input features.

In a few of the scenarios, a hybrid modeling approach provides a better performance when compared with a single global model. This approach involves modeling several internal submodels and these local submodels are trained with a specific cluster of the dataset. Thus, the whole dataset is divided into several clusters, and regression models are trained for each cluster (local model). Thus, these hybrid models are able to provide performance for biomass conversion to hydrogen production.

In the majority of data-driven experiments, it has been observed that downdraft gasifier is most widely used due to its easy operation at a small-scale level. The performance of the varied algorithms is evaluated with many performance indexes such as regression coefficient (R^2), mean squared error, mean absolute error, etc. These results showcase the applicability of different algorithms for the predication of output parameters such as product gas composition such as H_2, CO, CO_2, CH_4. In addition to this, the relative importance of the input variables is also studied using different methods such as Garson's equation, Pearson's ranking, etc. A summary of reported ML models for prediction of hydrogen yield using different gasification reactors and gasifying agents for non-catalytic gasification processes is illustrated in Table 1.2.

1.4.1.5 Conclusions and Future Directions

ML-based gasification research fundamentally focuses on parametric studies, process optimization, catalyst screening for hydrothermal gasification, and prediction of char formation during conventional gasification. For further research, efforts are needed in the following areas: (i) selecting appropriate algorithms and determining dataset size for developing standardized models with a practical approach. More case studies are needed to be studied/researched based on different feedstock, conversion technologies, and products. (ii) The quality and availability of data need to be enhanced for effective applications of AI/ML techniques through experimental studies with improved data sharing among broad science and engineering communities. (iii) A holistic perspective in supporting sustainable development is needed, as the recent studies have focused on a single aspect of sustainability, for example

Table 1.2 Reported ML studies for prediction of hydrogen yields and by-products with different gasification reactors and gasifying agents for non-catalytic gasification processes

I. Gasifying agent: Air

S.No	ML Algorithm	Input parameters	Output parameters	ML Model Performance	Reference
2	ANN-LM & ANN-BR	Proximate and ultimate analysis, and operating conditions: T, ER, and LHV biomass	CCE, CGE, LHV of gas, gas yield, and gas composition	R^2 of between 79 - 98% and 95–96%	[74]
II. Gasifying agent: Steam					
3	LRM, RLRM, ILRM, LSVM, QSVM, CSVM, QGPRM, SQGPRM, MGPRM, EGPRM, ANN-LM, and ANN-BR	Temperature, steam to biomass ratio, ash content, oxygen content, biomass weight, the flow rate of the gasifying agent, ash weight, feedstock weight, adsorbent to biomass ratio, superficial velocity, biomass particle size, coal content, and mass	Syngas production	LMANN and BRANN models displayed superior performance in all the gasification and co-gasification processes with $R^2 > 0.9$	[75]
4	ANN	Three inputs: X1 (gasification temperature), X2 (pyrolysis temperature), and X3 (steam to biomass ratio)	gas yield (Y1), Residue (Y2), tar yield (Y3), H2 yield (Y4), CO yield (Y5), CO2 yield (Y6) and CH4 yield (Y7	$R^2 > 0.99$	[76]
5	RBF and MLP	HDPE particle size, RSS particle size, gasification temperature, and the amount of plastic in the mixture	H2 production	$R^2 > 0.987$ for RBF	[77]

(Continued)

Table 1.2 (Continued) Reported ML studies for prediction of hydrogen yields and by-products with different gasification reactors and gasifying agents for non-catalytic gasification processes

I. Gasifying agent: Air

S.No	ML Algorithm	Input parameters	Output parameters	ML Model Performance	Reference
III. Gasifying agent: Air-steam					
6	ANN and GBR	ultimate and proximate analysis	CO, CO2, H2, CH4, and N2	$0.80 < R^2 < 0.89$ range for the ANN model, while for GBR $0.81 < R^2 < 0.93$	[78]
IV. Gasifying agent: SCWG					
7	ML based TDSS and TRS	Temperature (T in oC), Pressure (P in MPa), Solvent to Biomass ratio (S/B), Catalyst Loading (Cat. Load in wt. %), and Time (t in min), ultimate analysis	H2 yield	94% accuracy	[79]
8	ANN	Feedstock compositions: C, H, N, O, and ash; Operational conditions: SD, T, P, time, and catalyst ratio; Catalyst descriptors: molecular mass, atomic mass, radius, valency, ionization energy, electron affinity, and conductivity	H2 yield	R^2 of ML models developed from the updated non-catalyst, alkali catalyst, transition metal catalyst, and catalyst combination dataset were as high as 0.96, 0.85, 0.93, and 0.88, respectively	[80]
V. Gasifier type: Fixed bed reactor					
11	Hybrid Intelligent model: six local internal submodels that combine ANN & SVM	CO, CO2, CH4, CnHm, O2	H2	mean absolute prediction error for the hydrogen concentration was only 0.134 (vol%).	[81]

12	Linear and quadratic expressions and LASSO method	T gas, ER,MC, H, O, C, Ash,Gr, Fs, bulk density, biomass void percentage	H2, CO, CO2, CH4,N2, Gas/fuel ratio		[82]
13	PR, SVR, DTR & MLP	Fuel flow rate (FR), equivalence ratio (ER), T, ultimate and proximate analysis	CO, CO2, CH4, H2 and HHV outputs	$R^2 > 0.9$	[83]
14	SVM and multi-class RF classifiers	Fuel flow rate (FR), equivalence ratio (ER), T, ultimate and proximate analysis	CO, CO2, CH4, H2 and HHV outputs	accuracy over 96	[84]
15	ANN and NARX-NN model	Fuel flow rate (FR), equivalence ratio (ER), T, ultimate and proximate analysis	CO, CO2, CH4, H2 and HHV outputs	$R^2 > 0.99$	[85]
16	ANN & GBR	ultimate and proximate analysis	CO, CO2, H2, CH4, and N2	$0.80 < R^2 < 0.89$ range for the ANN model, while for GBR $0.81 < R^2 < 0.93$	[78]
18	ANN (6-1-1)	Proximate and ultimate analysis and reduction zone temperature	CH4%, CO%, CO2% and H2%	$R^2 > 0.99$ in the cases of CH4 and CO model and $R^2 > 0.98$ in the case of CO2 and H2 model	[86]
19	ANN	Proximate analysis, Ultimate/elemental analysis, and operating parameters: air to fuel ratio (AFR) and gasifier temperature (T).	Net Output Power (kW)	R^2 higher than 0.999	[87]

(Continued)

Table 1.2 (Continued) Reported ML studies for prediction of hydrogen yields and by-products with different gasification reactors and gasifying agents for non-catalytic gasification processes

I. Gasifying agent: Air

S.No	ML Algorithm	Input parameters	Output parameters	ML Model Performance	Reference
VI. Gasifier type: Fluidized bed reactor					
20	ANN based LM (6-12-1)	C, H, O, Fuel rate, Steam rate, Gasifier T	LHV of syngas	$R^2 > 0.99$	[83]

"**Abbreviations:** ANN-artificial neural network; LM-Levenberg-Marquardt backpropagation; BR-Bayesian regularization backpropagation; LRM-linear regression model; RLRM-robust linear regression model; ILRM-interaction linear regression model; LSVM-linear support vector machine; QSVM-quadratic support vector machine; CSVM-cubic support vector machine; QGPRM-rotational quadratic Gaussian process regression model; SQGPRM-squared quadratic Gaussian process regression model; MGPRM-Matern 5/2 Gaussian process regression model; EGPRM-exponential Gaussian process regression model; RBF-radial basis function; MLP-multilayer perceptron; GBR-gradient boosting regression; TDSS-tunable decision support system; TRS-tunable recommendation system; SVMR-support vector machines regression; GPR-Gaussian process regression; RF-random forest; techniques, i.e., PR-polynomial regression, SVR-support vector regression, DTR-decision tree regression; NARX-nonlinear autoregressive exogenous; GBR-gradient boos regression; KNN-K nearest neighbors; Proximate analysis of feedstocks: moisture content (M), volatile materials (VM), fixed carbon (FC), and ash (A) Ultimate/ elemental analysis of feedstocks: carbon (C), oxygen (O), hydrogen (H), nitrogen (N), sulfur (S)" on biomass conversion and economic evaluation, and (iv) Catalyst design and process optimization using ML modeling and optimization techniques.

1.4.2 Hydrogen Generation from Photocatalytic Water Splitting

Hydrogen is an energy carrier that is locked up in nature which when extracted from the compounds can be used as an energy source for different applications. Sunlight-directed photocatalytic water splitting is an irreproachable way of producing clean hydrogen energy [88]. This drew the attention of the researchers to develop a photocatalyst but the necessity to meet the tough requirements such as thermodynamic potential, narrow band gap, and resistance against photocorrosion have become obstacles along the path. Usually, the overall splitting of water can be achieved when a photocatalyst is supported/loaded with a suitable cocatalyst. Therefore, it is important to study the material properties and material science of the cocatalyst to associate it with the photocatalyst to develop a better material. In-depth, studies have shown that the photocatalyst activity is greatly influenced by Band Gap energy, Structure/surface area, light intensity, Temperature, pH, oxygen vacancies, and sacrificial reagent. In the process of photocatalytic splitting of water, on absorbing the UV light the electrons excite from the valence band to the conduction band generating an electron-hole pair followed by an oxidation-reduction reaction which gives H_2 and O_2. Photocatalytic water splitting systems is deeply investigated in two approaches- one-step excitation and the two-step excitation system also called the Z-scheme water splitting inspired by the natural process of photosynthesis in the plants [89].

TiO$_2$ was the first semiconductor used for water splitting by Fujishima and Honda in 1972 was a remarkable breakthrough in science. Since then, it was the most investigated photocatalyst and the material development against its limitations has seen a significant progress. TiO$_2$ faces difficulty in faster charge recombination rate and the photocatalytic activation only under UV light which is just 4–5% of the solar spectrum. Therefore, hindrance of the charge recombination and the photocatalytic activity under visible light are the main considerations in the further development and modification of the material.

1.4.2.1 Materials Development Photocatalytic Water Splitting

TiO$_2$ modifications include metal-modified TiO$_2$, non-metal-modified TiO$_2$, semiconductors coupling to TiO$_2$, and ternary TiO$_2$ photocatalysts. A summary of TiO2-based photocatalysts along with operating conditions and hydrogen production rate are reported in Table 1.3.

Table 1.3 Summary of various photocatalysts for hydrogen production [90–92]

Material Class	Catalyst	Reactor/Parameter	Hydrogen production $(mmol\ g^{-1}\ h^{-1})$
Metal Modified TiO$_2$	1wt% Pd/TiO$_2$	UV λ = 365nm	47.5
	2wt% Au/TiO$_2$	100 W F lamp λ = 365nm–UV	32.4
	1.5wt% Au/ TiO$_2$ (P25)	Spectroline model SB-100P/F Lamp—UV	27.9
Semiconductor Coupled TiO$_2$	CdS/TiO$_2$	Pyrex Reactor 300 W Xe Lamp, λ > 400 nm	128.3
	10wt% ZnO-TiO$_2$	Pyrex Reactor Hg Lamp, λ = 254 nm	12.97
	TiO$_2$/CuO	Pyrex Reactor 500 W Xe Lamp	8.23
Ternary TiO$_2$	g-C3N4- TiO$_2$/rGO	Borosilicate reactor 250 W Xenon lamp, 200 nm < l < 800 nm	23.143
	Cu/N/TiO$_2$	s400 W halide lamp, λ max = 360 nm-UV	27.4
	Ir-C-N-TiO$_2$	250 W Xe lamp	6

1.4.2.1.1 Metal-Modified TiO$_2$

Various metals such as Pt, Au, Ag, Ni, and Pd have been widely studied over recent years. Metal loading onto TiO$_2$ will minimize the faster charge recombination rate. The photocatalysis process can be enhanced by doping TiO$_2$ with noble metal nanoparticles through surface plasmon resonance (SPR effect). Zhu et al. (2016) have reported that Pt/TiO$_2$ is a favorable photocatalyst and produces H$_2$ efficiently at room temperature [93]. Metal-modified photocatalyst is a good approach to improve the performance of TiO$_2$ by transfer of electrons to the metal and thereafter reducing the electron/hole pair recombination.

1.4.2.1.2 Non-Metal-Modified TiO$_2$

A narrow band gap is necessary for the photocatalytic water splitting under visible radiation since it emits lesser energy to excite the electrons from the VB to the CB. When the semiconductor is doped with a non-metal, the band gap becomes narrow also with an additional advantage of the hindrance of the rapid recombination rate. This adds to the benefit, thus exhibiting a better property of the material compared to the other techniques. Cui, et al., (2009), reported that the N-doped semiconductor narrowed the band gap from 3.2eV to 2.65eV [94].

1.4.2.1.3 Semiconductor Coupling TiO₂

The rate of hydrogen production using TiO_2 is lower even under UV light irradiation due to fast electron-hole recombination and coupling TiO_2 with binary composites (e.g., WO_3, SiO_2, Al_2O_3, SnO_2CdS, PbS, Bi_2S_3) and transition metal oxides such as Cu_2O, Fe_2O_3, ZnO, NiO have improved the performance of TiO_2 because of change in properties of the material such as surface area, lowering band gap, its absorption ability, and stability.

1.4.2.1.4 Ternary TiO₂

Ternary photocatalyst consists of three materials each of which has its own role to improve the performance of the photocatalyst. Mostly, ternary composites constitute a heterojunction of two semiconductors and are deposited with a metal. It is already noted that doping metal to TiO_2 increases the hydrogen production rate. Coupling the same with a heterojunction of two narrow band gap semiconductors enhances the photocatalytic activity under visible light. Xie et al. (2017) reported that Pt/TiO_2-ZnO (Ti/Zn=10) gave a maximum hydrogen production rate of 2150 $mmolg^1h^{-1}$. Pt nanoparticles help in trapping the electrons to produce H_2 [95]. This mechanism provides a solution to the current challenges.

1.4.2.1.5 Carbon-Based Photocatalyst

Carbon has attracted much attention since it is a low-cost and abundant element in nature. Carbon-based g-C_3N_4, graphene, carbon nanotubes (CNTs), and other related materials have also been reported as efficient photocatalysts for water splitting. However, pristine g-C_3N_4 has shown a low activity compared to TiO_2. This low performance is a result of fast recombination rates, low surface area, and grain boundary effect. Thus, the modification is done on the basic understanding of the cause such as reaction parameters, synthesis process, crystallinity, structural defects, and surface area. Morphological modifications increase the number of active sites for reaction. Experiments done on modified g-C_3N_4 are summarized in Table 1.4.

On hydrogenation, TiO_2 can turn from white to black. Additionally, the hydrogenated black TiO_2 demonstrates superb photocatalytic activity for splitting water to produce H_2. 0.02 g black TiO_2 nanocrystals with 0.6 wt% Pt produced 0.2 mmol of H_2 per hour (i.e., 10 $mmolg^{-1}h^{-1}$) from water with methanol as the sacrificial reagent under simulated sun irradiation (about 1 Sun power). When compared to the majority of semiconductor photocatalysts, this hydrogen production rate is roughly two orders of magnitude higher. A novel substance, hydrothermally produced platinum ion-exchanged titania nanotubes (Pt(IE)/TiNT), was discovered to be functional when exposed to visible light. For the stoichiometric production of hydrogen

Table 1.4 Summary of photocatalyst activity of various classes of doping materials for hydrogen production [96–98]

Doping	Catalyst	Feed	Reactor/Parameter	H_2 production ($\mu mol\ g^{-1}h^{-1}$)
Semiconductor Doping g-C_3N_4	Ni2P/g-C_3N	20 vol% TEOA	Quartz reactor, 300 W Xe arc lamp, λ max = 420 nm	1503
	MoS2/ g-C_3N_4	25 vol% CH3OH	300 W Xe lamp, λ > 420 nm	867.6
	ZnS/ g-C_3N_4	Na2S and Na2SO3	Pyrex reactor, 300 W Xe lamp, λ = 420 nm	713.68
Metal Doping g-C_3N_4	Pt/g-C_3N_4	10 vol% TEOA	Pyrex reactor, 350 W Xe lamp	4210.8
	Pt/g-C_3N_4	10 vol% TEOA	Uv-vis lamp, λ > 380 nm	3900
	Cu/g-C_3N_4	10 vol% TEOA	Pyrex reactor, 300 W Xe lamp, λ > 420 nm	3643
Non-Metal Doping g-C_3N_4	P/g-C_3N_4	10 vol% TEOA	Pyrex reactor, 300 W Xe lamp, λ > 420 nm	2020
	O/g-C_3N_4	10 vol% TEOA	Pyrex reactor, 300 W Xe lamp, λ = 420 nm	1968
	S/g-C_3N_4	25 vol% TEOA	Pyrex reactor, 300 W Xe lamp, λ > = 420 nm	1511.2

and oxygen by the splitting of water under visible light at one sun, the platinum nanoparticles well embedded in nanotube matrixes in the ionized samples were highly photoactive materials, resulting in hydrogen evolution rates of 14.6 and 2.3 mol/h in aqueous methanol and pure water, respectively.

1.4.2.2 ML Aided Photocatalyst Development

From the above discussion, it is evident that a wide range of different classes and types of materials were employed for photocatalytic splitting of water. It is a tedious task to experiment on all the materials to find an efficient catalyst for further research. AI-ML technology reduces human effort with respect to the same and also helps in giving a new novel combination of the material which has not been in use. AI-ML framework involves the steps of Data Extraction, model construction and validation, and material prediction.

Data Mining or Data Extraction is a method of gathering all the experimental data from the research papers in the form of data points. More data points will help in improving the accuracy of the model. This step is followed by data cleaning and feature engineering. Feature engineering is the process of ranking the features according to their significant importance and removing those features that do not contribute to the performance of the model. This will help to overcome the problem of overfitting, thereby improving the accuracy of the model. The developed model's performance is determined by its ability to give good predictions for unknown data. The total data is divided into two sets-train data set and test data set. The model gets trained with the train dataset and checks if it is able to fit the unknown data with the test dataset. The performance of these models is evaluated using RMSE (Root Mean Square Error), Correlation Coefficient, Absolute Average Deviation, etc. Cross Validation is another method used to enhance the performance and accuracy of the model. This technique divides the total dataset into "n" number of sets where n-1 sets are used as train dataset and the nth set is used as test dataset and the same process is repeated for n times. The collected data is trained using ML models, which are then used to perform inverse design. Through the use of high throughput virtual screening (e.g., molecular dynamic simulation/DFT computation) or mathematical optimization (e.g., AI-based global optimization approaches), inverse design is used to find the best operating conditions as well as novel materials.

Recently, Mai et al. (2022) designed a photocatalyst through ML approach. Data from 160 ABO_3-type perovskite photocatalytic were collected from 43 experimental literature [99]. In photocatalytic water splitting, the E_g is an important parameter to decide on the light absorption capacity of a photocatalyst. Therefore, two different datasets and models were constructed and developed for both E_g and RH_2 of sample sizes 124 and 77, respectively. The primary target of photocatalyst water splitting is to utilize visible light since it contributes to the major portion of the solar spectrum. The goal is to design new perovskite photocatalytic materials with increased H_2 production and satisfactory E_g values. The dataset was split into two sets in the ratio 4:1, i.e., 80–20 train data-test data respectively. Back-propagation ANN (BPANN), SVR, GBR, and RF were the four models used to build the models. LOOCV was performed to evaluate the performance of each model. Pearson correlation coefficient(R) and Root Mean Square Error (RMSE) were incorporated as evaluation indices. RMSE and R were used to calculate the error and correlation coefficient respectively. An optimization model was developed to search for optimal operating conditions to obtain the maximum hydrogen production. Conclusions drawn from the model are discussed as follows (i) A three-dimension coupling mathematical model for a photocatalytic reactor is built and validated by the experimental data, (ii) The Sobol' sensitivity analysis method is suggested to provide a rank ordering of the critical components and measure the degree to which a particular factor affects the hydrogen generation in order to find the factor prioritizing. According to the sensitivity indices, the volume fraction of the photocatalyst and the inlet velocity of the suspensions are crucial factors in hydrogen production under simulated conditions. (iii) To simplify the computation required for optimization, a GPR surrogate model is constructed. The best operating conditions for the solar water splitting system are solved using a new memetic algorithm that combines the performance benefits of the WO technique with the SA algorithm. (iv) When the inlet velocity of the suspensions and the volume percent of the photocatalyst are 0.08 m/s and 0.01, respectively, the maximum hydrogen generation approximates 49.07 mol/(m^{3}h) and the maximum energy conversion efficiency to 2.12 %. When compared to traditional optimization methods, the suggested solution cuts the computing work from several days to a few seconds [100]. A database of 540 cases was constructed from 151 published papers on photocatalytic splitting of water over perovskites and analyzed using machine learning tools. Further studies were developed by decision tree analysis and predictive models were developed by random forest regression. Perovskites are doped to A-site and B-site and its effect on band gap is seen. About 80% of cases contain co-catalysts of which Pt is the most common one. The RMSE and R2 for training were 558.1 and 0.95 respectively and RMSE (1194) and R2 (0.79) for testing for hydrogen production.

1.4.2.3 Conclusions and Future Directions

Hydrogen production through water splitting reaction using solar energy is one of the most promising technologies to generate hydrogen energy in a sustainable way. After the first development of photocatalyst by Fujishima and Honda, significant progress was seen, and the research studies have proved that the solar-hydrogen-conversion efficiency is governed by the properties of the semiconductors. Therefore, further improvement in developing the photocatalyst must be based on an understanding of the structure and defect chemistry of the photocatalyst surface as well as the molecular reaction mechanisms in oxidation and reduction reaction and the charger transfer mechanism. Thus, it can be concluded that discovering semiconductors that help in narrowing the band gap for the photocatalytic utility under visible sunlight and reducing the rapid recombination rate would give better hydrogen production and AI-ML established technology would serve the same purpose.

1.4.3 Geothermal Energy Applications

Geothermal energy (GE) is a renewable energy source that is generated from the heat flux of the earth's core. GE is non-carbon-based renewable energy. It has a lot of potential and it is one of the dependable energy sources. In tectonically active nations, GE is seen as a crucial element of changes toward sustainable ESs. The world community has recognized GE as playing a significant role in the transition to sustainable ESs. It can support a country's energy security because it is an indigenous resource and has comparatively low carbon emissions. For many years, GE has mostly been used in places where the geothermal gradient is high and active hydrothermal or volcanic systems exist, to name a few, Iceland in Europe and Geysers in the United States. Along with such regions, GE that is stored in hydrocarbon reservoirs also has a lot of promise since not only there is a lot of GE present in oil and gas reservoirs, but also oilfields have many advantages when it comes to developing GE.

Compared to traditional energy sources (which are based on fossil fuels), GE has very less impact on the environment [101], however, concerns raised during the construction of certain projects have resulted in the creation of certain frameworks for evaluating the sustainability of GE projects [102]. According to estimates, there will be 10 GW of installed GE in total in the near future, with eight nations – United States, Iceland, Italy, Indonesia, Japan, Mexico, New Zealand, and the Philippines – producing 90% of the world's energy [103]. GE plants have a negligible impact on the environment, in contrast to fossil fuel power plants that may generate GHG emissions. The negative effects of GE have been greatly decreased thanks to improved technology and increased awareness of the necessity for environmental protection [104]. Since geothermal power facilities typically have high investment costs and longer payback times (approximately 5–7 years) compared to other renewable-energy power plants, the situation is more complicated in the case of GE [105].

The seismicity concerns are one of the biggest obstacles to using GE. Various tools have been developed in recent years to help mitigate the dangers associated with land subsidence and earthquakes by predicting them as accurately as possible. It is anticipated that the development of big data and AI over the past ten years will assist geothermal power plants in minimizing their harm. The development of operational procedures and more efficient power plants, such as hybrid power plants, can further help to reduce environmental effects. On the other hand, management and planning strategies on how to improve efficient energy use will greatly influence whether or not environmental impacts are reduced or increased. More research and development projects are urgently needed in the areas of exploration data, drilling technology, and reservoir operation and maintenance. To further improve the quality, efficiency of GE and to increase the capacity of the ES, an integrated system such as a solar geothermal hybrid energy conversion system, should be supported.

In order to ensure GE is harnessed and used sustainably, cascade technology for improved geothermal systems must be promoted [106]. Economic viability is required for better GE optimization. Other factors like life cycle environmental impact and thermodynamic efficiency need to be carefully considered [107]. The usage of renewable energy has increased globally because of the urgent requirement to decrease fossil fuel emissions, and GE is seen as a promising renewable energy source.

1.5 CHALLENGES OF AI IN THE RENEWABLE ENERGY INDUSTRY

Digital technological advancements have the potential to significantly alter our energy usage, trade, and supply. The AI technology underpins the new digitalization model. Intelligent software that optimizes decision-making and operations will automatically control the integration of energy supply, demand, and renewable sources into the power grid. AI will be crucial to reaching this objective. The major challenges of AI in the renewable energy industry are as follows.

1.5.1 Lack of Theoretical Background

Decision-makers' inadequate understanding of AI technology is one factor in the industry's sluggish adoption of AI. Many businesses lack the technical knowledge to comprehend how adopting AI might enhance their operations. Instead of taking a chance on a novel approach, conservative stakeholders prefer to remain with tried-and-true strategies and techniques [108]. Decision-makers in the energy sector are now paying attention to AI as different sectors, including education, banking, healthcare, and transportation, embrace the possibilities of this technology.

1.5.2 Lack of Practical Expertise

AI is still a young field of study and few experts are in it. Many professionals have an extensive theoretical understanding of the topic. However, finding experts who can create reliable AI-powered software with actual utility is extremely difficult. Additionally, the energy industry has very traditional values. Energy firms monitor and collect data, but digitizing it with cutting-edge tech solutions is difficult. Data loss, poor customization, system failure, and illegal access are present hazards [109]. The high cost of error in the energy sector makes many businesses wary of taking a chance to experiment with novel ideas.

1.5.3 Outdated Infrastructure

The most significant barrier to the modernization of the energy sector is out-of-date infrastructure. Utility firms are drowning in a sea of data they acquire and have no idea how to manage it. Even though the industry has more data than most, it is frequently dispersed, disorganized, stored only locally, and in many formats. Despite enormous revenues, the sector loses money because of obsolete systems' weaknesses.

1.5.4 Financial Pressure

The wisest action in the energy sector may involve implementing cutting-edge innovative technology, but it will not be cheap. It takes a lot of time and money to look for an expert software services provider, develop and customize software, and then manage and monitor it. Businesses in the energy sector must be prepared to set aside a sizable budget and incur the risks of updating their antiquated systems before they can gain from adopting AI, ML, and DL into their plans [110].

The energy sector is no exception to the modern economy's pervasive use of cutting-edge technology like AI. This industry can be globally revolutionized by AI. Soon enough, AI is anticipated to transform from a valuable tool to the most effective decision-maker the energy sector has ever had. It is anticipated to decrease manual labor, lower hazards, and enhance data and asset management. However, several obstacles must be overcome before the promising future can materialize and AI can completely transform the energy industry.

1.6 OUTLOOK AND FUTURE PERSPECTIVES

The market for renewable energy is expanding, which is an excellent way to increase environmental sustainability. The capability of data analytics is being increased by the integration of AI across critical industries. Due to the unpredictable nature of the weather, suppliers may be forced to turn to conventional energy sources in order to satisfy client demand. In order to give energy suppliers the information they need to respond to variations that could negatively affect operations and make plans appropriately, AI-driven energy forecasting solutions may show potential.

As indicated by the G7 and G20's vows to hasten implementation and boost overall energy efficiency, 2015 was a boom year for renewable energy sources [111]. However, persistent proof of benefits, particularly in the economic and political spheres, will be needed to get beyond the obstacles to widespread and speedy implementation. In the near future, platforms that can reliably identify cost reductions and energy efficiency for customers and businesses will be valuable.

REFERENCES

[1] R. J. Kolbjørnsrud, V. Amico, and R. Thomas, "The promise of artificial intelligence," *Accenture: Dublin, Ireland*, 2016.

[2] S. Marih, L. Ghomri, and B. Bekkouche, "Evaluation of the wind potential and optimal design of a wind farm in the Arzew industrial zone in Western Algeria," *Int. J. Renew. Energy Dev.*, vol. 9, no. 2, pp. 177–187, Jul. 2020, doi: 10.14710/ijred.9.2.177-187.

[3] W. Cai et al., "Optimal sizing and location based on economic parameters for an off-grid application of a hybrid system with photovoltaic, battery and diesel technology," *Energy*, vol. 201, p. 117480, Jun. 2020, doi: 10.1016/J.ENERGY.2020.117480.

[4] N. Kannan and D. Vakeesan, "Solar energy for future world: - A review," *Renew. Sustain. Energy Rev.*, vol. 62, pp. 1092–1105, Sep. 2016, doi: 10.1016/J.RSER.2016.05.022.

[5] J. Khan and M. H. Arsalan, "Solar power technologies for sustainable electricity generation – A review," *Renew. Sustain. Energy Rev.*, vol. 55, pp. 414–425, Mar. 2016, doi: 10.1016/J.RSER.2015.10.135.

[6] J. de Beer and C. Depew, "The role of process engineering in the digital transformation," *Comput. Chem. Eng.*, vol. 154, p. 107423, 2021, doi: 10.1016/j.compchemeng.2021.107423.

[7] M. R. Maghami, H. Hizam, C. Gomes, M. A. Radzi, M. I. Rezadad, and S. Hajighorbani, "Power loss due to soiling on solar panel: A review," *Renew. Sustain. Energy Rev.*, vol. 59, pp. 1307–1316, Jun. 2016, doi: 10.1016/j.rser.2016.01.044.

[8] H. H. Lou, R. Mukherjee, Z. Wang, T. Olsen, U. Diwekar, and S. Lin, "A new area of utilizing industrial Internet of Things in environmental monitoring," *Front. Chem. Eng.*, vol. 4, no. December, pp. 1–6, Mar. 2022, doi: 10.3389/fceng.2022.842514.

[9] F. Petropoulos et al., "Forecasting: Theory and practice," *Int. J. Forecast.*, vol. 38, no. 3, pp. 705–871, Jul. 2022, doi: 10.1016/j.ijforecast.2021.11.001.

[10] A. Subeesh and C. R. R. Mehta, "Automation and digitization of agriculture using artificial intelligence and internet of things," *Artif. Intell. Agric.*, vol. 5, pp. 278–291, 2021, doi: 10.1016/j.aiia.2021.11.004.

[11] S. K. Jha, J. Bilalovic, A. Jha, N. Patel, and H. Zhang, "Renewable energy: Present research and future scope of Artificial Intelligence," *Renew. Sustain. Energy Rev.*, vol. 77, pp. 297–317, Sep. 2017, doi: 10.1016/J.RSER.2017.04.018.

[12] A. H. Sodhro, S. Pirbhulal, V. Hugo, and C. De Albuquerque, "Artificial intelligence-driven mechanism for edge computing-based industrial applications; Artificial intelligence-driven mechanism for edge computing-based industrial applications," *IEEE Trans. Ind. Informatics*, vol. 15, no. 7, p. 4235, 2019, doi: 10.1109/TII.2019.2902878.

[13] International Energy Agency, "International energy agency," *IEA Digitalisation and Energy*, 2017.

[14] M. K. Deshmukh and S. S. Deshmukh, "Modeling of hybrid renewable energy systems," *Renew. Sustain. Energy Rev.*, vol. 12, no. 1, pp. 235–249, Jan. 2008, doi: 10.1016/J.RSER.2006.07.011.

[15] O. Elgerd, *Electric Energy Systems Theory: An introduction.* New York, NY, USA: McGraw-Hill, 1982.

[16] P. Palensky, S. Member, and D. Dietrich, "Demand side management: Demand response, intelligent energy systems, and smart loads," *IEEE Trans. Ind. Informatics*, vol. 7, no. 3, 2011, doi: 10.1109/TII.2011.2158841.

[17] M. Torabi, S. Hashemi, M. R. Saybani, S. Shamshirband, and A. Mosavi, "A hybrid clustering and classification technique for forecasting short-term energy consumption," *Environ. Prog. Sustain. Energy*, vol. 38, no. 1, pp. 66–76, Jan. 2019, doi: 10.1002/ep.12934.

[18] M. Hosseini Imani, S. Zalzar, A. Mosavi, and S. Shamshirband, "Strategic behavior of retailers for risk reduction and profit increment via distributed generators and demand response programs," *Energies*, vol. 11, p. 1602, 2018, doi: 10.3390/en11061602.

[19] K. Amasyali and N. M. El-Gohary, "A review of data-driven building energy consumption prediction studies," *Renew. Sustain. Energy Rev.*, vol. 81, pp. 1192–1205, Jan. 2018, doi: 10.1016/J.RSER.2017.04.095.

[20] Y. Peng, A. Rysanek, Z. Nagy, and A. Schlüter, "Using machine learning techniques for occupancy-prediction-based cooling control in office buildings," *Appl. Energy*, vol. 211, pp. 1343–1358, Feb. 2018, doi: 10.1016/J.APENERGY.2017.12.002.

[21] M. Arabloo, A. Bahadori, M. M. Ghiasi, M. Lee, A. Abbas, and S. Zendehboudi, "A novel modeling approach to optimize oxygen–steam ratios in coal gasification process," *Fuel*, vol. 153, pp. 1–5, Aug. 2015, doi: 10.1016/J.FUEL.2015.02.083.

[22] M. Arikan and C. Ozdemir, "Classification of power quality disturbances at power system frequency and out of power system frequency using support vector machines," *Prz. Elektrotech*, vol. 89, 2013.

[23] J. Ma, H. Jiang, K. Huang, Z. Bi, and K. L. Man, "Novel field-support vector regression-based soft sensor for accurate estimation of solar irradiance," *IEEE Trans. CIRCUITS Syst. Regul. Pap.*, vol. 64, no. 12, 2017, doi: 10.1109/TCSI.2017.2746091.

[24] J. Zhang, G. G. Walter, Y. Miao, and W. N. W. Lee, "Wavelet neural networks for function learning," *IEEE Trans. Signal Process.*, vol. 43, no. 6, pp. 1485–1497, 1995, doi: 10.1109/78.388860.

[25] B. Doucoure, K. Agbossou, and A. Cardenas, "Time series prediction using artificial wavelet neural network and multi-resolution analysis: Application to wind speed data," *Renew. Energy*, vol. 92, pp. 202–211, Jul. 2016, doi: 10.1016/J.RENENE.2016.02.003.

[26] J. Gu, J. Wang, C. Qi, C. Min, and B. Sundén, "Medium-term heat load prediction for an existing residential building based on a wireless on-off control system," *Energy*, vol. 152, pp. 709–718, Jun. 2018, doi: 10.1016/J.ENERGY.2018.03.179.

[27] Q. He, J. Wang, and H. Lu, "A hybrid system for short-term wind speed forecasting," *Appl. Energy*, vol. 226, pp. 756–771, Sep. 2018, doi: 10.1016/J.APENERGY.2018.06.053.

[28] J. A. Aguado, A. José, S. Racero, and S. De La Torre, "Optimal operation of electric railways with renewable energy and electric storage systems; Optimal operation of electric railways with renewable energy and electric storage systems," *IEEE Trans. Smart Grid*, vol. 9, no. 2, p. 993, 2018, doi: 10.1109/TSG.2016.2574200.

[29] D. C. L. Costa, M. V. A. Nunes, J. P. A. Vieira, and U. H. Bezerra, "Decision tree-based security dispatch application in integrated electric power and natural-gas networks," *Electr. Power Syst. Res.*, vol. 141, pp. 442–449, Dec. 2016, doi: 10.1016/J.EPSR.2016.08.027.

[30] S. Kamali and T. Amraee, "Blackout prediction in interconnected electric energy systems considering generation re-dispatch and energy curtailment," *Appl. Energy*, vol. 187, pp. 50–61, Feb. 2017, doi: 10.1016/J.APENERGY. 2016.11.040.

[31] P. Moutis, S. Skarvelis-Kazakos, and M. Brucoli, "Decision tree aided planning and energy balancing of planned community microgrids," *Appl. Energy*, vol. 161, pp. 197–205, Jan. 2016, doi: 10.1016/J.APENERGY.2015. 10.002.

[32] Y. Deng, B. Peng, D. Zhang, and H. Qian, "An intelligent hybrid short-term load forecasting model optimized by switching delayed PSO of micro-grids," *J. Renew. Sustain. Energy*, vol. 10, 2018.

[33] L.-L. Peng, G.-F. Fan, M.-L. Huang, and W.-C. Hong, "Hybridizing DEMD and Quantum PSO with SVR in Electric Load Forecasting," 2016, doi: 10.33 90/en9030221.

[34] Z. Qu, K. Zhang, J. Wang, W. Zhang, and W. Leng, "A Hybrid Model Based on Ensemble Empirical Mode Decomposition and Fruit Fly Optimization Algorithm for Wind Speed Forecasting," 2016, doi: 10.1155/2016/3768242.

[35] E. Chemali, P. J. Kollmeyer, M. Preindl, and A. Emadi, "State-of-charge estimation of Li-ion batteries using deep neural networks: A machine learning approach," *J. Power Sources*, vol. 400, pp. 242–255, Oct. 2018, doi: 10.1016/J.JPOWSOUR.2018.06.104.

[36] I. M. Coelho, V. N. Coelho, E. J. D. S. Luz, L. S. Ochi, F. G. Guimarães, and E. Rios, "A GPU deep learning metaheuristic based model for time series forecasting," *Appl. Energy*, vol. 201, pp. 412–418, Sep. 2017, doi: 10.1016/ J.APENERGY.2017.01.003.

[37] J. Kim, T.-T.-H. Le, and H. Kim, "Nonintrusive Load Monitoring Based on Advanced Deep Learning and Novel Signature," 2017, doi: 10.1155/2017/-4216281.

[38] H. Wang *et al.*, "Deterministic and probabilistic forecasting of photovoltaic power based on deep convolutional neural network," *Energy Convers. Manag.*, vol. 153, pp. 409–422, Dec. 2017, doi: 10.1016/J.ENCONMAN. 2017.10.008.

[39] C. Yu, Y. Li, Y. Bao, H. Tang, and G. Zhai, "A novel framework for wind speed prediction based on recurrent neural networks and support vector machine," *Energy Convers. Manag.*, vol. 178, pp. 137–145, Dec. 2018, doi: 10.1016/J.ENCONMAN.2018.10.008.

[40] Y. L. Hu and L. Chen, "A nonlinear hybrid wind speed forecasting model using LSTM network, hysteretic ELM and Differential Evolution algorithm," *Energy Convers. Manag.*, vol. 173, pp. 123–142, Oct. 2018, doi: 10.1016/J.ENCONMAN.2018.07.070.

[41] P. Hajela and C.-Y. Lin, "Genetic search strategies in multicriterion optimal design," *Struct. Optim.*, vol. 4, no. 2, pp. 99–107, 1992, doi: 10.1007/BF01 759923.

[42] D. E. Goldberg, *Genetic Algorithms in Search Optimization and Machine Learning.* Addison-Wesley, 1989.

[43] Y. P. Cai, G. H. Huang, Z. F. Yang, Q. G. Lin, and Q. Tan, "Community-scale renewable energy systems planning under uncertainty—An interval chance-constrained programming approach," *Renew. Sustain. Energy Rev.*, vol. 13, no. 4, pp. 721–735, May 2009, doi: 10.1016/J.RSER.2008.01.008.

[44] S. E. Fleten, K. M. Maribu, and I. Wangensteen, "Optimal investment strategies in decentralized renewable power generation under uncertainty," *Energy*, vol. 32, no. 5, pp. 803–815, May 2007, doi: 10.1016/J.ENERGY. 2006.04.015.

[45] K. Mitchell, M. Nagrial, and J. Rizk, "Simulation and optimisation of renewable energy systems," *Int. J. Electr. Power Energy Syst.*, vol. 27, no. 3, pp. 177–188, Mar. 2005, doi: 10.1016/J.IJEPES.2004.10.001.

[46] S. D. Pohekar and M. Ramachandran, "Application of multi-criteria decision making to sustainable energy planning—A review," *Renew. Sustain. Energy Rev.*, vol. 8, no. 4, pp. 365–381, Aug. 2004, doi: 10.1016/J.RSER.2003. 12.007.

[47] J. J. Wang, Y. Y. Jing, C. F. Zhang, and J. H. Zhao, "Review on multi-criteria decision analysis aid in sustainable energy decision-making," *Renew. Sustain. Energy Rev.*, vol. 13, no. 9, pp. 2263–2278, Dec. 2009, doi: 10.1016/ J.RSER.2009.06.021.

[48] S. Zhou *et al.*, "Sustainable hydrothermal self-assembly of hafnium–lignosulfonate nanohybrids for highly efficient reductive upgrading of 5-hydroxymethylfurfural," 2019, doi: 10.1039/c8gc03710h.

[49] Y. Zhai *et al.*, "Synergetic Effect of B and O Dopants for Aerobic Oxidative Coupling of Amines to Imines," 2018, doi: 10.1021/acssuschemeng.8b05217.

[50] M. Ni, D. Y. C. Leung, M. K. H. Leung, and K. Sumathy, "An overview of hydrogen production from biomass," *Fuel Process. Technol.*, vol. 87, no. 5, pp. 461–472, May 2006, doi: 10.1016/J.FUPROC.2005.11.003.

[51] A. Demirbaş, "Biomass resource facilities and biomass conversion processing for fuels and chemicals," *Energy Convers. Manag.*, vol. 42, no. 11, pp. 1357–1378, 2001, doi: 10.1016/S0196-8904(00)00137-0.

[52] M. M. J. Larminie and A. Dicks, *Fuel Cell Systems Explained*. Wiley, 2003.

[53] T. Tabata, "Waste-to-energy incineration plants as greenhouse gas reducers: A case study of seven Japanese metropolises," *Waste Manag. Res.*, vol. 31, no. 11, pp. 1110–1117, Sep. 2013, doi: 10.1177/0734242X13502385.

[54] P. Parthasarathy and K. S. Narayanan, "Hydrogen production from steam gasification of biomass: Influence of process parameters on hydrogen yield – A review," *Renew. Energy*, vol. 66, pp. 570–579, Jun. 2014, doi: 10.1016/ j.renene.2013.12.025.

[55] M. Siedlecki, W. de Jong, and A. H. M. Verkooijen, "Fluidized bed gasification as a mature and reliable technology for the production of bio-syngas and applied in the production of liquid transportation fuels-a review," *Energies*, vol. 4, no. 3, pp. 389–434, 2011, doi: 10.3390/en4030389.

[56] T. Yoshida, Y. Oshima, and Y. Matsumura, "Gasification of biomass model compounds and real biomass in supercritical water," *Biomass and Bioenergy*, vol. 26, no. 1, pp. 71–78, Jan. 2004, doi: 10.1016/S0961-9534 (03)00063-1.

[57] L. Cao *et al.*, "Optimizing xylose production from pinewood sawdust through dilute-phosphoric-acid hydrolysis by response surface methodology," *J. Clean. Prod.*, vol. 178, pp. 572–579, Mar. 2018, doi: 10.1016/ J.JCLEPRO.2018.01.039.

[58] X. Xiong, I. K. M. Yu, L. Cao, D. C. W. Tsang, S. Zhang, and Y. S. Ok, "A review of biochar-based catalysts for chemical synthesis, biofuel production,

and pollution control," *Bioresour. Technol.*, vol. 246, pp. 254–270, Dec. 2017, doi: 10.1016/J.BIORTECH.2017.06.163.

[59] A. G. Ebadi, H. Hisoriev, M. Zarnegar, and H. Ahmadi, "Hydrogen and syngas production by catalytic gasification of algal biomass (Cladophora glomerata L.) using alkali and alkaline-earth metals compounds," *Environ. Technol.*, vol. 40, no. 9, pp. 1178–1184, Apr. 2019, doi: 10.1080/0959333 0.2017.1417495.

[60] P. Qiu, C. Du, L. Liu, and L. Chen, "Hydrogen and syngas production from catalytic steam gasification of char derived from ion-exchangeable Na- and Ca-loaded coal," *Int. J. Hydrogen Energy*, vol. 43, no. 27, pp. 12034–12048, Jul. 2018, doi: 10.1016/J.IJHYDENE.2018.04.055.

[61] R. Ryczkowski, M. Niewiadomski, B. Michalkiewicz, El_ Zbieta Skiba, A. M. Ruppert, and J. Grams, "Effect of alkali and alkaline earth metals addition on Ni/ZrO 2 catalyst activity in cellulose conversion," doi: 10. 1007/s10973-016-5465-z.

[62] and R. Z. Yongjie and Y. C. Mingqiang, "Exploring energy from biomass—the gasification of residues from hydrolyzed sawdust," *Acta Energiae Solaris Sin.*, vol. 17, 1996.

[63] L. Chuangzhi, W. Xiuli, Y. Bingyan, X. Zhengfan, & L. Ping, "The performance study of biomass gasification with oxygen-rich air," *Acta Energiae Solaris Sin.*, vol. 18, 1996.

[64] W. D. Y. Xia, "Study of gasification treatment of biomass in fixed bed gasifier," *Mei Qi Yu Re Li 20*, vol. 243, 2000.

[65] S. Rapagnà, N. Jand, and P. U. Foscolo, "Catalytic gasification of biomass to produce hydrogen rich gas," *Int. J. Hydrogen Energy*, vol. 23, no. 7, pp. 551–557, Jul. 1998, doi: 10.1016/S0360-3199(97)00108-0.

[66] T. Y. J. Jian-chun, J. Chun, Z. Jin-Ping, Y. Hao, D. Wei-di, "Study on industrial applied technology for biomass catalytic gasification," *Chem. Ind. For. Prod.*, vol. 21, 2001.

[67] L. D. W. Zhiwei, T. Songtao, S. Xueyong, L. Zian, C. Congming, "A study on model for biomass pyrolysis and gasification in fluidized bed," *J. Fuel Chem. Technol.*, vol. 30, 2002.

[68] S. Rapagná, H. Provendier, C. Petit, A. Kiennemann, and P. U. Foscolo, "Development of catalysts suitable for hydrogen or syn-gas production from biomass gasification," *Biomass and Bioenergy*, vol. 22, no. 5, pp. 377–388, May 2002, doi: 10.1016/S0961-9534(02)00011-9.

[69] R. C. Brown, "Biomass-derived hydrogen from a thermally ballasted gasifier," 2007. doi: No.DOE/GO/11091-5. Iowa State Univ., Ames, IA (United States).

[70] P. Mishra, S. Krishnan, S. Rana, L. Singh, M. Sakinah, and Z. Ab Wahid, "Outlook of fermentative hydrogen production techniques: An overview of dark, photo and integrated dark-photo fermentative approach to biomass," *Energy Strateg. Rev.*, vol. 24, no. June 2018, pp. 27–37, Apr. 2019, doi: 10. 1016/j.esr.2019.01.001.

[71] V. Laxman Pachapur *et al.*, "energies Seed Pretreatment for Increased Hydrogen Production Using Mixed-Culture Systems with Advantages over Pure-Culture Systems," doi: 10.3390/en12030530.

[72] C. Gai *et al.*, "Hydrochar supported bimetallic Ni-Fe nanocatalysts with tailored composition, size and shape for improved biomass steam reforming performance †," 2018, doi: 10.1039/c8gc00433a.

[73] S. Basu, Narayan, and C. Pradhan, "Selective production of hydrogen by acetone steam reforming over Ni-Co/olivine catalysts," vol. 127, pp. 357–373, 2019, doi: 10.1007/s11144-019-01542-8.

[74] M. Ozonoh, B. O. Oboirien, A. Higginson, and M. O. Daramola, "Performance evaluation of gasification system efficiency using artificial neural network," *Renew. Energy*, vol. 145, pp. 2253–2270, 2020, doi: 10.1016/j.renene.2019.07.136.

[75] A. Bahadar *et al.*, "Elucidating the effect of process parameters on the production of hydrogen-rich syngas by biomass and coal Co-gasification techniques: A multi-criteria modeling approach," *Chemosphere*, vol. 287, p. 132052, Jan. 2022, doi: 10.1016/J.CHEMOSPHERE.2021.132052.

[76] H. O. Kargbo, J. Zhang, and A. N. Phan, "Optimisation of two-stage biomass gasification for hydrogen production via artificial neural network," *Appl. Energy*, vol. 302, p. 117567, Nov. 2021, doi: 10.1016/j.apenergy.2021.117567.

[77] B. V. Ayodele, S. I. Mustapa, R. Kanthasamy, M. Zwawi, and C. K. Cheng, "Modeling the prediction of hydrogen production by co-gasification of plastic and rubber wastes using machine learning algorithms," *Int. J. Energy Res.*, vol. 45, no. 6, pp. 9580–9594, May 2021, doi: 10.1002/er.6483.

[78] H.-T. Wen, J.-H. Lu, and M.-X. Phuc, "Applying Artificial Intelligence to Predict the Composition of Syngas Using Rice Husks: A Comparison of Artificial Neural Networks and Gradient Boosting Regression," 2021, doi: 10.3390/en14102932.

[79] P. V. Gopirajan, K. P. Gopinath, G. Sivaranjani, and J. Arun, "Optimization of hydrothermal gasification process through machine learning approach: Experimental conditions, product yield and pollution," *J. Clean. Prod.*, vol. 306, p. 127302, Jul. 2021, doi: 10.1016/J.JCLEPRO.2021.127302.

[80] J. Li, L. Pan, M. Suvarna, and X. Wang, "Machine learning aided supercritical water gasification for H2-rich syngas production with process optimization and catalyst screening," *Chem. Eng. J.*, vol. 426, p. 131285, Dec. 2021, doi: 10.1016/j.cej.2021.131285.

[81] R. Aguado, J.-L. Casteleiro-Roca, D. Vera, and J. L. Calvo-Rolle, "A hybrid intelligent model to predict the hydrogen concentration in the producer gas from a downdraft gasifier," *Int. J. Hydrogen Energy*, vol. 47, no. 48, pp. 20755–20770, Jun. 2022, doi: 10.1016/j.ijhydene.2022.04.174.

[82] M. Binns, H. Muhammad, U. Ayub, S. Yeomans, M. Kozlova, and D. Musmarra, "Model Reduction Applied to Empirical Models for Biomass Gasification in Downdraft Gasifiers," 2021, doi: 10.3390/su132112191.

[83] F. Kartal and U. Özveren, "A deep learning approach for prediction of syngas lower heating value from CFB gasifier in Aspen plus®," *Energy*, vol. 209, p. 118457, 2020, doi: 10.1016/j.energy.2020.118457.

[84] A. Y. Mutlu and O. Yucel, "An artificial intelligence based approach to predicting syngas composition for downdraft biomass gasification," *Energy*, vol. 165, pp. 895–901, Dec. 2018, doi: 10.1016/J.ENERGY.2018.09.131.

[85] O. Yucel, E. S. Aydin, and H. Sadikoglu, "Comparison of the different artificial neural networks in prediction of biomass gasification products," *Int. J. Energy Res.*, vol. 43, no. 11, pp. 5992–6003, Sep. 2019, doi: https://doi.org/10.1002/er.4682.

[86] D. Baruah, D. C. Baruah, and M. K. Hazarika, "Artificial neural network based modeling of biomass gasification in fixed bed downdraft gasifiers," *Biomass and Bioenergy*, vol. 98, pp. 264–271, Mar. 2017, doi: 10.1016/j.biombioe.2017.01.029.

[87] S. Safarian, S. M. Ebrahimi Saryazdi, R. Unnthorsson, and C. Richter, "Artificial neural network integrated with thermodynamic equilibrium modeling of downdraft biomass gasification-power production plant," *Energy*, vol. 213, p. 118800, Dec. 2020, doi: 10.1016/J.ENERGY.2020.118800.

[88] S. Shiva Kumar and V. Himabindu, "Hydrogen production by PEM water electrolysis – A review," *Mater. Sci. Energy Technol.*, vol. 2, no. 3, pp. 442–454, Dec. 2019, doi: 10.1016/j.mset.2019.03.002.

[89] K. Maeda, "Z-Scheme Water Splitting Using Two Different Semiconductor Photocatalysts," *ACS Catal.*, vol. 3, no. 7, pp. 1486–1503, Jul. 2013, doi: 10.1021/cs4002089.

[90] A. T. Montoya and E. G. Gillan, "Enhanced Photocatalytic Hydrogen Evolution from Transition-Metal Surface-Modified TiO 2," *ACS Omega*, vol. 3, no. 3, pp. 2947–2955, Mar. 2018, doi: 10.1021/acsomega.7b02021.

[91] H. H. Do et al., "Recent progress in TiO2-based photocatalysts for hydrogen evolution reaction: A review," *Arab. J. Chem.*, vol. 13, no. 2, pp. 3653–3671, Feb. 2020, doi: 10.1016/j.arabjc.2019.12.012.

[92] N. R. Reddy et al., "Photocatalytic hydrogen production by ternary heterojunction composites of silver nanoparticles doped FCNT-TiO2," *J. Environ. Manage.*, vol. 286, p. 112130, May 2021, doi: 10.1016/j.jenvman.2021.112130.

[93] Z. Zhu, C.-T. Kao, B.-H. Tang, W.-C. Chang, and R.-J. Wu, "Efficient hydrogen production by photocatalytic water-splitting using Pt-doped TiO 2 hollow spheres under visible light," *Ceram. Int.*, vol. 42, no. 6, pp. 6749–6754, May 2016, doi: 10.1016/j.ceramint.2016.01.047.

[94] Y. Cui, H. Du, and L. Wen, "Origin of visible-light-induced photocatalytic properties of S-doped anatase TiO2 by first-principles investigation," *Solid State Commun.*, vol. 149, no. 15–16, pp. 634–637, Apr. 2009, doi: 10.1016/j.ssc.2009.01.021.

[95] M.-Y. Xie, K.-Y. Su, X.-Y. Peng, R.-J. Wu, M. Chavali, and W.-C. Chang, "Hydrogen production by photocatalytic water-splitting on Pt-doped TiO2–ZnO under visible light," *J. Taiwan Inst. Chem. Eng.*, vol. 70, pp. 161–167, Jan. 2017, doi: 10.1016/j.jtice.2016.10.034.

[96] M. Wang, Y. Zeng, G. Dong, and C. Wang, "Br-doping of g-C3N4 towards enhanced photocatalytic performance in Cr(VI) reduction," *Chinese J. Catal.*, vol. 41, no. 10, pp. 1498–1510, Oct. 2020, doi: 10.1016/S1872-2067(19)63435-2.

[97] W. Yan, L. Yan, and C. Jing, "Impact of doped metals on urea-derived g-C3N4 for photocatalytic degradation of antibiotics: Structure, photoactivity and degradation mechanisms," *Appl. Catal. B Environ.*, vol. 244, pp. 475–485, May 2019, doi: 10.1016/j.apcatb.2018.11.069.

[98] W. Xing, G. Chen, C. Li, Z. Han, Y. Hu, and Q. Meng, "Doping effect of non-metal group in porous ultrathin g-C 3 N 4 nanosheets towards synergistically improved photocatalytic hydrogen evolution," *Nanoscale*, vol. 10, no. 11, pp. 5239–5245, 2018, doi: 10.1039/C7NR09161C.

[99] H. Mai, T. C. Le, D. Chen, D. A. Winkler, and R. A. Caruso, "Machine Learning for Electrocatalyst and Photocatalyst Design and Discovery," *Chem. Rev.*, vol. 122, no. 16, pp. 13478–13515, Aug. 2022, doi: 10.1021/acs.chemrev.2c00061.

[100] F. Cus and J. Balic, "Optimization of cutting process by GA approach," *Robot. Comput. Integr. Manuf.*, vol. 19, no. 1–2, pp. 113–121, Feb. 2003, doi: 10.1016/S0736-5845(02)00068-6.

[101] H. Kristmannsdóttir and H. Ármannsson, "Environmental aspects of geothermal energy utilization," *Geothermics*, vol. 32, no. 4–6, pp. 451–461, Aug. 2003, doi: 10.1016/S0375-6505(03)00052-X.

[102] R. Shortall, B. Davidsdottir, and G. Axelsson, "Geothermal energy for sustainable development: A review of sustainability impacts and assessment frameworks," *Renew. Sustain. Energy Rev.*, vol. 44, pp. 391–406, Apr. 2015, doi: 10.1016/J.RSER.2014.12.020.

[103] G. W. Huttrer, "Geothermal power generation in the world 2015-2020 update report," *Proc. World Geotherm. Congr.*, 2020.

[104] R. DiPippo, *Geothermal Power Plants: Principles, Applications, Case Studies and Environmental Impact.* Butterworth-Heinemann, 2012.

[105] S. Y. Pan, M. Gao, K. J. Shah, J. Zheng, S. L. Pei, and P. C. Chiang, "Establishment of enhanced geothermal energy utilization plans: Barriers and strategies," *Renew. Energy*, vol. 132, pp. 19–32, Mar. 2019, doi: 10.1016/J.RENENE.2018.07.126.

[106] L. Gerber and F. Maréchal, "Environomic optimal configurations of geothermal energy conversion systems: Application to the future construction of Enhanced Geothermal Systems in Switzerland," *Energy*, vol. 45, no. 1, pp. 908–923, Sep. 2012, doi: 10.1016/J.ENERGY.2012.06.068.

[107] S. Borović and I. Marković, "Utilization and tourism valorisation of geothermal waters in Croatia," *Renew. Sustain. Energy Rev.*, vol. 44, pp. 52–63, Apr. 2015, doi: 10.1016/J.RSER.2014.12.022.

[108] L. Belenguer, "AI bias: exploring discriminatory algorithmic decision-making models and the application of possible machine-centric solutions adapted from the pharmaceutical industry," *AI Ethics*, Feb. 2022, doi: 10.1007/s43681-022-00138-8.

[109] L. Cheng, F. Liu, and D. D. Yao, "Enterprise data breach: causes, challenges, prevention, and future directions," *Wiley Interdiscip. Rev. Data Min. Knowl. Discov.*, vol. 7, no. 5, p. e1211, Sep. 2017, doi: 10.1002/widm.1211.

[110] A. Sharma, A. Jain, A. Kumar Arya, and M. Ram, Eds., *Artificial Intelligence for Signal Processing and Wireless Communication.* De Gruyter, 2022.

[111] IRENA, "World energy transitions outlook," *Irena*, pp. 1–54, 2021, [Online]. Available: https://irena.org/publications/2021/March/World-Energy-Transitions-Outlook.

Chapter 2

Recent Advancements in Artificial Intelligence and Machine Learning in Sustainable Energy Management

Chiranjit Biswas, Abanishwar Chakraborti, and Swanirbhar Majumder

CONTENTS

2.1 INTRODUCTION

In recent days the urban populations of the countries are increasing day by day because the young generations are coming to urban areas to get jobs. Due to the job-seeking generation, the urban areas are increasing and carbon emission is also increasing due to the use of more power. The demand for electricity is also increasing due to the increase in users. In recent days the main challenge is to maintain the carbon emission and fulfill the power demand. Conventional power generation plants are using fossil fuels for generating electricity which is the cause of the emission of greenhouse gases in the environment, because of greenhouse gases the atmosphere temperature is increasing continuously. Renewable energy sources are less effective for the environment. Renewable energies are economically beneficial, green and clean energy, environment friendly and it is beneficial for human society development. The demand for the uses of renewable energy is increasing day by day because of the low-cost operation and ease

DOI: 10.1201/9781003356639-2

of installation [1]. To hold on to the environment, using clean renewable energy is best. Demand for renewable energies due to the negative effect of conventional energy sources and their involvement in climate change. Due to the influence of this conventional energy source on the environment, interest in using electricity is shifting towards renewable sources [2]. Due to urbanization, the level of comfort, the growing population, and construction the requirement and demand for energy sources of electricity are continuously increasing worldwide. Conventional energy sources are the cause of the emission of sulfur oxides, carbon oxides, CO_2, nitrogen oxide, etc. The availability of renewable energy sources is suitable for power generation in many countries [3]. Using the optimization models is beneficial for renewable energy management systems. Predicting models are helpful for the prediction, forecasting, and optimization techniques of energy management systems.

2.2 LITERATURE SURVEY

Here we are reviewing some papers of others who are working on the advanced energy management system:

Zhou Wu, Zhile Yang, Gan Luo,Kang Li, Yuanjun Guo and Yusheng Xue have discussed the prediction models for forecasting wind energy. The main prediction models are based on the RNN, DBN, CNN, etc. but prediction models have their own disadvantages and advantages under various prediction tasks. Like the CNN models are good for bring out the multiplex time-series correlation and the RNN is good for bring out time-series dependencies, the advanced neural network is developed for the forecasting of wind energy [1].

Muhammad Fahim, Tuan-Vu Cao, Vishal Sharma, Trung Q. Duong, and Berk Canberk proposed a framework for the 5G-NG-RAN (5G-Next Generation-Radio Access Network) which is a model cloud-based for the analysis and understanding of wind farms. There are two components used in this model one is based on a (TCN) temporal convolutional neural network for wind speed forecasting and another is the forecasting of the speed of the wind for the prediction of power generation for a month. This framework gives the advantage of monitoring real-time wind turbines. This framework uses the KNN regression and CNN for forecasting the power generation and speed of the wind. This framework supports the solution of sustainable energy and is also available for monitoring offshore farms of wind [2].

Janusz Jaglarz and Przemysław Korasiak are presenting a PVE (photovoltaic emulator) algorithm for the test and teaching of low voltage, single-phase photovoltaic inverter. the main aim is to emulate the characteristics of PV with high accuracy [3].

Bartosz Fetlinski, Piotr Kapler, Mirosław Parol, and Paweł Piotrowski are analyzing the 5-minute short-time PV system power generation. Verifying the input values, air temperature, wind speed, wind direction, and solar irradiance. Explain the ten reliable methods for short-time PV power generation [4].

Min Ding, Ibrahim Al-Wasabi, Zhijian Fang, Tarek Kandil, Hassan M. Hussein Farh, Abdullah M. Al-Shaalan, and Abdulrahman A. Al-Shamma'a present a new algorithm CSA-PID for tracking the PV (photovoltaic) global peak, modulating the converter duty cycle and tracking the speed of CSA (Cuckoo Search Algorithm) [5].

Kwok Tai Chui and Miltiadis D. Lytras overviewed the recent development of renewable energy with AI and ML (machine learning). The development of renewable energy is helpful for energy users [6].

Muhannad Alaraj, Ibrahim Alsaidan, and Mohammad Rizwan developed a model of solar energy forecasting for a short time. Here the ground is used for forecasting the energy. It is helpful for the energy storage control and management system for the grid connection [7].

Sami G. Al-Ghamdi, Muammar Koc, mar Alrawi, and Islam Safak Bayram are analyzing the system of energy storage of PV systems. PV energy charging and discharging management. Analysis of the energy data in various areas [8].

Benjamin Bowler, Mojgan Hojabri, Govinda Upadhyay, and Samuel Kellerhals are investigating the eight various faults for the performance check of the classification and fault detection. They check that the training data changed during the various weather conditions [9].

Innocent Ewan Davidson, Akinyemi Ayodeji Stephen, and Kabeya Musasa proposed a method of IC+IR to the extract highest output value of the PV array. The main aim is to track the accurate value. the proposed model is decreasing the output voltage oscillation of solar PV [10].

Rajasekar Natarajan and Ezhilmaran Ranganathan represent an SHO (Spotted Hyena Optimizer) algorithm for the tracking of the highest power at short-term and global peaks. It is helpful for power storage savings [11].

David Haughton, Lauren Burnham-King, Andres L. Su arez-Cetrulo, and Ricardo Simon Carbajo are presenting work on forecasting the wind power for power mapping and training the data set, and to get accurate values for power storage. Through this method, the expected power is known easily [12].

Huanxin Chen, Tanveer Ahmad, Yonghua Song, Dongdong Zhang, Hongcai Zhang, Ningyi Dai, and Chao Huang are analyzing the development of AI with energy. They discuss the use of AI in demand management, supply chain, and power generation [13].

Eng. Mariam Aerabe, Dr. Ahmed Al-Gindy, Eng. Aya Al-Chikh Omar and Dr. Ziad Elkhatib are analyzing the recent development in technologies which is helpful for sustainable cities. They discuss the IoT (Internet of Things), intelligence systems, control systems, AI, etc. they analyze the difficulties and challenges of sustainable cities [14].

Chiranjit Biswas, Swanirbhar Majumder, and Jayanta Pal are exploring the optimization of energy systems with quantum computing and different challenges. The smart energy system, smart grid security, and process of energy production also discuss here. This study will be helpful for those readers who are working on the optimization of energy management systems [15].

From the above review, we find that the authors use different algorithms for the optimization of energy management like supervised learning, reinforced learning, deep learning, etc.

2.3 DIFFERENT FORMS OF SUSTAINABLE ENERGY

There are many types of sustainable sources of energy surroundings of us but the major source is solar, wind, geothermal, hydropower, biomass, wood waste and wood, solid waste, biodiesel, ethanol, biogas, etc. The generated power from the sources of wind and solar energy are used in maximum are in many countries as renewable energy.

2.3.1 Solar Energy/Solar Farms

In a photovoltaic cell, electricity is produced through solar radiation. The photovoltaic cell is built with p-type and n-type semiconductors. The current carriers are generated through the solar radiation fluxes which are pairs of electron-hole. When the current carriers separate then the voltage is generated, then the current flows through the external circuit. The current produced in a single photovoltaic cell is very low. But the photovoltaic (PV) panel has a huge number of series or parallel connected photovoltaic cells. The electricity generated from the PV panels is enough for the demand of supply. More numbers of connected cells do not change the characteristics of output, but the (ISC) short-circuit current and VOC (open circuit voltage) shift to larger values. It means the generated voltage and current are dependent on the PV panel surface, solar flux, radiation, etc. [3]. The solar irradiance and temperature of a cell are one of the main parameters which affect the photovoltaic system; if the temperature is increased then the PR (performance ratio) and voltage of the open circuit are decreased. Spectral effects cause bandgap losses and heating of PV modules [4–9,16]. Photovoltaic cells are provided dc sources of voltage. It is also expressed as a forwarding diode and fixed current source parallel connection; the photon current is proportional to the area of the photovoltaic cell [5–11,16]. It is easy to include solar PV cells in a panel due to the demand response, there are many types of solar cell installation methods like rooftop installation (there are groups of solar panels), solar farms (there are arrays of solar panel groups), etc.

2.3.2 Wind Energy

The atmospheric movement is called wind; it is solar energy's featured form. When create difference in atmospheric pressure then the air goes to an area of lower to higher pressure. It is caused by three events: the earth's rotation, irregularities in the earth's surface, and the earth's atmosphere heating due to the sun. When the air flows through the turbine blades then the blade creates the difference in pressure and produces drag and lift. When the drag is weaker than the lift then the rotor rotates to produce the electricity. If p denotes the wind power, ρ denotes air density, V is wind speed, A is wind turbine swept area then the wind power is

$$p = (1/2) \ \rho A V 3 \qquad (2.1)$$

Accurate wind speed produces higher power [1–12,16].

Figure 2.1 show both wind and solar energy management system which are sources of renewable energy.

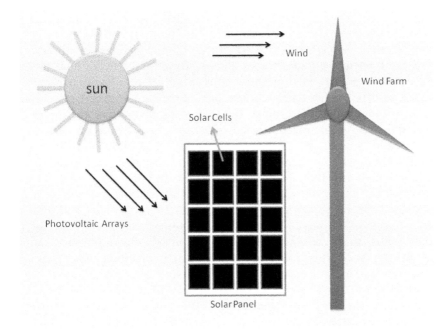

Figure 2.1 Solar panels and wind turbines.

2.4 SUSTAINABLE ENERGY MANAGEMENT

The sustainable development progress in energy is the main motive of the whole world because it is related to the economic, environmental, cultural, etc. In recent days the demand for energy is increasing due to the increase of population, industries, domestic lifestyle etc. Because of this, the sustainable development progress in energy is increased due to the increase in energy demand. The management of energy is essential for the losses of energy in many fields, carbon emission from many conventional generating units, heating and cooling systems, buildings, industry, forestry, agriculture, etc. [6,16]. Sources of renewable energy are the best option to fulfill the demand of conventional sources of energy. The main motives of the management of sustainable energy are advances in renewable energy to focus on the neutrality of carbon and electrification, energy transition solutions extend the area of research with new findings and approaches for urban performance optimizing, cooling, and heating of electric vehicles and districts. The main aim of the technology of wind power systems is to predict the proper speed of wind; the heat engines analyze the waste heat of low-temperature. There are many types of energy management systems like controlling the wastewater sources combustion model for biomass gasification, to prevent thermal runaway and produce green hydrogen using battery cycling. In recent days renewable energy behaves as an alternative to conventional energy. The main focus of energy management is harvesting the efficiency and reliability of energy. There are some other topics to focus is acoustic energy, vibration energy, and energy of water waves. Present days every person have their own personal phone, so cloud storage is more familiar to Smartphone; because of this the big data, storage, and processing of smart grids are easy to manage with Smartphone. Because of all advantages, the interest in using the fuel is decreased. And also increase the use of hybrid electric vehicles and sources of renewable energy [7]. The main aim of solar power technologies is to predict the performance of photovoltaic (pv) modules under critical temperature distribution and operating conditions, also check the data-driven and photovoltaic (pv) module hotspots, learn about the compact design of thermo-chemical energy storage and granular materials properties. Forecasted measurements of solar energy give proper guidance to decision-makers, system operators, and electric participants for proper management and effective planning. Choose the Forecasted horizon for ensuring the performance of applications. If the generated power of PV plant is known through forecasting, then it is an advancement for the power distribution company to exceed the power, and also helpful for the customer to save power and control local over-voltage [8].

2.5 RECENT ADVANCEMENTS IN ENERGY MANAGEMENT USING AI AND ML

The rapid development in engineering and computer science enables the adaptation of AI algorithms in different applications of energy systems. The energy systems aim to develop the recent advance in sustainable and smart energy system applications.

The basic aims of the energy management system are as follows: applications and theories of the algorithm of ML of smart grid developed the design and applications and design of deep learning for the smart grid, for smart grids use various optimization algorithms, for metering infrastructure using AI, for load monitoring use disaggregation techniques, simulation and modelling for smart grid, analytics of data-driven (prescriptive, predictive and diagnostic, descriptive) for smart grid, smart grid and Internet of Things (IoT), For security use AI techniques, demand response for smart grid, predictive maintenance, and Fraud detection, interoperability for smart grid, management approach of peak load for smart grid, manage the smart grid using cloud computing, development, design, and application of vehicle-to-grid.

2.5.1 Solar Related Methodological Approaches

There are various methodological approaches for the different applications related to the solar system: ANN (artificial neural network algorithm) uses for SYM (Static Young's Modulus) estimation for rheological properties, prediction (calcium chloride brine-based mud) and sandstone formation, conditional random fields of linear-chain are used for energy disaggregation, concatenate CNN (convolutional neural network) used for energy disaggregation, faster region-CNN (convolutional neural network) used for the power transmission insulation detection and images of transformation inspection, for the electric grid price and load used the logistic regression, for energy disaggregation used the decision tree and memory of long short time, algorithm of distributed genetics is used in the wireless sensor network applications, for optimizing the energy consumption of residentially used flower pollination and optimization of bacterial foraging, in energy disaggregation used the multiple kernel learning, genetic algorithm, support vector machine [7].

For solar energy forecasting, the basic model for the prediction of energy and irradiation is a fuzzy logic algorithm, the fuzzy logic algorithm is used fuzzy variables like very high, high, moderate, low, and very low and these are represented by the membership functions. And the ANN is used the connecting the simple units together working simultaneously. Solar energy forecasting is helpful for the making of predicting models and it is decreasing the error of percentage [8].

2.5.2 Related Models of Predicting Algorithms

There are various models for the predicting algorithms: The integrated CSA (Cuckoo Search Combined) with PID technique has a fast combination for catching the PV systems GP. The inputs of the CSA system are used for PV SYSTEM current and voltage. The error percentage is gained by using the CSA and using the proper value of the duty cycle to increase the efficiency of the system efficiency. This system provides the opportunity to work with very low oscillation [5]. The persistence model is the simplest one which needs few periods of values, multiple linear regression models (are the linear models which adopt a linear union between the multiple inputs and single inputs), K-Nearest Neighbors Regression (this method is used in classification tasks and regression, where the output is the objective property value), MLP-type ANN (it is the popular method which is based on the hidden layers and output layers, this method used the algorithm of back-propagation in the process of supervised learning), Regression of Support Vector model (it is based on the several hyper-parameter), Interval Fuzzy Logic System of Type-2(it is the extension of fuzzy set-1, for the computational complexity it is used in the practice), Random Forest Regression(it is based on the single decision tree instead of the value of average target), Gradient-Boosted Trees for Regression (it is the combination of weak learners), weighted Averaging Ensemble [9]. The PVE (photovoltaic emulator) model is the modified voltage/current stabilizer. This emulated model has the ability to emulate the V-I curves. Works of this PVE depend on the operation mode, and dependency on the mode of operation this model works as likewise a voltage or current stabilizer. NN (neural network) is able to detect the various PV faults, the accuracy of classification is too accurate but for the building and pole shading, the accuracy is not satisfactory. To track the top PowerPoint the integral (IC+IR) (incremental conductance and integral regulator) strategy is useful and also useful for the maximize the PV system output. This (IC+IR) strategy prevents the system from high phase voltage/current surge, grid fault, and faults of solar PV panels. It is also provided stability of grid voltage, solar temperature, and irradiance [10]. The determined playback period is used to examine the economic viability of PV systems. The decay rate affecting materials are the PV panels, installation site, the weather, and installation type. For the unconstrained and constrained optimization problems use the best algorithm is swarm-based SHO (Spotted-Hyena Optimizer), the main advancement is fast convergence, avoidance of settlement of local power, and the convergence time is optimum [11].

2.5.3 Wind System Related Methodological Approaches

There are various methodological approaches for the different applications related to the wind system: Wind speed forecasting is the main issue the wind power systems. the methods of wind forecasting are five types:

physical method, persistence method, method of conventional statistical, shallow structure method of ML, with deep structure method of ML (deep learning) [1]. There is a new modern deep neural network approach the TCN (temporal convolutional neural) network, the data stream of wind speed is used as input in TCN; it gives better results since the sequence modelling. TCN is a combination of residual block and dilated convolution power, it also predicts the power generation with an easy algorithm (k-nearest neighbor regression) [12]. The forecasting-based AI (artificial intelligence) techniques are used for forecasting wind power. There are many supervised techniques used in the SVR (Support Vector Regression), NN (Neural Networks), switching models of Markov, Bayesian approaches, genetic algorithms, fuzzy logic systems, and ensemble systems. there are many deep learning methods applied for the wind power system a convolutional neural network (CNN), recurrent neural network (RNN), restricted Boltzmann machine (RBM), the other networks of generative adversarial are extreme learning machine (ELM), stacked denoising auto-encoders (SDAE), stacked auto-encoder (SAE), etc. Multilayer Perceptron, Feed-Forward Neural Networks, and many newest approaches used ELM (Extreme Learning Machines), RNN (Recurrent Neural Networks), and LSTMs (Long-Short Memory Networks) for very short-term and short-term forecasting. CNNs (Convolutional Neural Networks) are used for the features exhibition of wind power of time series. All these algorithms used for forecasting wind power are Bagging Neural Networks, Random Forest, Adaptive Boosting, and Gradient Boosting Machines. With diversity adding to the improving the accuracy of forecasting, hybrid models are integrating the above algorithms, and optimization algorithms, and cover the unsupervised and supervised algorithms combinations [14].

Quantum computing-based approaches are helpful for energy systems. There are many algorithms to solve the problems like Integer Quadratic Fractional Program, Mixed-integer Linear Program, Improved Radial Basis Function Networks, Mixed-integer Quadratic Program, and many more. The quantum computer is comfortable with prediction problems. If the power of quantum computer is increased then it handles large-scale optimization problems [15].

Figure 2.2 shows that the papers are based on different AI algorithms. The bright evolution of the energy system of renewable energy sources with AI and ML is helpful for predicting energy uses. From the above discussion, it is clear that the price of renewable energy sources is not able to compute with conventional sources because the sources of renewable energy are not constant. There is a need to forecast accurate air quality, solar irradiance, temperature, weather condition, etc. There is an opportunity for renewable energy with AI to give operating independence with microgrids and distributed energy sources.

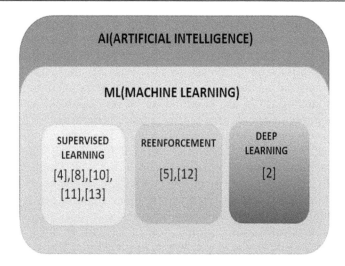

Figure 2.2 Papers related to different AI algorithms.

2.6 PROS AND CONS OF CURRENT SCENARIO

Renewable energy has advantages and it has disadvantages. Renewable energy is helpful for those areas where the bigger power plant is not easy to set up, it is more cost efficient than other conventional sources of energy, it is eco-friendly, easy to use and if have a good storage system then it is used for supplying to others. There are some challenges to the current scenario of renewable energy: It is too difficult to find the win power accurate resources and improve penetration of wind. Real-time monitoring is not easy to predict. Predict the wind power. Ensure stable and safe power system operation. To maintain the demand for power supply while Connection between wind power and the grid [1,2]. To enhance the efficiency and accuracy of the PV characteristics [3]. To increase the horizon of forecast and examine the error of forecast. Decrease the operating cast, separate series of time [4]. Modulating the converter duty cycle, tracking the PV global peak (pk), increases the speed of the search algorithms [5]. Store the energy and detect the energy consumption [9]. Fault detection (PID fault, connector fault, activated bypass diode /condition of partial shading, condition of pole shading, condition of building shading, soiling, short circuit, glass breakage, classification, normal condition). Reducing the oscillation in the output voltage of solar [10]. Tracking the highest power in a short time and global peak [11].

2.7 CONCLUSION

Renewable energy is an alternative source to conventional sources. The demand for renewable energy is increasing day by day because of its efficient characteristics. This paper discusses solar and wind power renewable energies and their applications, loopholes, and energy management system; because these power sources are the elite renewable energy sources. This paper provides the proper information about energy management systems and also discusses energy management algorithms. the pros and cons of renewable energy are discussed which are helpful for further studies, due to this discussion it is easy to know what challenges are faced by the AI and ML algorithms while it is used.

REFERENCES

[1] Z. Wu, G. Luo, Z. Yang, Y. Guo, K. Li, Y. Xue, "A comprehensive review on deep learning approaches in wind forecasting applications," *CAAI Transactions on Intelligence Technology*, vol. 7(2), pp. 129–143. 2021.

[2] M. Fahim, V. Sharma, T. V. Cao, B. Canberk, T. Q. Duong, "Machine learning-based digital twin for predictive modeling in wind turbines," *IEEE Access*, vol. 10, pp. 14184–14194, 2022.

[3] P. Korasiak, J. Jaglarz, "A new photovoltaic emulator designed for testing low-power inverters connected to the LV grid," *Energies*, vol. 15(7), pp. 2646, 2022.

[4] P. Piotrowski, M. Parol, P. Kapler, B. Fetliński, "Advanced forecasting methods of 5-minute power generation in a PV system for microgrid operation control," *Energies*, vol. 15(7), pp. 2645, 2022.

[5] I. Al-Wesabi, Z. Fang, H. M. Farh, A. A. Al-Shamma'a, A. M. Al-Shaalan, T. Kandil, M. Ding, "Cuckoo search combined with PID controller for maximum power extraction of partially shaded photovoltaic system," *Energies*, vol. 15(7), pp. 2513, 2022.

[6] M. D. Lytras, K. T. Chui. "The recent development of artificial intelligence for smart and sustainable energy systems and applications," *Energies*, vol. 12 (16), pp. 3108, 2019.

[7] I. Alsaidan, M. Rizwan, M. Alaraj, "Solar energy forecasting using intelligent techniques: A step towards sustainable power generating system," *Journal of Intelligent & Fuzzy Systems*, vol. 42(2), pp. 885–896, 2022.

[8] O. Alrawi, I. S. Bayram, M. Koc, S. G. Al-Ghamdi, "Economic viability of rooftop photovoltaic systems and energy storage systems in Qatar," *Energies*, vol. 15(9), pp. 3040, 2022.

[9] M. Hojabri, S. Kellerhals, G. Upadhyay, B. Bowler, "IoT-based PV array fault detection and classification using embedded supervised learning methods," *Energies*, vol. 15 (6), pp. 2097, 2022.

[10] A. A. Stephen, K. Musasa, I. E. Davidson, "Modelling of solar PV under varying condition with an improved incremental conductance and integral regulator," *Energies*, vol. 15 (7), pp. 2405, 2022.

[11] E. Ranganathan, R. Natarajan, "Spotted hyena optimization method for harvesting maximum PV power under uniform and partial-shade conditions," *Energies*, vol. 15 (8), pp. 2850, 2022.

[12] A. L. Suárez-Cetrulo, L. Burnham-King, D. Haughton, R. S. Carbajo, "Wind power forecasting using ensemble learning for day-ahead energy trading," *Renewable Energy*, vol. 191, pp. 685–698, 2022.

[13] T. Ahmad, D. Zhang, C. Huang, H. Zhang, N. Dai, Y. Song, H. Chen, "Artificial intelligence in sustainable energy industry: Status Quo, challenges and opportunities," *Journal of Cleaner Production*, vol. 289, p. 125834, 2021.

[14] A. Al-Gindy, A. A. Omar, M. Aerabe, Z. ElKhatib, "Conceptualizing smart sustainable cities: Crossing visions and utilizing resources in Africa," *International Journal of Advanced Computer Science and Applications*, vol. 12 (5), 2021.

[15] C. Biswas, J. Pal, S. Majumder, "An overview of quantum computing approach in the present-day energy systems," *Advances in Smart Energy Systems*, pp. 39–54, 2023.

[16] S. Kılıç, G. Krajačić, N. Duić, M. A. Rosen, "Accelerating mitigation of climate change with sustainable development of energy, water and environment systems," *Energy Conversion and Management*, vol. 245, pp. 114606, 2021.

Chapter 3

Role of Machine Learning in Renewable Energy

*A. Subarna Kiruthiga, S. Arunkumar, R. Thirisha, and
J. Felicia Lilian*

CONTENTS

3.1 INTRODUCTION

Renewable energy sources have existed since the beginning of civilization; however, only in recent decades has technology been a primary focus as people's concerns about energy shortages and the threat of climate change have started growing [1]. Only from the beginning of the 1970s, did all the renewable energy sources have started to grow dramatically [2]. The oil crisis of 1973 and 1979, as most people point out, was the driving force for why they first began to think more seriously about renewable energy [1]. Throughout history, numerous renewable resources have been discovered. In 200 BC, for example, Waterwheels were discovered [1]. They were the first type of hydropower, converting the energy of moving water into mechanical or electrical energy. At the end of the sixteenth century, windmills came into existence [2].

Windmills were at their peak in popularity in the Netherlands by the 1950s. These were a little like the highly technical wind turbines of today [3]. Various renewable energy systems, solar cells, and wind turbines were established in the mid-nineteenth century [2]. After the invention of the wind turbine at the end of the nineteenth century, there was a great deal of interest both in and out of Europe [3]. In 1888, a year after the invention of a wind turbine, the first windmill to generate electricity was invented on a farm in Cleveland [3]. In the twentieth century, the Hoover Dam was built, and solar power was used as a backup power source for a US satellite. Let us now observe the need for renewable energy after reviewing its history [1].

One of the significant characteristics of renewable energy is its plentiful supply [1]. It is limitless. As Renewable energy sources have an almost negligible environmental impact, they are also termed clean energy sources. Renewable energy is ecologically sound when compared to fossil fuels [2]. Renewable energy sources do not release harmful gases for energy production, unlike fossil fuels [1]. This poses a significant risk of global warming caused by the interaction of hydrocarbons, oil, and methane gas [2]. So, it is recommended that we move to renewable energy sources which are cleaner and do not discharge pollutants and hazardous gases [3]. This shift needs to be accelerated as fossil fuels are non-renewable and thus come to an end at some point in the future [3].

Renewable energy releases an almost negligible amount of hydrocarbons and thus helps to combat the climatic and environmental changes caused by the use of fossil fuels [2]. It is worth noting that a classic solar PV system can save between one and a half to two tonnes of CO_2 per year [3]. The usage of fossil fuels and other nonrenewable sources can be considered risky as the reserves of coal and natural gas are buried deep underground or available under the oceans [3]. Therefore making it is difficult to find a new reserve after one becomes exhausted. Contrastingly, the availability of renewable energy sources like wind and sunlight is a surplus [1]. As the cost of renewable energy is independent of the price of coal and natural gas keeps on fluctuating, it can be of great use to mankind by lowering the price of electricity [2]. It equalizes the overall cost of energy consumption [1].

3.2 MACHINE LEARNING

With the use of machine learning (ML), which is a form of artificial intelligence (AI), software programs attempt to mimic how people learn and may anticipate outcomes more precisely without having to be specifically instructed to do so [3]. The first mathematical model of neural networks published in a scholarly publication in 1943 marks the beginning of the history of ML. A groundbreaking foundation of machine-learning research, Donald Hebb's thoughts on how behavior relates to neural networks and brain activity, were presented in a book in 1949 [1]. Alan Turing develops the "Turing Test" in 1950 to evaluate if a system possesses true intelligence. A computer must be able to deceive a person into thinking it is also human to pass the test. The perceptron, the first neural network for computers that mimics the workings of the human brain, was created in 1957 [2]. In 1967, the "nearest neighbor" method was developed. Neocognitron, a hierarchical multilayered network designed to identify patterns and the precursor of convolutional neural networks, the modern systems used mostly for image analysis, was developed by Kunihiko Fukushima and published [1]. The Stanford cart project, which has been in development since the 1960s, made significant progress in 1979. It was a robotic device that could be controlled remotely and navigate the environment in three dimensions [3]. In 1990, boosting algorithm was and in 1995 Random decision forests were introduced. In 2011, the deep neural network of Google Brain evolved, enabling it to find and classify items in a manner similar to that of a cat. In the Go tournament in 2016, the AlphaGo algorithm created by Google DeepMind was successful in winning five of the five games. One of the most popular uses of ML is image identification [1]. Face recognition and human identification in photos are handled by a Facebook initiative called "Deep Face." When using Google, we have the option to "Search by voice," which falls under speech recognition and is a well-known machine-learning application [2]. Speech recognition technology is used by Alexa, Google Assistant, Siri, Cortana, and Microsoft Cortana to carry out voice commands. Amazon, Netflix, and other e-commerce and entertainment businesses frequently utilize ML to propose products to users [2]. By identifying fraudulent transactions, ML makes our online transactions safe and secure. The Feed Forward Neural Network assists us by determining if the transaction is legitimate or fraudulent. This function is offered by Google's GNMT (Google Neural Machine Translation), which uses neural ML to automatically convert text into our native tongue [3].

3.3 RENEWABLE ENERGY

Even though the sources of renewable energy are naturally replenishing, they are bounded [2]. The output energy of renewable sources that is obtainable

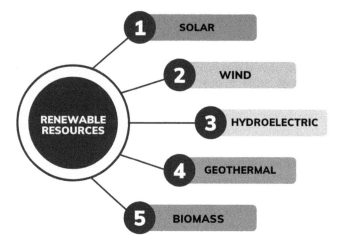

Figure 3.1 Types of renewable energy sources.

per unit of time is restricted when compared to the immeasurable availability and lifespan of these sources [3]. Renewable energy sources can also be referred to as "alternative energy" [3]. The planet covers a wide variety of renewable resources [2]. The five primary types of renewable energy are classified in Figure 3.1.

The combustion of fossil fuels accounts for approximately 98 percent of carbon emissions [3]. The overall CO_2 production and emission level of pollutants can be brought down drastically by decreasing the use of fossil fuels. In the current times, the estimated cost of reducing carbon emissions has been raised accountably due to the availability of carbon-reducing and carbon-free technologies [3]. Such technologies include energy efficiency and conservation types of equipment.

The cost factors can be handled by reducing the overall energy consumption or by switching to alternative energy sources [2] (Table 3.1).

Table 3.1 Usage of renewable energy

Renewable Energy	Usage and energy alternatives
Solar Energy	Solar cooker, Solar home system, Dryer
Geothermal Energy	Power generation, Urban heating
Wind Energy	Windmill, Power generation
Hydrothermal Energy	Power generation, Barrage, Tidal stream
Biomass	Pyrolysis, Heat generation

3.4 SOLAR ENERGY

One of the abundant and marvelous resources giving all of its access to inhabitants in the sanitary form of renewable energy is the sun [4]. Catching the radiant energy of the sun and transforming it into heat, electricity, or hot water is how solar energy is created. In order to convert direct radiation into energy, photovoltaic systems employ solar cells [5,6]. More energy is sent to our planet by the sun in an hour than is used by all of humanity in a year. The input to the photovoltaic is solar energy and outputs the usage of electrical current. Solar energy is used wherever since it is generated by the sun, which illuminates the entire planet [7]. If batteries are used to store energy, solar electric systems may be disconnected from the utility grid, making them an affordable option for remote locations. Solar modules require less maintenance and provide electricity for a longer period of time because they don't have any moving parts and there is no need to drill, refine, or transport petroleum-based fuels to the area [8]. The potential to harness the unlimited supply of solar energy might render fossil fuels unnecessary. It also benefits the ecology and public health to use solar energy instead of fossil fuels [9].

3.4.1 Current Usage of Solar Energy

Most solar energy is used for water heaters and heating systems. Because we use hot water often every day, one of the finest applications of solar energy is to heat water. The popular home and commercial options include solar water heating, solar lighting, solar ventilation, and portable solar mobility [5]. Solar energy may be utilized for a number of functions, including heating, drying, cooking, and providing power in rural regions of India. It may also be found in satellites, calculators, large motor boats, cars, planes, and many other gadgets, making it perfect for city people [5]. Outdoor economical lighting, often known as security lights or flood lights, converts sunlight into electricity and may be utilized in the event of a power outage [4]. Chemical-using sectors like those in food, heated greenhouses, textiles, cow barns, and swimming pools may all profit from the heat produced by solar energy [8]. The battery chargers can be powered by stored energy at night after being charged during the day using sunlight. It is also possible to use solar energy to power electrical devices [5].

3.4.2 Role of ML in Solar Power Forecasting

In order to lessen the effects of solar variability, solar power forecasting is the process of gathering and gaining access to data to estimate the power consumed by a solar planet across a number of periods [8]. Solar power projections are used for power trading as well as to increase the effectiveness of the electric system. Issues of intermittency and dependability have

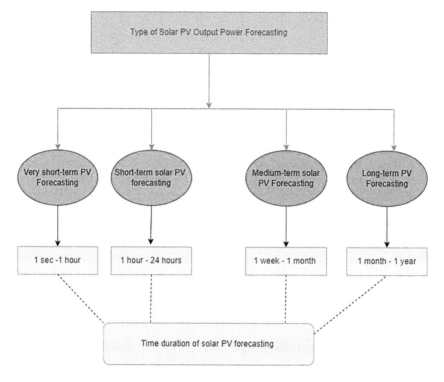

Figure 3.2 Types of PV forecasting.

come to the forefront as important impediments to the deployment of solar energy, such as resource pricing and a low conversion ratio, which continue to decrease [9]. Volatility has been addressed and controlled in a number of circumstances using solar forecasting. Predictions for solar energy often take into account the Sun's course, the state of the atmosphere, light scattering, and the features of the solar energy plant [8] (Figure 3.2).

Although there are many various approaches to dealing with the forecasting problem in the literature, one widely known methodology has been identified to classify the forecasting horizon into three groups so that applications can be differentiated conveniently [4]. These three forecasting techniques cover time periods from a few hours to a week, months, and years in the future. Forecasting in the very short and near term aids decision-making in grid operations and is beneficial to electric market regulators [8]. This technique makes use of predicted atmospheric resources from diverse time and geographical areas [9]. The numerical weather prediction model and the global forecast system are the two most common models utilized in this forecasting. Energy producers can engage with financial institutions involved in the distribution of energy, which is often done on a smaller scale, with the help of long-term forecasts [4]. Mesoscale

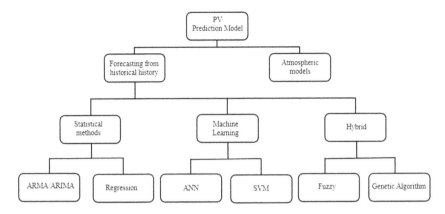

Figure 3.3 Methods of PV forecasting.

re-analyzed data is frequently fed into this method's models, and a range of statistical and machine-learning techniques are used to handle the result [9] (Figure 3.3).

Time series analysis may be used in the statistical approach of PV prediction to understand the behavior of observed data series or to estimate future values of these series. These techniques can be used to forecast PV electricity generation in the near future [7]. In the statistical techniques, regression models and autoregressive models are used. PV power generation is a dependent variable in regression models that are explained by meteorological data. For PV estimation utilizing temporal data, Auto Regressive Moving Average (ARMA) and Auto-Regressive Integrated Moving Average (ARIMA) are extensively used algorithms [7]. These methods show that the series' future values, often known as the series' history, are influenced by a mix of Auto-Regressive (AR) and Moving Average (MA) features [7].

Machine-learning approaches frequently need a substantial amount of data in order to provide an accurate estimate of PV energy generation. These are used in SPV Forecasting including Artificial Neural Networks (ANN), Multilayer Perceptron Type (MLP), and Support Vector Machines (SVM). ANNs are built using a mathematical model of the nervous system of humans. The great majority of investigations are done using MLP [7]. Nonlinear interactions between input and output data may be approximated using an MLP. ANN-based techniques for solar power prediction have sparked a lot of attention. SVM are supervised learning techniques for classification and regression issues [5].

They are used to estimate PV power using a time series analytic methodology, and there is rising interest in these methods. Hybrid models blend physical and statistical models in order to maximize the benefits of both techniques in order to improve PV power estimation accuracy [8]. Neuro-fuzzy systems, for example, integrate a neural network's supervised learning capability with a fuzzy inference system's knowledge representation.

Adaptive Neuro-Fuzzy Inference Systems (ANFIS) is a common term for this sort of system, and it has been used to estimate PV power [7]. The use of neural networks optimized using genetic algorithms, the use of ARMA models with neural networks, the union of several types of neural networks, and the combination of atmospheric models such as MM5 for radiation prediction with fuzzy logic or neural networks for power prediction are all examples of hybrid models [4].

Atmospheric models integrate the numerical forecast values of meteorological variables received from several meteorological institutions' numerical prediction systems. These inputs may also be supplemented by those mentioned in the preceding group. MM5 National Center for Atmospheric Research and WRF-NMM Atmospheric/National Centers for Environmental Prediction is the most extensively used models in this category [7].

3.5 WIND ENERGY

Wind energy is a unique renewable energy that captures wind energy at greater altitudes than traditional wind turbines using avian devices. Up to the centenary, there was no longer a systematic organization of automation. Although a variety of harvesting methods have been investigated, the most popular method is an avian device that conducts rapid crosswind movements and then passes the resulting driving force to a ground station through a cable [10].

The Knot is a twirl of the drum-generator module at the base station, which converts the driving force into electrical energy, when the device reaches its maximum knot length, the gadget's flight path is adjusted, and the knot is twirled back in, it is just using a little amount of the energy that was previously generated. This concludes the operation of a pumping wind energy system [11].

In comparison to horizontal wind turbines, wind energy systems have several advantages. In addition to significantly lesser material utilization for the tower construction as well as the foundations, as well as reduced transit costs, installation, and upkeep expenses. In classical wind turbines, the curving moment of the modernized laden rotors is shared with the base via the tower and foundation. One or more knots are used in wind energy systems to transfer forces of equal size. As a tensile structure, the design uses less material, resulting in reduced system costs and a smaller environmental imprint. It also enables dynamic modification of the operational height to accessible wind resources, as a result, the capacity factor has increased significantly [12].

The tip of the rotor blades creates about 30% of the power in a horizontal wind turbine, whereas the remainder of the rotor provides mostly a support framework for the blade's crosswind movement. It has a greater capacity factor, an wind energy system produces a greater annual production than horizontal wind turbines for the same rated power. The larger capacity factor is due to the wind being more consistent and persistent at higher elevations [10].

3.5.1 Current Use of Wind Energy

Wind turbines operate on a basic concept: rather than utilizing electricity to create wind, They create electricity using the wind. Wind shoves a turbine's shove-like blades around a rotor. It powers a generator and produces energy [11].

The wind is a type of solar energy produced by three concurrent events:

1. The sun heats the atmosphere unevenly.
2. Surface irregularities of the earth
3. The planet's rotation.

Patterns of the wind and the speeds vary greatly across the US and are influenced by bodies of water, flora, and adjustments in topography. Wind flow, or motion energy, is utilized by humans in a variety of ways, involving sailing, kite flying, and even energy generation.

Both wind energy and wind power refer to the process of generating mechanical or electrical energy from the wind. This mechanical power can be used for specific tasks or transformed into energy using a generator [11].

Wind turbine rotor blades transform wind energy into electricity using the same modified force as an airplane wing or a helicopter rotor blade. When the blade is blown across by the wind, One side's air pressure falls. The air pressure difference between the two sides of the blade causes lift and drag. The rotor rotates because the lift force exceeds the drag force. The rotor is connected to the generator either directly or indirectly, allowing for a smaller generator. When modernized force is converted to generator rotation, energy is produced [12].

3.5.2 Role of ML in Wind Energy

The goal of forecasting comprises wind speed, wind strength, wave duration, and wave intensity from several published research and It is also no longer rare to execute a thorough analytical procedure [12]. Meanwhile, The records used in forecasting may also include historical datasets from meteorological, remote sensing, and geographic records in wind speed, wind direction, wave top, wave period, and wave direction, as well as many corresponding factors with temperature, device parameters, weather condition, sea ground salinity, ocean depth, pressure, humidity, orographic and dynamic atmosphere as computation resources [12] (Figure 3.4).

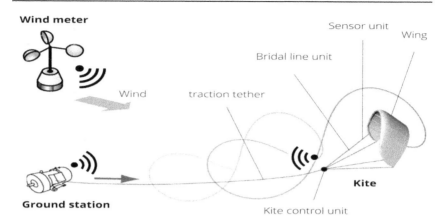

Figure 3.4 Working of wind energy.

Meanwhile, The dataset should include at least a one-time series, spatial, or remote sensing picture [12]. If the reviewed paper is a historical dataset with meteorological parameters, it is necessary to calculate the wave and wind strength predictions using equations using key parameters, including wave top, wave period, wind speed, wind turbine hub top, and device pitch attitude parameters [10].

Calculated electricity is much less variable and tough to create than without delay amassed or measured information. Indirect factors inclusive of temperature, salinity, pressure, and precipitation, on the other hand, are probably hired for forecasting and prediction, in addition to correlation investigation [11]. If the associated elements may be utilized for forecasting in place of parameters that are direct. It can be a valuable and useful strategy for anomalous information ease and version enhancement in terms of calculation and effort [10].

The 2D wind aircraft prediction changed into completed the usage of a mixed auto-encoder of CNN and LSTM, and the dataset utilized withinside the case take a look at included NREL gathered meteorological information from the Wind Integration National Dataset, that is housed from 2010 to 2012, a ten via way of means of 10 wind array changed into mounted in Indiana, USA [10]. The decision changed to finish in five minutes. Raw information changed used to create a series, which changed into then converted right into a two-hour time period [11]. The uncooked information is composed of a three-year span and yielded a complete of 1314,000 points. The percent of schooling information vs checking out information changed into The CNN-LSTM version is fed and assessed in a 4:1 ratio [11].

The dataset frequently becomes time-sensitive during collection [12]. Wave height, wind speed, air stress at sea level, floor temperature, floor wind speed/path, and instant most floor windspeed/path were used as

Table 3.2 Applications of wind energy

MODEL	APPLICATION	PROS
CNN	Wind speed/turbulent, offshore wind speed	Ability to develop an internal representation of a two-dimensional Image; feature extraction
RNN	Wind turbine data uncertainty, Wave energy period,	In short, It deals with time series data
LSTM	Wind Power, Wind farm cluster power, Wave Condition, Wind velocity	Processes long-term time series data
GRU	Wave height, Wind speed, Wind power	Less reminiscence than LSTM, easy to design faster, handles long-time period data; mitigates the vanishing gradient problem
DBN	Single variables forecasting	Good at unsupervised super extraction
HYBRID	Wind speed/power, wind scenario forecasting; typhoon hurricane forecasting; power system optimization; energy storage size optimization	

datasets and characteristic organization for the gated recurrent unit neural network (GRU) and CNN function and time collection extraction enter and used as wind-speed-prediction fashions and extended four wave-height-prediction fashions primarily based entirely on the effects of wind [12]. The contrast was obtained with input units: one comprised uncooked records from meteorological records and the large wave top dataset individually, whilst the opposite blanketed the primary institution with the outcomes of wind pace prediction models, respectively [12] (Table 3.2).

3.6 HYDROELECTRIC POWER

Using moving water to generate electricity is known as hydropower or hydroelectricity [13]. As a renewable energy source, hydroelectricity has become the most influential and accessible. Pumped storage hydroelectricity is the process by which water flows through a dam's turbines to generate electricity [14]. This process of energy production is called dumped-storage hydropower. The redirection pattern of flowing water or the difference in elevation created by the dam is used to generate hydroelectric power [13]. Hydropower is an environmentally friendly source of energy as it does not contribute to pollution. This energy can be promising as it acts as a backup power source during major power outages [13]. Other significant uses of hydroelectric power are irrigation support, flood control, and water control.

3.6.1 Current Use of Hydroelectric Power

Hydroelectric power is currently used for a variety of purposes, including generating clean electricity, managing flood risk, providing recreational facilities, enabling agricultural irrigation, and providing business benefits [14]. Turbines, dams, and rivers are considered the main component of hydroelectric power. The generation of electricity is the central usage of hydropower energy [14]. The hydropower plant uses the dams as a reservoir to store water.

It can be seen from a business perspective. They have favorable conditions for the hydro sites to be located as it is abundant and cheap [13]. As hydroelectric power is environmentally friendly, it has a major role in the clean energy scheme of these corporate companies [14]. One of the most significant community benefits of hydropower plants is that the facilities are required by law to be open to the public, and many plants offer a variety of recreational activities such as swimming, fishing, and boating [14].

Hydroelectric plants contribute to a major part of the prevention and control of flooding [4]. A single water body can be controlled easily in comparison to multiple water bodies. The availability of a dam makes the water body stored in a single place [4]. Hence, the maintenance and monitoring processes have become easier using damming. The possibility of flooding has dropped drastically as these dams have higher retention rates [13]. This can be proved with an example. In a district called Kaprun Ache placed in Australia, the probability of flooding has decreased from once every 10 years to once every 75 years [14]. This massive change happened due to the construction of a hydropower plant along with a reservoir.

3.6.2 Role of ML in Hydroelectric Energy

For the dataset prediction in the field of hydroelectric energy, various machine-learning methodologies are primarily used [14]. SVM, linear regression, ANN, support vector regression, clustering, and fuzzy clustering are some majorly used methodologies. These methodologies can be divided into "supervised learning" and "unsupervised learning" [14]. SVR, LR, and SVM fit into the category of "supervised learning", while clustering and fuzzy clustering fall into the category of "unsupervised learning" [14] (Figure 3.5).

The input and output variables are both obtainable in the supervised learning approach [14]. It is a machine-learning strategy in which an algorithm is used to map the input to the respective output. The name

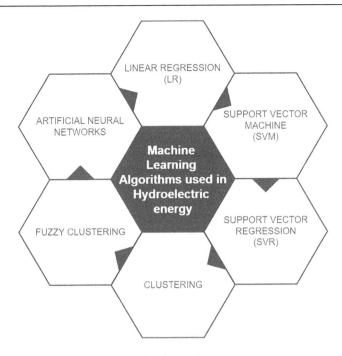

Figure 3.5 Various ML algorithms used in hydroelectric energy.

"supervised learning" is given to this approach as only trained datasets are given to this algorithm. When new input data is given, the algorithm must be able to obtain a decent approximation of the mapping function to allow the forecast of output variables [4].

To establish a relationship between dependent and independent variables, the LR best fit straight line is used [4]. Linear regression has only one input, whereas multivariate linear regression has numerous input variables. Some examples of applications of Linear regression in the hydropower field are annual streamflow trend assessment, hydropower generation projections, hydropower cascade, simulation, and control, as well as optimization [14].

Considering the long course of yearly water flow, a new approach to trend flow is designated by the annual streamflow trend assessment [4]. The current and future predictions of hydroelectric energy are improved by collaborating LR with a novel linear moving window approach. The existing and observed n years' predictions of annual flow are used as input. Improvement in the predictability of influx to the reservoir can be done by a modified SVM framework from the previous data [14]. In flow forecasting, genetic algorithms are used to optimize SVM parameters for daily flow forecasting [14].

A modified SVM model for investigating streamflow forecasting uses monthly streamflow forecasting. Streamflow forecasting uses a combination

Table 3.3 Role of ML algorithms in predicting hydroelectric energy

ML Algorithm	Role
LR	Annual streamflow trend assessment, Hydropower generation projections, Hydropower cascade, Control and optimisation
SVM	Streamflow forecasting, Flow forecasting, Streamflow forecasting
SVR	Hydropower consumption forecasting, Streamflow forecasting
Clustering	Hydro energy inflow forecasting, Streamflow forecasting
Fuzzy Cluster	Streamflow forecasting
ANN	Reservoir operation scheme, River streamflow forecasting, Reservoir runoff forecasting, Reservoir inflow, Reservoir storage

of SVM and various time series decomposition methods to improve streamflow estimation [14]. One of the main advantages of SVR is that its computational complexity is not dependent on the dimensionality of input space. Elevated forecasting precision and outstanding generalization potential are some of the features of SVM [13]. Hydropower consumption forecasting is an example of an application in which SVR is used instead of SVM. The SVM also shows a positive note in intricate time series predicting seasonality, even though it has set it the main objective to predict hydropower consumption [4]. After SVM, the clustering method is used to add values to the state of affairs tree node by segregating statistics into clusters [14]. The current real-time streamflow forecasting uses the clustering approach to produce its streamflow production for every month [14].

Assigning data to multiple clusters is known as fuzzy clustering. The streamflow production based on fuzzy clustering can also be used as an alternative to the clustering techniques [4]. The technique groups data patterns using fuzzy c-means clustering and classifies prediction patterns using fuzzy clustering [4]. The input and output relationship can be found accurately using ANNs [4]. For a single-unit hydropower plant, ANN has been used to map the enter facts for charge and influx at once to the most appropriate manufacturing styles [4]. The challenges associated with rainfall-runoff models' non-linearities are forecasted using the ANN technique. This technique is also used to forecast daily reservoir runoff [4].

It has been shown that combining particle swarm optimization with ANN has shown improved accuracy [4]. The ANN model results show a positive relationship with a fairly high correlation between actual and forecasted reservoir inflow [4] (Table 3.3).

3.7 BIOMASS

Biomass is considered a renewable biological source [15]. It acts as a base to the production of bioenergy. To understand bioenergy, the term biomass must be understandable [2]. It can be defined as a substance derived from biotic plants and organisms [15]. The most common and frequent application of biomass in the home is the use of a fireplace. There are numerous methods for generating energy from biomass [15]. Acquiring methane gas and burning biomass are such methods to generate energy from biomass. Methane gas can be obtained by the decay of organic or biotic ponds or landfill [16].

Biomass manufacturing in power generation produces Carbon dioxide which can be compensated by the restoration of vegetation, as it consumes identical amounts of CO_2 [15]. This mechanism provides equilibrium to the atmosphere. Biomass may be utilized in some extraordinary approaches in our day-by-day lives, now no longer handiest for private use, but for corporations as well [16].

3.7.1 Current Usage of Biomass

The use of products made from biomass has increased drastically [2]. We have started to use them unconsciously [16]. We do not realize that the daily products that we use, like skin care products, gasoline, and nutritional supply are made from biomass. Personal care products like shampoo, skin creams, and mascara are made from biobased feedstocks [16].

Fermenting plant sugar and palmitic acid produces acetone which is used in conditioners. It is considered to be the most saturated fatty acid found in biological organisms [16]. This conditioner provides silky and shiny hair [16].

Biomass is also used in the production of food additives and nutritional supplements [15]. Some companies produce nutrition supplements directly from algae by extracting omega-3 fatty acids. These supplements are found in fish oil. Renewable fuels are also being produced from algae oil [15].

3.7.2 Role of ML in Biomass Gasification

Some important dynamics in the biomass gasification process are temperature distribution, fuel flow rate, and equivalence ratio [16]. These factors are considered for the machine-learning module to run properly.

Dependent variables of biomass gasification are carbon dioxide, carbon monoxide, methane, hydrogen, and oxygen [16]. The regression technique in ML is fed with an independent variable where distance measure is used to predict the dependent variable levels, according to the similarity in the features [15]. Domination of large-valued features is prevented by normalizing the dataset with linear scaling in the scale-sensitive computation of metrics such as Euclidean or Manhattan distance [13]. The feature component with minimum and maximum variance in a given dataset can be found using Principal Component Analysis [14].

Aside from the algorithms mentioned above, a few others are used in the prediction process of biomass gasification. The best studying approach for increasing prediction trends on the basis of primary logical statements is the Decision Tree [14].

In addition to the machine-learning process, DTR can be used as a potential device to predict the biomass gasification process [16].

3.7.3 Role of ML in Biomass Production in the Wastewater Treatment System

The cultivation of carbohydrate-rich microalgae biomass in wastewater is considered a powerful method of producing biofuels [16]. Machine-learning algorithms are explored in order to create a model for predicting biomass production in treating wastewater [15]. Five machine-learning methods were used to model carbohydrates (Figure 3.6).

Both solar energy and inorganic compounds are converted and stored in the cyanobacteria [15]. They are photosynthetic prokaryotic microalgae. The intercommunication between the process of the microalgae growth and treatment of wastewater is compared to the internal metabolite accumulation such as carbs are anticipated using machine-learning techniques [16].

Carbohydrate accumulation and a sudden biomass surge are predicted using computational models [15]. The performance, cultivation device boom for commercialization viability, and operating conditions are improved by various developing scenarios [15].

Initially, datasets are prepared, and a suitable machine-learning algorithm setup is established. The biological brain acts as an inspiration to ANNs [4]. Deep learning standards, it is a simple architecture. A larger model requires more data to be trained adequately whereas the cyanobacteria data produces outstanding results [15].

There are two portions of a Convolutional Neural Network: a regressor or a classifier and a feature extractor [4]. One dimensional convolutional layer and a One-dimensional max-pooling layer act as a base for the feature extractor [4]. A Neural Network that has the ability to recollect Preceding significant information is called a Long Short-Term Memory Network [4]. A supervised learning algorithm and an ensemble machine-learning method called K -Nearest Neighbours and Random Forest respectively are also used in biomass production [15].

It can be seen and noted that ML can be used to monitor carbohydrate growth behavior [2]. As the problem of contamination caused by physical

Figure 3.6 Various ML algorithms used in biomass prediction.

tests has been overcome, it becomes an added advantage [16]. For large-scale carbohydrate production, the optimization process can be critical for the profitable usage of microalgae or cyanobacteria-based wastewater treatment. By this method, the fermentation process can be done on biomass, which can then be converted into valuable biofuels [15].

3.8 GEOTHERMAL ENERGY

A renewable energy source that originates from the Upper mantle is geothermal energy [17]. It is created by the radioactive decay of constituents and thermal conduction that occurs during planet formation [3]. This thermal energy is kept in the form of fluids and rocks in the inner crust. The heat from the Planet's core is what causes surface phenomena like lava flows, fumaroles, hot springs, geysers, and mud pots [17]. The radioactive decay of potassium, thorium, and uranium inside the friction at continental plate borders, in addition to the Earth's mantle and core, is the primary mechanism by which the heat is produced [17].

This heat can occasionally spontaneously release massive amounts of energy all at once, leading to good occurrences like geysers and volcanic eruptions [17]. Geothermal power plants may sometimes offer baseload electricity as well as support facilities for short and long-term mobility because of their exceptionally elevated power requirements and lack of reliance on the weather [17].

3.8.1 Current use of Geothermal Energy

In many places, it has been used for warming and food preparation for hundreds of years. It is possible to produce power as well as heat and cool spaces using geothermal stockpiles [17]. The geothermal water has been utilized to aid plant growth in greenhouses, as well as for district heating in homes and businesses [17].

Most Frequent usage of geothermal energy includes industrial processes, large-scale snow melting, pasteurizing milk, and cooking. In the heating system, hot water is widely utilized for many of these processes [2]. When the fluid includes dangerous minerals and gases, such as Sulphur dioxide, it may also be used in combination with a heat exchanger, which transfers heat [3].

A heat exchanger and a pump that uses geothermal energy make up a geothermal heat pump system. The fluid, frequently water or a solution of water and antifreeze, runs through the pipes of the heat exchanger to transfer heat energy from the land to the air at the surface [17]. Due to the temperature and hydraulic movement, geothermal energy may be used to generate electricity.

3.8.2 Role of ML in Geothermal Oil and Gas Well Subsurface Temperature Prediction

Geothermal scientists were able to produce a flow of heat, which was then utilized to find possibly geothermally active locations, using bottom-hole temperature data from petroleum well records [17]. The two models that can predict subsurface temperature with the greatest accuracy are XGBoost and Random forest [17]. The XGBoost model is used to generate 2D constant temperature mapping at three different depths in the areas surrounding the sites, identifying potentially geothermally active locations [17]. Furthermore, the specified algorithms were evaluated using additional datasets to demonstrate their best performance [17].

The major algorithms used in predicting the geothermal oil and gas well subsurface temperature are:

1. Decision Tree Regression
2. Adaptive Booster Regression
3. Random Forest Regression
4. Support Vector Regression

An unsupervised learning approach, with an emphasis on characterization rather than detection, can be used to deploy machine-learning techniques that forecast geothermal heat flux results based on geologist variables [17]. It contains information on bedrock, topography, crustal thickness, and other geologic variables for a specific area, as well as geothermal heat flux data from around the world [3].

3.9 CONCLUSION

This chapter delves into the various types of renewable energy and explains why they are necessary. The long history of renewable energy is described, allowing us to comprehend the origins and onset of renewable energy resources. Every renewable energy source is specified for use. To be successful with renewable energy resources, one must understand how to use them to their full potential. To get the most out of these renewable energies, we need to be able to predict and guess them.

This chapter discussed and explained the methods for predicting renewable energy using machine-learning algorithms. It is worth noting that different algorithms are used to forecast the five major types of renewable energy. A few algorithms are used in all of these renewable energies, but the purposes of use for each of these energies differ. For example, the ANN algorithm is used to predict each reservoir influx and streamflow forecasting in hydroelectric power generation. The methods fortab predicting renewable energy are reviewed in general.

REFERENCES

[1] Zeng, Shihong, et al. "A review of renewable energy investment in the BRICS countries: History, models, problems and solutions." *Renewable and Sustainable Energy Reviews* 74 (2017): 860–872.

[2] Shahzad, Umair. "The need for renewable energy sources." *Energy* 2 (2012): 16–18.

[3] Sørensen, Bent. "A history of renewable energy technology." *Energy Policy* 19.1 (1991): 8–12.

[4] Qiu, Yiwei, et al. "Stochastic online generation control of cascaded run-of-the-river hydropower for mitigating solar power volatility." *IEEE Transactions on Power Systems* 35.6 (2020): 4709–4722.

[5] Kannan, Nadarajah, and Divagar Vakeesan. "Solar energy for future world: A review." *Renewable and Sustainable Energy Reviews* 62 (2016): 1092–1105.

[6] Kelly, Geoff. "History and potential of renewable energy development in New Zealand." *Renewable and Sustainable Energy Reviews* 15.5 (2011): 2501–2509.

[7] Gutiérrez, Leidy, Julian Patiño, and Eduardo Duque-Grisales. "A comparison of the performance of supervised learning algorithms for solar power prediction." *Energies* 14.15 (2021): 4424.

[8] Mishra, Manohar, et al. "Deep learning and wavelet transform integrated approach for short-term solar PV power prediction." *Measurement* 166 (2020): 108250.

[9] Kumar, Utkarsh, Sukumar Mishra, and Sreedhar Madichetty. "An efficient SPV power forecasting using hybrid wavelet and genetic algorithm based LSTM deep learning model." *2020 21st National Power Systems Conference (NPSC)*. IEEE, 2020.

[10] Rushdi, Mostafa A., et al. "Power prediction of airborne wind energy systems using multivariate machine learning." *Energies* 13.9 (2020): 2367.

[11] Gu, Chengcheng, and Hua Li. "Review on deep learning research and applications in wind and wave energy." *Energies* 15.4 (2022): 1510.

[12] Stetco, Adrian, et al. "Machine learning methods for wind turbine condition monitoring: A review." *Renewable Energy* 133 (2019): 620–635.

[13] Rayess, Al, Hesham Majed, and Asli Ülke Keskin. "Forecasting the hydroelectric power generation of GCMs using machine learning techniques and deep learning (Almus Dam, Turkey)." *Geofizika* 38.1 (2021): 1–14.

[14] Bordin, Chiara, et al. "Machine learning for hydropower scheduling: State of the art and future research directions." *Procedia Computer Science* 176 (2020): 1659–1668.

[15] Elmaz, Furkan, Özgün Yücel, and Ali Yener Mutlu. "Predictive modeling of biomass gasification with machine learning-based regression methods." *Energy* 191 (2020): 116541.

[16] Rodríguez-Rángel, Héctor, et al. "Machine learning methods modeling carbohydrate-enriched cyanobacteria biomass production in wastewater treatment systems." *Energies* 15.7 (2022): 2500.

[17] Kshirsagar, Ameya, and Parth Sanghavi. "Geothermal, oil and gas well subsurface temperature prediction employing machine learning." Proceedings of the 47th workshop on geothermal reservoir engineering. https://pangea.stanford.edu/ERE/db/GeoConf/papers/SGW/2022/Kshirsagar.pdf. 2022.

Chapter 4

Smart Home Energy Management Using Non-intrusive Load Monitoring

A Deep Learning Perspective

L.N. Sastry and Sri Phani Krishna Karri

CONTENTS

4.1 INTRODUCTION

The rapid increase in the demand for the energy and purchase of energy from cloud storage [1] motivates users to monitor energy consumption data for individual appliances. There are numerous numbers of services offered by smart cities to users [2]. With the existence of smart meters [3] and smart appliances users were able to identify the power consumption for individual devices thereby, they manage the power bill. Smart electrical outlets on each of the equipment provide good energy analysis; however, this contributes to the cost and implementation complexity. The smart energy meters give an

DOI: 10.1201/9781003356639-4

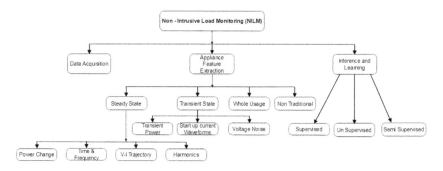

Figure 4.1 Functional block diagram of NILM.

aggregated consumption analysis of a whole building. This technological shift to monitor the energy usage of individual appliances, encourage users an improved energy saving, fault detection, demand forecast, etc. Non-intrusive load monitoring (NILM) provides various features like voltage, current, active power, reactive power, power factor, harmonic components, V-I trajectory, load signatures, Eigen-values, energy usage pattern of the loads, etc [4].

NILM is the process of extracting the consumption and operating conditions of various electrical appliances from a composite load measurement taken from the electric meter of a building. The NILM process consists of three major steps as shown in Figure 4.1. Data acquisition is the first step, where power measuring devices or sensors collect the aggregated consumption data on all phases with a predefined sampling rate. The second step is appliance feature extraction, where the state changes of appliances are identified using real and reactive power [5]. These state changes are known as events. Recent approaches also use harmonics of current, transients, and usage patterns of various devices as features. These features are categorized into four types: transient-state, steady-state, whole usage, and non-traditional appliance features. In steady-state features, sampling rates are fixed and are ranging from 1 Hz to 0.02 Hz approximately. Whereas in transient features, current harmonics are involved with an increased sampling rate of 1 kHz [6]. Finally, the inference and learning stage uses supervised, unsupervised, and semi-supervised algorithms to perform the disaggregation process.

4.1.1 Supervised Algorithms

In supervised algorithms, the model was trained using labeled known data and identifying the instances based on this model. These algorithms have an advantage of increased calculation speed, less space, and analyzing the result with high accuracy [7]. Optimization algorithms to address the disaggregation problem by calculating the error difference between the observed power measurement and combinations of signals [5,8,9]. Various optimization techniques like integer programming [6], and genetic algorithms [10] are proposed by many researchers. In the case of optimization methods, electrical appliances with similar power consumption, noise, unknown loads, cannot be recognized. The problems in the optimization algorithms are addressed by developing a new method for optimization by modifying a post process [11]. In a three-phase environment, the harmonic content of electrical loads can be determined by measuring the harmonic energy of the non-zero harmonics of the fundamental current [12]. Temporal patterns of appliances are obtained by integrating with Bayesian networks [13] and the state transition information by Hidden Markov Models (HMMs). Classifiers are trained by a database with known signatures of electrical appliances and the recognition of appliances.

4.1.2 Unsupervised Algorithms

The unsupervised algorithm performs classification without information on samples. These algorithms have the ability to detect new data without re-training and also have a limitation of low accuracy [14]. The Blind Source Separation Technique [15] employs groups of steady-state active and reactive power fluctuations, which are then fed into a matching pursuit algorithm. Another method for extracting frequent power change patterns from electrical equipment is motif mining [16]. Motifs are also known as basic forms and often occurring patterns. The statistical data computation of on- and off-durations of electrical equipment is an extension of motif mining [17]. A novel technique [18] applies statistical aspects to the Factorial HMMs (FHMM), such as the connection between appliances, state duration probability, and time of day. A difference HMM [19] utilizes prior models of general appliances. Factorial additive HMMs [20] employs an enhanced HMM inference technique. This method uses a computationally efficient convex formulation of approximation inference that avoids local optima and outperforms previous approaches in practice. A suitable Bayesian non-parametric extension of the HMM is the Hierarchical Dirichlet Process Hidden Semi-Markov Model (HDP-HSMM) [21].

4.1.3 Semi-Supervised Algorithm

Semi-Supervised Learning (SSL) is a collection of learning methods that either provide external information to an unsupervised component or support a supervised learning method with unidentifiable observations [22,23]. The fundamental goal of SSL tools is to deal with the shortage of external data. For eventless disaggregation, data available is both sub-metered loads and hand-categorized events for event-based NILM structures [19]. In recent days researchers apply various machine learning algorithms to NILM, including HMM [24–28] and its variants, K- Nearest Neighbors (KNN) [29–31], and the Support Vector Machine (SVM)

[29,32] that have high performance. These traditional algorithms have a limitation of only two classes in the classification of appliances. This can be reduced by converting the networks to nonlinear. The above-mentioned state-of-the-art algorithms are applied to various publicly available NILM datasets.

This chapter presents the implementation of various deep neural network algorithms listed in the literature [14,33,34] on four publicly available datasets namely REDD, UK-DALE, REFIT, and SynD. The main contributions of the work are as follows:

1. A review of state-of-the-art deep learning algorithms developed by various researchers is presented.
2. The use of various deep learning algorithms for four publicly available datasets is elaborated.
3. The survey gives experimental validation of deep learning algorithms and their comparison on four datasets.
4. A detailed comparison of results is attempted in terms of the metrics recall, precision, accuracy, F1-Score, and Mean Absolute Error (MAE).
5. The paper clearly demonstrates the advantage and use of NILMTK-contrib API for the implementation of algorithms, a comparative study on various appliances. The complete code using Tensorflow and Keras on four publicly available datasets is given on GitHub (https://github.com/sastry3009/nilmtk-contrib) for better reproducibility of results and comparative study.

4.2 DATASETS AND ALGORITHMS

NILM is to figure out the power consumption of appliances individually from a resultant power outcome in a domestic building. Thus, the problem is identified as the power consumption of each appliance from a superimposition of power of N appliances is given as follows

$$(t) = P_{noise}(t) + \sum_{i=1}^{N} p_i(t), \quad t \in \{1, T\} \tag{4.1}$$

where p_i is the power of each appliance and P_{noise}, is the power of the unwanted signal.

4.2.1 Datasets

4.2.1.1 REDD

The Reference Energy Disaggregation Data set (REDD) [35] was the most popular dataset in the area of NILM, released in the year 2011. It has the details of power usage for six homes in the USA. Each of the six homes consists of aggregated power data along with the individual appliance features as ground truth data. It provides the dataset for both low frequency and high frequency. The REDD contains approximately twenty categories in ten variants of residential appliances. The appliances include lighting, electronics, refrigerator, disposal, dishwasher, crazy-washer, furnace, washer-dryer, smoke-alarms, bathroom GFI, outlets, microwave oven, heater, stove, clothes-dryer, AC, cooking utilities, cooker. In this work, REDD is considered as a low frequency dataset for analysis and comparison.

4.2.1.2 UK – DALE

The United Kingdom – Domestic Appliance-Level Electricity (UK-DALE) Data set [36] was the open-access UK-based dataset, released in the year 2014. This data set was most widely used by the researchers for cross-domain validation with NILMTK. It contains aggregated and individual appliance data like REDD for five homes. Among five houses there are approximately forty categories with fewer variants (1 to 3) of residential appliances available. UK-DALE consists of data from aggregated homes with a frequency of 16 KHz and individual appliances with the frequency of 1/6 Hz.

4.2.1.3 REFIT

The Personalized Retrofit Decision Support Tools for UK Homes using Smart Home Technology (REFIT) Data set [37] was a UK-based dataset, released in the year 2017. It was an electrical load measurement dataset consists of whole home aggregated, nine individual appliances data with a sampling frequency of 8 sec per appliance. The appliances include Television, Wi-Fi, fridge, microwave, cooker hood, kettle, toaster, washing machine, washer dryer, tumble dryer, dishwasher, computer, router, electric mixer, blender, heater, lamp, pond pump, dehumidifier, bread maker.

4.2.1.4 SynD

The Synthetic Energy Dataset (SynD) [38] was a synthetic data set with a focus on residential buildings, released in 2020. It contains aggregated and individual appliance power consumption data for two houses and twenty-one appliances with a sampling frequency of 5 Hz. The appliances are Fridge, Dishwasher, Electric heater, Washing machine, Toaster, Fan, Microwave, Iron, Hot air gun, Router, Coffee machine, TV, Printer, Laptop computer, Lamp, Gaming PC, Pocket radio, Monitor, Electric oven, Hair dryer, Water kettle.

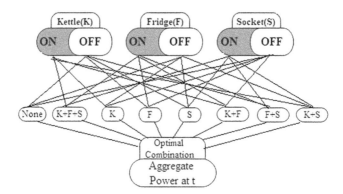

Figure 4.2 Application of CO to non-intrusive load monitoring.

4.2.2 Algorithms

4.2.2.1 Combinatorial Optimization (CO)

Combinatorial optimization is the process of selecting the best thing from a limited number of options [5]. It is applicable to optimization issues when the set of possible options is discrete or can be reduced to discrete, and the goal is to discover the optimal answer. An application of CO in the problem of NILM is shown in Figure 4.2. CO will give appropriate appliance states. This will reduce the variation between the total consumption of each appliance and the aggregated power [39].

4.2.2.2 Factorial HMM

The hidden state in an HMM [18] is a single discrete variable that reflects previous information. As a result, time series data is often modeled with HMMs. According to a generalization of HMMs, this state is separated into numerous state variables and therefore represented in a dispersed manner. A general graphical model is shown in Figure 4.3. Each appliance's power usage may be represented as the measured value of an HMM. The statuses of the appliances constitute a hidden element of these HMMs. A factorial HMM [40] is ideally suited for energy disaggregation since it involves collectively decoding the power demand of n appliances.

4.2.2.3 Denoising Auto Encoder (DAE)

The general network topology for NILM using denoising autoencoder is shown in Figure 4.4. One or more one-dimensional convolution layers are used in the encoder stage of DAE [41] to transform an input signal into a set of feature maps. The DAE has the structure of *Convolution → linear activation → maximization → convolution → pooling layer → fully connected layers*. If max pooling is used with NILM, it reduces the size of the

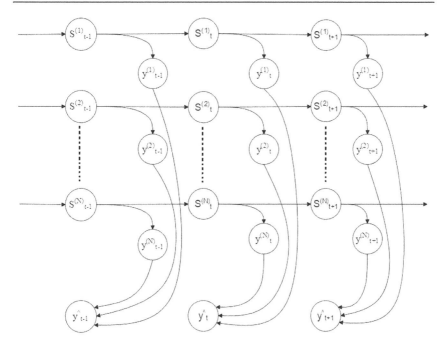

Figure 4.3 Graphical representation of FHMM.

feature maps, thereby reducing the number of training parameters. Negative values of the disaggregated active power are less likely to occur with the ReLu activation function. In the disaggregation, input signals are analyzed by sliding windows with lengths depending on the dimension of device activations. Using DAE the MSE between output and the state of single equipment was minimized.

4.2.2.4 Recurrent Neural Network (RNN)

Recurrent Neural Network (RNN) is the variation of feed-forward neural networks that is used to process sequential data. As given in Figure 4.5, the bidirectional long short-term memory (LSTM) [41] unit is used in NILM because of its nature to predict current value based on previous and future information. LSTM also has longer memory unit to handle vanishing gradient and the exploding gradient problems. RNN used in the application of NILM receives a sequence of mains reading and outputs a single value of power consumption of the target appliance.

4.2.2.5 Gated Recurrent Unit (GRU) and Window GRU

The Gated Recurrent Unit (GRU) [42] is a new type of Neural Network shown in Figure 4.6, that aims to reduce computational load. GRU has

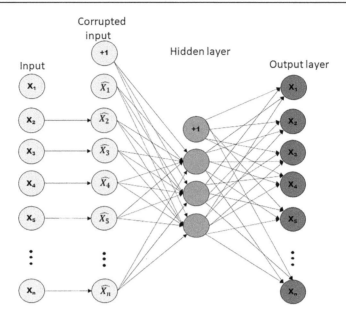

Figure 4.4 Architectural model for DAE.

gained better performance by replacing the LSTM units with lightweight Gated Recurrent Units (GRU) and reducing the recurrent layer widths to decrease duplication and the possibility of a vanishing gradient. They are a short-term memory solution with internal devices known as gates that may control the flow of information. These gates figure out which parts of the data are the most critical and send that information down the long chain of sequences. As shown in Figure 4.6 there are only two gates on it: a reset gate and an update gate. The reset gate regulates how much previous knowledge should be forgotten; whereas the update gate determines what information

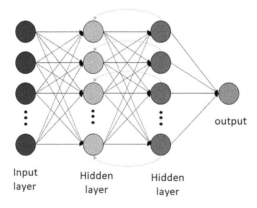

Figure 4.5 Architecture of RNN.

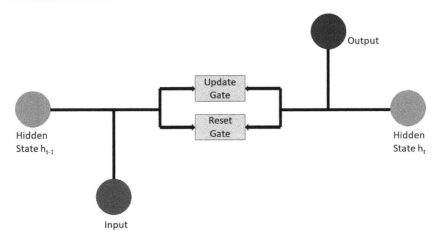

Figure 4.6 Architectural model for GRU.

should be discarded and what new information should be added. When the reset gate is near to zero, GRU continues to function in such a manner that the hidden state is confined to disregard the previous hidden state and is reset with the current input. This enables the concealed state to delete any data that is subsequently determined to be irrelevant.

The number of neurons per layer was reduced in Window GRU [43]. The precision of the network remains the same with recurrent layers half the size, as per tests. This resulted in a 60 percent reduction in the number of trainable parameters. Finally, overfitting was eliminated by inserting dropout between the layers. This is especially beneficial when using data from numerous homes to train an appliance model. Dropout is also useful if any of the input values are missing.

4.2.2.6 Short Sequence to Point (SS2P)

Sequence-to-point learning (seq2point) [44] depicts the network's input as a mains window and the output as the middle element of the target appliance's corresponding window. The idea behind this strategy is that the target appliance's midpoint should have a strong relationship with the mains data before and after that point. Seq2point learning can be thought of as a type of nonlinear regression.

4.2.2.7 Sequence to Sequence (S2S)

The sequence-to-sequence (S2S) [44] learning model is one of the deep learning concepts that is used to convert between two sequences. It has an encoder RNN that understands the input sequence and a decoder RNN that decodes the thought vector, resulting in the creation of an output sequence as

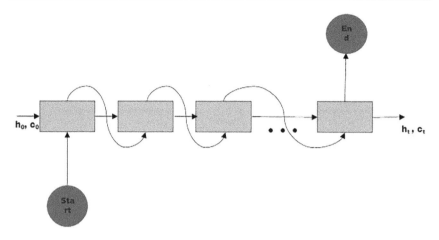

Figure 4.7 Architecture of Seq2Seq.

shown in Figure 4.7. An encoder network compresses an input sequence into a vector, which is then unfolded into a new sequence by a decoder network. Recurrent Neural Networks are the common element for input and output structures in the sequence-to-sequence paradigm. The decoder takes as input the encoder's final state, which should contain all of the information encoded within the input sentence, and then passes it on to each subsequent phase, which seeks to predict the output using a discrete probability distribution and the loss function. The major goal here is to create a regression map from the mains sequence to the target appliance sequence.

4.2.2.8 Bidirectional Encoder Representation for Transformers (BERT)

As illustrated in Figure 4.8, BERT [45] was able to identify individual household appliances with the same form output by using an embedding module, layers of transformers, and a multi-layer perceptron as output layer. A comparison of electrical appliances was also used to calculate threshold values.

By employing a convolutional layer on top of the one-dimensional input array, it was able to recover and increase the hidden size of the features from the design. The BERT model uses an iterative procedure to calculate the least prediction error for the supplied training data using a supervised learning method. The error is the difference between the model's projected output and the actual/target output, which is supplied as part of the training data.

4.3 EXPERIMENTAL RESULTS AND DISCUSSION

Non- Intrusive Load Monitoring (NILM) has 42 publicly available datasets. These datasets are classified as low-frequency and high-frequency datasets.

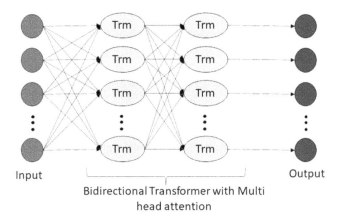

Input | Bidirectional Transformer with Multi head attention | Output

Figure 4.8 Architectural model for BERT.

The complete specifications and the list of appliances available in each of the datasets are clearly given in [46]. An open-source toolkit for non-intrusive load monitoring (NILMTK), was released and facilitates the authors to reproduce state-of-the-art algorithms and easy comparison. Further, NILMTK was modified and released as the disaggregation API, NILMTK-contrib which removes the barrier for both developers and the contributors to add new algorithms with less complexity. The work is carried out by using two basic algorithms Combinatorial Optimization (CO), Factorial HMM (FHMM) also six Deep neural network algorithms, namely Denoising Auto Encoder (DAE), Gated Recurrent Unit (GRU), Recurrent Neural Network (RNN), Short Sequence -to- Point (SS2P), Window GRU, and Bidirectional Encoder Representations from Transformers (BERT). This paper focuses on four datasets: REDD, UK-DALE, SynD, and REFIT. The work was carried out by splitting 80% as training data and 20% as testing data of the same building in all the datasets. The tests are run using Tensorflow and Keras framework for deep learning, and the specification of the workstation for training is with CPU: Intel core i7 Cooler Master; GPU: GeForce RTX 2080 Ti (Ö1); RAM: 32 GB.

The relative metrics use d to evaluate the algorithmic performance are as follows

$$Precision\,(P) = \frac{TruePositive}{TruePositive + FalsePositive}$$

$$Re\,call\,(R) = \frac{TruePositive}{TruePositive + FalseNegative}$$

$$Accuracy\,(Acc) = \frac{TruePositive + TrueNegative}{TruePositive + FalsePositive + TrueNegative + FalseNegative} \quad (4.2)$$

$$F_1 - Score\,(F_1) = \frac{2*P*R}{P+R}$$

$$MeanAbsoluteError\,(MAE) = \frac{1}{T}\sum_{t=1}^{T}|\hat{x}_t - x_t|$$

Where $\hat{x}_t$ is the disaggregated power of the devices at time t, and x_t is the device true power at time t. The four publicly available datasets used in this work namely REDD, UKDALE, SynD, and REFIT in various geographic are trained and tested for various benchmark algorithms using NILMTK-contrib API. The results are presented as follows.

The predictions of all algorithms are reported using metrics recall, precision, accuracy, F1-score, and Mean Absolute Error (MAE) for each of the targeted appliances in four publicly available datasets.

Figures 4.9–4.12 shows the performance of four datasets in terms of five metrics for all nine algorithms. The figures can be viewed as vertical columns representing the result of each algorithm; among them, each colored stack represents the performance of individual appliances. The horizontal rows depict the performance of target appliances in a dataset for each of the metrics.

4.3.1 Case 1: REDD with Five Appliances (Fridge, Light, Sockets, Microwave, and Dishwasher)

Table 4.1 corresponds to the results produced on REDD dataset for each of the five appliances, fridge, light, sockets, microwave, and dishwasher. It is evident that the device microwave gave a better performance in SS2P with respect to the accuracy of the metric, F1-score, and MAE, whereas the same device performed well in Window GRU and S2S for recall. In all the algorithms with respect to the metrics recall, precision, accuracy, F1-score, and MAE, comparatively less performance except in S2S for recall was reported by the appliance fridge. The device sockets outperformed all the DNN algorithms with respect to all the metrics namely Recall, accuracy, precision, F1-score, and MAE. It is shown that all the DNN algorithms produced comparable results greater than 0.9 on a target device light in Recall. The same device gave a better performance in the algorithm DAE with respect to precision, accuracy, and F1-score. The device dishwasher performed equally well in the algorithms DAE, RNN, and Window GRU with respect to recall and the same device gave comparatively less performance in precision, accuracy, F1-score, and MAE.

4.3.2 Case 2: UK – DALE with Five Appliances (Washer Dryer, Kettle, Fridge Freezer, Microwave, and Dish washer)

Table 4.2 shows the results produced on UK-DALE dataset for the five appliances washer dryer, kettle, fridge freezer, microwave, and dish washer. It is clear that except for the device fridge freezer all the appliances did better in S2S in terms of accuracy and MAE. In the same manner, except for the appliance fridge freezer, all the other devices score better results in terms of precision in FHMM algorithm. The metric recall got good performance

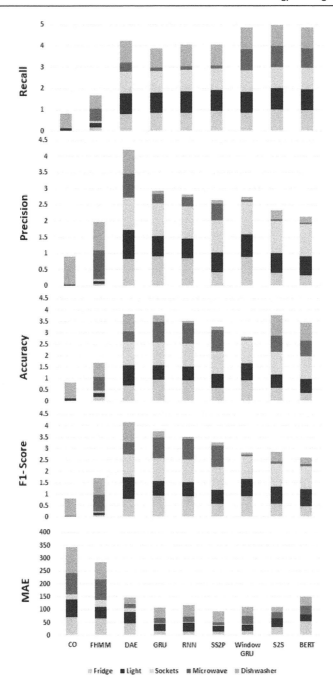

Figure 4.9 Comparison of various algorithms on REDD.

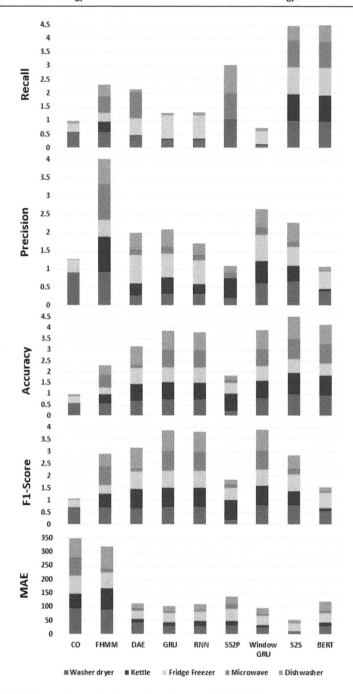

Figure 4.10 Comparison of various algorithms on UK-DALE.

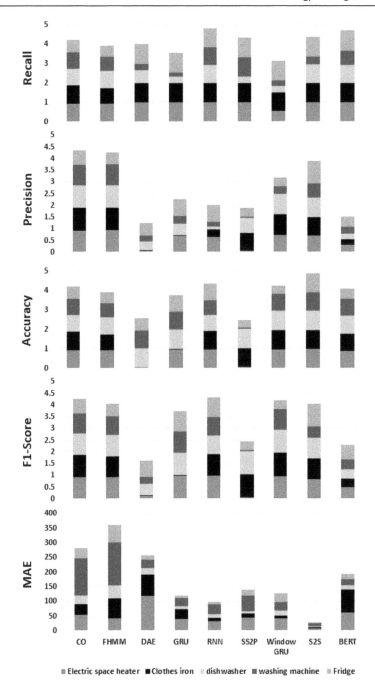

Figure 4.11 Comparison of various algorithms on SynD.

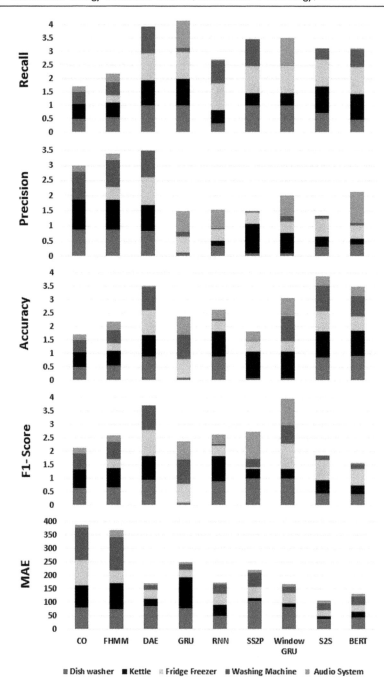

Figure 4.12 Comparison of various algorithms on REFIT.

Table 4.1 Comparison of various algorithms for REDD dataset

	CO [2]	FHMM [33]	DAE [34]	GRU [35]	RNN [34]	SS2P [37]	Window GRU [36]	S2S [37]	BERT [38]
Recall									
Fridge	0.0011	0.1857	0.7879	0.8589	0.8638	0.9346	0.859	**0.9988**	0.967
Light	0.1417	0.1857	0.9993	0.9435	–	0.9943	0.9859	–	0.9913
Sockets	0.0123	0.088	–	–	–	–	–	–	–
Microwave	0.0002	0.6119	0.4404	0.1811	0.1859	0.1469	–	–	0.9122
Dishwasher	0.6851	0.62	–	0.9048	–	0.9765	–	0.9847	0.9923
Precision									
Fridge	0	0.0547	0.8269	**0.8955**	0.8454	0.4108	0.885	0.4017	0.308
Light	0.0349	0.084	**0.894**	0.642	0.6089	0.6147	0.7047	0.5958	0.5988
Sockets	0.0005	0.053	0.9999	0.9999	0.9999	0.9999	0.9999	–	–
Microwave	0	**0.9023**	0.7442	0.2997	0.2783	0.5298	0.0661	0.0644	0.0574
Dishwasher	0.8728	**0.885**	0.7499	0.1029	0.0927	0.093	0.0917	0.2651	0.168
Accuracy									
Fridge	0.0011	0.1857	0.6958	**0.9282**	0.9125	0.5819	0.9248	0.5712	0.3646
Light	0.1417	0.1857	**0.8935**	0.6452	0.6089	0.6166	0.7396	0.5958	0.5991
Sockets	0.0123	0.088	0.9999	0.9999	0.9999	0.9999	0.9999	–	–
Microwave	0.0002	0.6119	0.4722	0.9178	0.9142	**0.9348**	0.0661	0.7148	0.7043
Dishwasher	0.6851	0.62	0.7499	0.2602	0.0927	0.1239	0.0917	**0.876**	0.7777
F1-score									
Fridge	0.0001	0.0793	0.8069	**0.9282**	0.9125	0.5819	0.9248	0.573	0.4672
Light	0.0559	0.1149	**0.9437**	0.6452	0.6089	0.6166	0.7396	0.7467	0.7466
Sockets	0.0011	0.0658	0.9999	0.9999	0.9999	0.9999	0.9999	–	–

(Continued)

Table 4.1 (Continued) Comparison of various algorithms for REDD dataset

	CO [2]	FHMM [33]	DAE [34]	GRU [35]	RNN [34]	SS2P [37]	Window GRU [36]	S2S [37]	BERT [38]
Recall									
Microwave	0	0.7292	0.5534	0.9178	0.9142	**0.9348**	0.0661	0.1211	0.1081
Dishwasher	0.7672	0.7292	**0.8571**	0.2602	0.0927	0.1239	0.0917	0.4178	0.2874
MAE									
Fridge	71.53	65.87	46.95	17.59	**14.55**	14.67	17.69	31.46	52.78
Light	69.19	43.75	44.14	26.01	33.48	**22.51**	24.05	34.01	27.41
Sockets	19.57	29.21	15.54	2.48	2.29	2.3	2.26	**0.62**	0.7
Microwave	82.66	80.18	15.51	22.24	23.44	**11.91**	32.36	25.67	35.62
Dishwasher	100.64	66	25.36	39.39	45.31	41.46	33.77	**18.73**	33.74

Table 4.2 Comparison of various algorithms for UK-DALE dataset

	CO [2]	FHMM [33]	DAE [34]	GRU [35]	RNN [34]	SS2P [37]	Window GRU [36]	S2S [37]	BERT [38]
					Recall				
Washer dryer	0.5941	0.5589	0.4201	0.2967	0.2918	**0.9998**	0.1072	0.9896	0.9627
Kettle	0.0008	0.4136	0.0503	0.0371	0.0632	0.0359	0.0359	**0.9735**	0.966
Fridge Freezer	0.2953	0.3026	0.609	0.8673	0.8423	0	0.5001	**0.9997**	0.9993
Microwave	0.0002	0.6345	1	0.0408	0.0628	0.9991	0.0484	0.989	0.9682
Dishwasher	0.0905	0.4026	0.0752	0.044	0.0582	**0.9998**	0.0427	0.5187	0.591
Precision									
Washer dryer	**0.8993**	0.9134	0.2821	0.3112	0.3137	0.2051	0.6169	0.6759	0.3867
Kettle	0	**0.9859**	0.3313	0.4603	0.272	0.5597	0.6083	0.4204	0.0694
Fridge Freezer	0.3617	0.454	**0.7783**	0.6486	0.6524	0	0.7311	0.5145	0.4869
Microwave	0	**0.9915**	0.1637	0.2147	0.1756	0.1637	0.207	0.1501	0.0367
Dishwasher	0.0243	**0.6783**	0.446	0.4548	0.2932	0.1742	0.483	0.5158	0.087
Accuracy									
Washer dryer	0.5941	0.5589	0.6617	0.721	0.7237	0.2052	0.8032	**0.9738**	0.9156
Kettle	0.0008	0.4136	0.7968	0.8055	0.7863	0.8082	0.8092	**0.9914**	0.9189
Fridge Freezer	0.2953	0.3026	**0.7155**	0.6955	0.6944	0.496	0.6554	0.6104	0.5649
Microwave	0.0002	0.6345	0.1637	0.8184	0.7982	0.1644	0.8138	**0.9764**	0.8935
Dishwasher	0.0905	0.4026	0.8225	0.8242	0.8114	0.1743	0.8252	**0.9786**	0.8545
F1 – Score									
Washer dryer	0.7155	0.6934	0.6617	0.721	0.7237	0.2052	**0.8032**	**0.8032**	0.5518
Kettle	0	0.5827	0.7968	0.8055	0.7863	0.8082	**0.8092**	0.5872	0.1295
Fridge Freezer	0.3177	0.3552	**0.7155**	0.6955	0.6944	0.496	0.6554	0.6794	0.6548

(Continued)

Table 4.2 (Continued) Comparison of various algorithms for UK-DALE dataset

	CO [2]	FHMM [33]	DAE [34]	GRU [35]	RNN [34]	SS2P [37]	Window GRU [36]	S2S [37]	BERT [38]
Recall									
Microwave	0	0.7737	0.1637	**0.8184**	0.7982	0.1644	0.8138	0.2607	0.0708
Dishwasher	0.0383	0.5052	0.8225	0.8242	0.8114	0.1743	**0.8252**	0.5172	0.1517
MAE									
Washer dryer	93.46	88.87	41.3	30.05	29.29	31.83	23.71	**9.48**	28.73
Kettle	54.59	78.35	15.19	14.88	20.33	16.42	10.61	**3.5**	15.65
Fridge Freezer	64.87	60.11	**28.6**	32.64	32.68	44.19	34.06	29.3	34.64
Microwave	69.06	13.59	12.24	7.84	7.61	20.85	8.66	**5.3**	9.88
Dishwasher	67.19	79.43	15.52	18.82	21.38	25.3	18.17	**6.08**	31.97

for the appliances washer dryer and dishwasher in SS2P algorithm, for the appliances kettle and fridge freezer in S2S algorithm. The same metric score better performance for the device microwave in DAE algorithm.

The algorithm Window GRU gives comparable results in terms of F1-score for the appliances washer dryer, kettle, and dishwasher. The device washer dryer gave equal performance in S2S algorithm for the same metric. The appliances fridge and microwave reported quite differently in terms of F1-score and gave a better performance in DAE and GRU, respectively.

4.3.3 Case 3: SynD with five appliances (Electric space heater, Clothes iron, Dish washer, Washing machine, and Fridge)

Table 4.3 gives the results corresponding to the SynD dataset for the selected five appliances electric space heater, clothes iron, dishwasher, washing machine, and fridge. Sequence-to-Sequence algorithm performs the best for all five appliances in terms of mean absolute error (MAE). The same algorithm reports comparatively better performance in terms of accuracy for all the devices except clothes iron, which gave good performance in Window GRU. The algorithm FHMM performs well in terms of precision for all the appliances except fridge, which gave a better performance in S2S algorithm. The metric recall score better value of unity, in DAE and SS2P algorithms for the appliance electric space heater, and in SS2P and Window GRU algorithms for the device fridge. The same metric got a comparable performance in DAE, S2S, and SS2P algorithms for the appliances clothes iron, dishwasher, and washing machine respectively. It is evident that the appliances clothes iron and dish washer got winning performance in terms of F1-score in Window GRU algorithm. In the same manner, devices electric space heater, washing machine, and fridge performed well in RNN, GRU, and S2S algorithms, respectively.

4.3.4 Case 4: REFIT with five appliances (Dish washer, Kettle, Fridge freezer, Washing machine, and Audio system)

Table 4.4 indicates the results obtained for REFIT dataset on all the deep learning algorithms for the appliances dishwasher, kettle, fridge freezer, washing machine, and audio system. It is shown that all the algorithms produce comparable results on targeted appliances except for the audio system. The appliance fridge freezer outperforms all the DNN algorithms in terms of recall. The same metric record better performance for the appliance dishwasher in SS2P and Window GRU algorithms; for the device kettle in GRU algorithm; for the appliance washing machine in DAE and SS2P algorithms.

Table 4.3 Comparison of various algorithms for SynD dataset

	CO [2]	FHMM [33]	DAE [34]	GRU [35]	RNN [34]	SS2P [37]	Window GRU [36]	S2S [37]	BERT [38]
Recall									
Electric space heater	0.9161	0.9223	—	0.9882	0.9939	—	0.5351	0.9954	0.9997
Clothes iron	0.9549	0.8112	**0.9999**	0.9975	0.9847	0.9737	0.9764	0.9946	0.9989
Dishwasher	0.8647	0.8685	0.6545	0.3397	0.9198	0.3577	0.3154	**0.9713**	0.9303
washing machine	0.848	0.7432	0.338	0.2236	0.9225	—	0.3234	0.4122	0.7424
Fridge	0.6287	0.5563	0.9923	0.982	0.9912	—	—	0.9991	0.9991
Precision									
Electric space heater	0.9341	**0.9417**	0.0576	0.7009	0.6488	0.0576	0.7327	0.716	0.3155
Clothes iron	**0.9707**	0.9638	0.0287	0.0285	0.3362	0.7605	0.8881	0.7803	0.2313
Dishwasher	0.957	**0.9587**	0.3603	0.4923	0.1128	0.6677	0.8746	0.8275	0.2657
washing machine	0.9016	**0.9092**	0.2933	0.342	0.21	0.0615	0.3269	0.6287	0.2951
Fridge	0.6086	0.5102	0.5082	0.7191	0.7077	0.3727	0.3727	**0.9395**	0.4424
Accuracy									
Electric space heater	0.9161	0.9223	0.0581	0.975	0.9686	0.0576	0.9619	**0.9772**	0.8765
Clothes iron	0.9549	0.8112	0.0287	0.0289	0.944	0.9904	**0.9958**	0.9916	0.9032
Dishwasher	0.8647	0.8685	0.9596	0.9729	0.8041	0.978	0.9804	**0.9938**	0.9299
washing machine	0.848	0.7432	0.9091	0.9257	0.7771	0.0615	0.9174	**0.9478**	0.8725
Fridge	0.6287	0.5563	0.6391	0.8503	0.8441	0.3727	0.3727	**0.9757**	0.5302
F1 – Score									
Electric space heater	0.925	0.9319	0.1089	**0.975**	0.9686	0.0576	0.9619	0.8329	0.4796
Clothes iron	0.9624	0.8803	0.0555	0.0289	0.944	0.9904	**0.9958**	0.8745	0.3757
Dishwasher	0.9085	0.9113	0.4648	0.9729	0.8041	0.978	**0.9804**	0.8937	0.4134
washing machine	0.8737	0.8175	0.3141	**0.9257**	0.7771	0.0615	0.9174	0.498	0.4224
Fridge	0.609	0.5312	0.6721	0.8503	0.8441	0.3727	0.3727	**0.9684**	0.6132

MAE

Electric space heater	52.78	40.57	116.85	38.97	30.73	43.7	40.72	**7.82**	60.59
Clothes iron	37.51	69.37	75.47	34.83	13.93	14.95	10.44	**3.6**	79.84
Dishwasher	31.35	44.65	22.55	9.66	12.3	7.72	18.51	**3.14**	14.24
washing machine	126.48	149.05	28.86	29.78	33.92	53.1	28.11	**12.36**	22.73
Fridge	35.28	59.04	15.54	6.36	7.22	21.67	29.69	**1.62**	17.52

Table 4.4 Comparison of various algorithms for REFIT dataset

	CO [2]	FHMM [33]	DAE [34]	GRU [35]	RNN [34]	SS2P [37]	Window GRU [36]	S2S [37]	BERT [38]
Recall									
Dish washer	0.5011	0.5399	0.9997	0.9884	0.337	—	—	0.7281	0.4577
Kettle	0.5404	0.5569	0.938	—	0.4899	0.4647	0.4788	0.9787	0.9906
Fridge Freezer	0.0219	0.2754	—	0.9918	—	—	—	0.9999	0.9988
Washing Machine	0.4486	0.5205	—	0.1689	0.8693	—	0.0357	0.4238	0.6407
Audio System	0.1924	0.2795	0	—	0.007	0	—	0	0.0059
Precision									
Dish washer	**0.8907**	0.8905	0.8371	0.0873	0.3396	0.0877	0.0877	0.3238	0.3974
Kettle	0.9797	**0.9831**	0.8645	0.0254	0.1801	0.983	0.6882	0.338	0.1912
Fridge Freezer	0.0014	0.4143	**0.9147**	0.5507	0.385	0.3845	0.3845	0.5826	0.4428
Washing Machine	0.9216	**0.9224**	0.8679	0.1613	0.0463	0.0502	0.1956	0.1078	0.1086
Audio System	0.2165	0.1911	0	0.6687	0.6063	0	0.67	0	—
Accuracy									
Dish washer	0.5011	0.5399	0.8729	0.0961	0.8847	0.0877	0.0877	0.8619	**0.9048**
Kettle	0.5404	0.5569	0.8194	0.0254	0.9302	**0.983**	0.9812	0.9733	0.9423
Fridge Freezer	0.0219	0.2754	**0.9147**	0.6852	0.385	0.3845	0.3845	0.7284	0.5233
Washing Machine	0.4486	0.5205	0.8679	0.9136	0.0897	0.0502	0.9442	**0.9733**	0.7831
Audio System	0.1924	0.2795	0.0427	0.6687	0.3329	0.3299	**0.67**	0.3368	0.3407
F1 – Score									
Dish washer	0.6408	0.6712	0.9321	0.0961	0.8847	**0.983**	0.9812	0.4483	0.4254
Kettle	0.6966	0.7106	0.8998	0.0254	**0.9302**	0.3845	0.3845	0.5025	0.3205
Fridge Freezer	0.0026	0.3199	**0.9554**	0.6852	0.385	0.0502	0.9442	0.7362	0.6136
Washing Machine	0.6033	0.6654	**0.9292**	0.9136	0.0897	0.3299	0.67	0.1719	0.1857
Audio System	0.1889	0.2269	0	0.6687	0.3329	0.983	**0.9812**	0	0.0118

MAE

Dish washer	81.26	73.5	85.77	78.72	50.55	104.51	82.89	**37.27**	44.24
Kettle	82.41	98.22	28.08	114.42	40.7	12.61	13.73	**12.36**	21.5
Fridge Freezer	94.06	47.78	34.11	27.88	40.59	40.59	40.16	**22.23**	26.31
Washing Machine	121.51	124.81	**16.73**	22.12	36.04	56.67	24.76	27.56	32.39
Audio System	7.78	24.28	**5.61**	6.12	7.27	6.8	6.12	9.49	8.86

Whereas the appliance audio system gave poor performance in all the algorithms except GRU and Window GRU. In the case of accuracy, it records the better performance of the appliances dishwasher, kettle, fridge freezer, washing machine, and audio system in the algorithms BERT, SS2P, DAE, S2S, and Window GRU respectively.

The appliances dishwasher, kettle, and fridge freezer got a winning performance in terms of MAE in S2S algorithm. The appliances washing machine and audio system gave a good performance for the same metric in DAE algorithm. The metric precision score high performance for the appliances kettle and washing machine in FHMM algorithm. The same metric, record better performance in CO, DAE, and BERT algorithms for the devices dish washer, fridge freezer, and audio system respectively. From the results, it is shown that the metric F1-score gave a good performance for the appliances dishwasher and audio system in SS2P algorithm. In a similar manner, the algorithm RNN performed well for the appliance kettle and the algorithm DAE perform comparatively high for the appliances washing machine and fridge freezer.

It is also shown from the results that different appliances use varying amounts of energy, the inaccuracies observed related to low energy use may be less considerable when compared to a high energy consumption load. Furthermore, because some end devices are used less frequently than others, metric data may not be predictive of efficiency if a statistically significant number of run times is not recorded. In light of these issues, it is advised that every metric evaluation include some form of energy leveling or another basis for comparing data across multiple end uses, such as a fixed energy usage per end use, a fixed number of real events per end use, or a fixed period.

4.4 CONCLUSION

In recent years, the NILM has emerged as a forward-thinking field that has produced promising results in terms of measuring energy usage at a cheap cost. The assessment looked at four publicly accessible NILM datasets for benchmarking algorithms for load detection and energy disaggregation. For the benefit of readers, it detailed the merits and drawbacks of current NILM algorithms, as well as an outlook on current issues and future research possibilities. All of the key elements of the NILM algorithms, datasets, and metrics under investigation are described in detail in figures to assist the community in selecting the most suited algorithms.

The experiments were carried out on four publicly available data sets namely REDD, UK-DALE, SynD, and REFIT. The results are produced on various deep learning algorithms concerning five metrics, namely recall, precision, accuracy, f1-score, and mean absolute error. This chapter also draws the usage of NILMTK-contrib, an API to perform NILM studies on various algorithms and datasets with lesser knowledge.

As the demand for energy and resources increases day by day, effective use is the only way to save them. Energy disaggregation can be an important component in energy conservation since it gives energy usage patterns for each of the appliances.

The NILM and the patterns of individual appliances are used for energy management, assisted living, and load forecasting. It is also used to identify the smart grid demand response, various equipment failures in large industries, and climatic changes.

REFERENCES

[1] J. Liu, N. Zhang, C. Kang, D. Kirschen, Q. Xia, "Cloud energy storage for residential and small commercial consumers: A business case study", *Applied Energy*, vol. 188, pp. 226–236, 2017.

[2] G. Betis, C. G. Cassandras, C. A. Nucci, "Smart cities [scanning the issue]", *Proceedings of the IEEE*, vol. 106 (4), pp. 513–517, 2018.

[3] Y. Wang, Q. Chen, T. Hong, C. Kang, "Review of smart meter data analytics: Applications, methodologies, and challenges", *IEEE Transactions on Smart Grid*, vol. 10 (3), pp. 3125–3148, 2019.

[4] M. Berg´es, E. Goldman, H. S. Matthews, L. Soibelman, "Training load monitoring algorithms on highly sub-metered home electricity consumption data", *Tsinghua Science & Technology*, vol. 13, pp. 406–411, 2008.

[5] G. Hart, "Nonintrusive appliance load monitoring", *Proceedings of the IEEE*, vol. 80 (12), pp. 1870–1891, 1992.

[6] K. Suzuki, S. Inagaki, T. Suzuki, H. Nakamura, K. Ito, "Nonintrusive appliance load monitoring based on integer programming", *2008 SICE Annual Conference*, pp. 2742–2747, 2008.

[7] Y. Liu, J. Wang, J. Deng, W. Sheng, P. Tan, "Non-intrusive load monitoring based on unsupervised optimization enhanced neural network deep learning", *Frontiers in Energy Research*, vol.9, p. 468, 2021.

[8] A. Zoha, A. Gluhak, M. A. Imran, S. Rajasegarar, "Non-intrusive load monitoring approaches for disaggregated energy sensing: A survey", *Sensors*, vol. 12, pp. 16838–16866, 2012.

[9] J. Liang, S. K. K. Ng, G. Kendall, J. W. M. Cheng, "Load signature study—Part I: Basic concept, structure, and methodology", *IEEE Transactions on Power Delivery*, vol. 25 (2) pp. 551–560, 2010.

[10] M. Baranski, J. Voss, "Genetic algorithm for pattern detection in nialm systems", In: *2004 IEEE International Conference on Systems, Man and Cybernetics (IEEE Cat. No.04CH37583)*, vol. 4, pp. 3462–3468, 2004.

[11] K. He, D. Jakovetic, B. Zhao, V. Stankovic, L. Stankovic, S. Cheng, "A generic optimization-based approach for improving non-intrusive load monitoring", *IEEE Transactions on Smart Grid*, vol. 10 (6), pp. 6472–6480, 2019.

[12] A. Cole, A. Albicki, "Nonintrusive identification of electrical loads in a threephase environment based on harmonic content", In: *Proceedings of the 17th IEEE Instrumentation and Measurement Technology Conference [Cat. No. 00CH37066]*, vol. 1, pp. 24–29, 2000.

[13] G. Yuan Lin, S. Chiang Lee, J. Y. Jen Hsu, W. Rong Jih, "Applying power meters for appliance recognition on the electric panel", In: *2010 5th IEEE Conference on Industrial Electronics and Applications*, pp. 2254–2259, 2010.

[14] J. Kelly, W. Knottenbelt, "Neural nilm: Deep neural networks applied to energy disaggregation", In: *Proceedings of the 2nd ACM international conference on embedded systems for energy-efficient built environments*, vol. 445, pp. 55–64, 2015.

[15] H. Gon̩calves, A. Ocneanu, M. Berǵes, "Unsupervised disaggregation of appliances using aggregated consumption data", 2011.

[16] H. Shao, M. Marwah, N. Ramakrishnan, "A temporal motif mining approach to unsupervised energy disaggregation: Applications to residential and commercial buildings", In: *Proceedings of the Twenty-Seventh AAAI Conference on Artificial Intelligence, AAAI'13*, AAAI Press, pp. 1327–1333, 2013.

[17] C. Elbe, E. Schmautzer, "Appliance-specific energy consumption feedback for domestic consumers using load disaggregation methods", In: *22nd International Conference and Exhibition on Electricity Distribution (CIRED 2013)*, pp. 1–4, 2013.

[18] H. Kim, M. Marwah, M. Arlitt, G. Lyon, J. Han, "Unsupervised disaggregation of low frequency power measurements", vol. 11, pp. 747–758, 2011.

[19] O. Parson, S. Ghosh, M. Weal, A. Rogers, "Non-intrusive load monitoring using prior models of general appliance types", In: *Proceedings of the Twenty-Sixth AAAI Conference on Artificial Intelligence, AAAI'12*, AAAI Press, pp. 356–362, 2012.

[20] J. Z. Kolter, T. Jaakkola, "Approximate inference in additive factorial hmms with application to energy disaggregation", In: N. D. Lawrence, M. Girolami (Eds.), *Proceedings of the Fifteenth International Conference on Artificial Intelligence and Statistics, Vol. 22 of Proceedings of Machine Learning Research, PMLR, La Palma, Canary Islands*, pp. 1472–1482, 2012.

[21] M. J. Johnson, A. S. Willsky, "Bayesian nonparametric hidden semi-markov models". *Journal of Machine Learning Research*, vol. 14, pp. 673–701, 2013.

[22] A. B. Goldberg, "New directions in semi-supervised learning", Ph.D. thesis, USA 2010.

[23] K. S. Barsim, B. Yang, "Toward a semi-supervised non-intrusive load monitoring system for event-based energy disaggregation", In: *2015 IEEE Global Conference on Signal and Information Processing (GlobalSIP)*, pp. 58–62, 2015.

[24] Y. F. Wong, Y. A. S̩ekercioğlu, T. Drummond, V. S. Wong, "Recent approaches to non-intrusive load monitoring techniques in residential settings", In: *2013 IEEE Computational Intelligence Applications in Smart Grid (CIASG)*, IEEE, pp. 73–79, 2013.

[25] M. Aiad, P. H. Lee, "Non-intrusive load disaggregation with adaptive estimations of devices main power effects and two-way interactions", *Energy and Buildings*, vol. 130, pp. 131–139, 2016.

[26] A. Cominola, M. Giuliani, D. Piga, A. Castelletti, A. E. Rizzoli, "A hybrid signature-based iterative disaggregation algorithm for non-intrusive load monitoring", *Applied Energy*, vol. 185, pp. 331–344, 2017.

[27] W. Kong, Z. Y. Dong, D. J. Hill, J. Ma, J. Zhao, F. Luo, "A hierarchical hidden Markov model framework for home appliance modeling", *IEEE Transactions on Smart Grid*, vol. 9 (4), pp. 3079–3090, 2016.

[28] J. A. Mueller, J. W. Kimball, "Accurate energy use estimation for non-intrusive load monitoring in systems of known devices", *IEEE Transactions on Smart Grid*, vol. 9 (4), pp. 2797–2808, 2016.

[29] M. B. Figueiredo, A. De Almeida, B. Ribeiro, "An experimental study on electrical signature identification of non-intrusive load monitoring (nilm) systems", In: *International Conference on Adaptive and Natural Computing Algorithms*, Springer, pp. 31–40, 2011.

[30] O. Kramer, O. Wilken, P. Beenken, A. Hein, A. Ḧuwel, T. Klingenberg, C. Meinecke, T. Raabe, M. Sonnenschein, "On ensemble classifiers for non-intrusive appliance load monitoring", In: *International Conference on Hybrid Artificial Intelligence Systems*, Springer, pp. 322–331, 2012.

[31] S. Giri, M. Berǵes, A. Rowe, "Towards automated appliance recognition using an emf sensor in nilm platforms", *Advanced Engineering Informatics*, vol. 27 (4), pp. 477–485, 2013.

[32] T. Hassan, F. Javed, N. Arshad, "An empirical investigation of VI trajectory based load signatures for non-intrusive load monitoring", *IEEE Transactions on Smart Grid*, vol. 5 (2), pp. 870–878, 2013.

[33] A. Verma, A. Anwar, M. Mahmud, M. Ahmed, A. Kouzani, "A comprehensive review on the nilm algorithms for energy disaggregation", *arXiv preprint 2102*.

[34] P. Huber, A. Calatroni, A. Rumsch, A. Paice, "Review on deep neural networks applied to low-frequency nilm", *Energies*, vol. 14 (9), pp. 2390, 2021.

[35] J. Kolter, M. Johnson, "Redd: A public data set for energy disaggregation research", *Artif. Intell.*, vol. 25, 2011.

[36] J. Kelly, W. Knottenbelt, "The UK-DALE dataset, domestic appliance-level electricity demand and whole-house demand from five UK homes", *Scientific Data*, vol. 2, no. 150007, 2015.

[37] D. Murray, L. Stankovic, V. Stankovic, "An electrical load measurements dataset of united kingdom households from a two-year longitudinal study", *Scientific Data*, vol. 4, no. 160122, 2017.

[38] C. Klemenjak, C. Kovatsch, M. Herold, W. Elmenreich, "A synthetic energy dataset for non-intrusive load monitoring in households", *Scientific Data 7*, vol. 1, 2020.

[39] N. Batra, J. Kelly, O. Parson, H. Dutta, W. Knottenbelt, A. Rogers, A. Singh, M. Srivastava, "Nilmtk: An open source toolkit for non-intrusive load monitoring", 2014.

[40] Z. Ghahramani, M. I. Jordan, "Factorial hidden Markov models", *Machine Learning*, vol. 29 (2), pp. 245–273, 1997.

[41] T. Wang, T. Ji, M. Li, "A new approach for supervised power disaggregation by using a denoising autoencoder and recurrent LSTM network", In: *2019 IEEE 12th International Symposium on Diagnostics for Electrical Machines, Power Electronics and Drives (SDEMPED)*, IEEE, pp. 507–512, 2019.

[42] J. Kim, H. Kim, "Classification performance using gated recurrent unit recurrent neural network on energy disaggregation", In: *2016 International Conference on Machine Learning and Cybernetics (ICMLC)*, Vol. 1, IEEE, pp. 105–110, 2016.

[43] O. Krystalakos, C. Nalmpantis, D. Vrakas, "Sliding window approach for online energy disaggregation using artificial neural networks", In: *Proceedings of the 10th Hellenic Conference on Artificial Intelligence*, pp. 1–6, 2018.

[44] C. Zhang, M. Zhong, Z. Wang, N. Goddard, C. Sutton, "Sequence-to-point learning with neural networks for non-intrusive load monitoring", In: *Proceedings of the AAAI Conference on Artificial Intelligence*, Vol. 32, 2018.

[45] Z. Yue, C. R. Witzig, D. Jorde, H.-A. Jacobsen, "Bert4nilm: A bidirectional transformer model for non-intrusive load monitoring", In: *Proceedings of the 5th International Workshop on Non-Intrusive Load Monitoring*, pp. 89–93, 2020.

[46] H. K. Iqbal, F. H. Malik, A. Muhammad, M. A. Qureshi, M. N. Abbasi, A. R. Chishti, "A critical review of state-of-the-art non-intrusive load monitoring datasets", *Electric Power Systems Research*, vol. 192, p. 106921, 2021.

Chapter 5

New Scheme of Cost-Load Optimization by Appliance Scheduling in Smart Homes

Govind Rai Goyal and Shelly Vadhera

CONTENTS

5.1 INTRODUCTION

Reduction of monthly electricity cost and peak power consumption are two major objectives of residential load management. Reduction of peak power demand leads to various advantages in the system such as reduced transmission cost and power losses, reduced consumption of fossil fuels as well as the emission of greenhouse gases (GHG), and reduction of equipment's overloading which helps to improve the reliability of the power system. The above two objectives of residential load management may be achieved with the help of demand-side management (DSM) (Nezhad et al. 2022). Two different approaches of DSM have been proposed in the literature viz. centralized management and distributed management (Anees et al. 2021). In the former case, a common utility function is optimized. But this model of optimization increases the diversity of system due to active involvement

DOI: 10.1201/9781003356639-5

of all the consumers. Solving the problems of DSM in a centralized fashion increases the complexity due to wide constraints of consumers. On the other hand in the distributed optimization models users can apply their strategy/ response without sharing the details of their power consumption (Goyal & Vadhera 2020). Most of the DSM programs that are in use since the last decade are focused on the interaction between the utility companies and each end user individually. Under these programs, each user is expected to respond independently to the dynamic pricing by shifting his/her power consumption. The objective for shifting the load demand can be different (Ahmad et al. 2020a). In view of the electricity suppliers, the objective can be to avoid the appearance of a high peak load demand or a long demand valley. It is desired that the load curve be as flat as possible. Flattening of the load curve is the reduction of power consumption at peak load hours and increasing the consumption during the low load periods. To flatten the load curve, it is required to bring the actual load curve as close to the objective load curve as possible. So, the objective becomes to minimize the difference between actual load curve and objective load curve (Sharma & Saxena 2019).

Reducing the power demand during peak hours and minimizing the peak power demand in the load curve for 24 hours a day are two different objectives. The former objective can be achieved by employing a high price during peak hours. As a consequence consumers shift their power consumption from high-price hours to low-price hours; which may also result in increased power demand during off-peak/mid-peak hours. So it becomes important to minimize the peak power demand during low load periods also. Peak power demand can be minimized by minimizing the objective function of peak to average ratio (PAR). PAR is the ratio of peak demand to the average power consumption in 24 hours of a day. The problem of minimization of monthly cost of power consumption and peak power demand has been solved by various researchers as single objective functions, or as a composite function (Goyal & Vadhera 2021). Some researchers have also solved the problems of minimizing of cost of power consumption, power consumption in peak hours, peak-to-average ratio, waiting time, etc. as multi-objective functions (Yahia & Pradhan 2020; Ahmad et al 2020b) or by converting into single-objective function (Hussain et al. 2018; Goyal & Vadhera 2019).

Decentralized energy generation can be defined as the energy generated & distributed closer to its end users. This has been integrated with DSM in order to reduce the cost of monthly electricity bill and peak power demand in residential and industrial loads (Samuel et al. 2018a). Saravanan (2015) implemented MS Excel solver for the minimization of the cost of electricity bill and maximization of the load factor for industrial consumers. Optimal utilization of storage systems with/without non-conventional energy sources has also been proposed in the minimization of monthly cost and peak power demand (Bedi et al. 2018; Hussain et al. 2018; Samuel et al. 2018b).

There are various conventional and artificial intelligence-based optimization algorithms available in literature like game theory, genetic algorithm (GA) (Yahia & Pradhan 2020), particle swarm optimization (PSO) (Ahmad et al. 2020), Jaya algorithm (Samuel et al. 2018a), Harmony search algorithm and their recent versions (Sharma & Saxena 2019; Singhal & Goyal 2018). These algorithms have been proposed for the solution of minimization of electricity bill cost and peak-to-average ratio. But due to the conflicting behavior of both objectives, it becomes difficult and confusing for the consumers to manually decide the optimal scheduling of appliances. To fulfill this requirement and to manage the residential load optimally a smart home energy management system (HEMS) is required. With this motivation, this research work is aimed to achieve both objectives simultaneously. This study is divided into three scenarios:

A. **Scenario 1:** Individual smart home residents reschedule his/her power consumption in order to minimize electricity bill cost.
B. **Scenario 2:** Individual smart home residents reschedule his/her power consumption in order to minimize the peak-to-average ratio (PAR).
C. **Scenario 3:** Individual smart home residents reschedule his/her power consumption in order to optimize the electricity bill cost and peak demand together through the proposed dynamic pricing scheme.

The proposed algorithm is tested on seven households of different monthly power consumption and real data of electricity pricing applicable in two utilities viz. **Waterloo North Hydro Inc., Canada** and **Gulf Power's Company, Northwest Florida** (Electricity prices in Canada 2019).

5.2 MATHEMATICAL MODELLING

Smart home appliances under HEMS are categorized as deferrable and non-deferrable. In the smart HEMS, consumers can define their preferences for the using appliances to energy controller.

5.2.1 Objective Functions

Minimization of the cost of the consumer's electricity bill and maximum power consumption simultaneously is the main objective of this research work. Total cost of electricity for 24 hours of a day is calculated by the following equation (Shakouri 2017).

$$Minimize \quad C_{DEC} = \sum_{t=1}^{T} x^t(d) * p^t(d) \quad T = 24 \tag{5.1}$$

$$x^t(d) = \sum_{\ell=1}^{\pounds} \xi_\ell^t y_\ell^t(d) T_\ell \quad t \in T \tag{5.2}$$

The vector $p(d)$ accumulates electricity prices for all the intervals on day $d \in N$. Here, p^t denotes the electricity price during time interval t, and $x^t(d)$ is the energy consumption schedule in time slot t of the day d, whereas   represents the power demand for a load $\ell \in \pounds$ in time slot t. Here, ξ_ℓ^t is the ON/OFF state and T_ℓ denotes the operational time of load ℓ.

Minimization of peak-to-average ratio (PAR) helps the utility to retain stability and ultimately leads to the cost reduction. It is minimized to reduce the peak power demand. Mathematical expression for PAR can be given by Eqn. (5.3) (Yahia & Pradhan 2020). Objective functions given by Eqn. (5.1) and Eqn. (5.3) are used to minimize the cost of electricity bill and peak power demand individually in scenario 1 and scenario 2, respectively.

$$Minimize \;\; PAR = \frac{\max\left\{\sum_{\ell=1}^{\pounds} \xi_\ell^t y_\ell^t(d)\right\}}{\frac{1}{T}\sum_{t=1}^{T}\sum_{\ell=1}^{\pounds} \xi_\ell^t y_\ell^t(d)} \quad t \in T \tag{5.3}$$

In scenario 3, household appliances are rescheduled with the aim to optimize the cost of monthly bill of electricity and maximum demand for power together. To achieve both objectives simultaneously a cost function is proposed for both cases. In the first case of **Waterloo North Hydro Inc., Canada**, the proposed function of electricity cost is given by Eqn. (5.4). In this function CPP price is also included in the calculation of the total cost of monthly power consumption.

$$Minimize \;\; C_{Total} = \sum_{d=1}^{N} \sum_{t=1}^{T} \left\{x_{(d)}^t\, p_{ToU}^t\right\} + \left\{x_{(d)}^{\max}\, p_{CPP}^t\right\} \tag{5.4}$$

While in the second case of **Gulf Power's Company, Northwest Florida** Eqn. (5.5) is suggested to minimize the total cost of electricity bill.

$$Minimize \;\; C_{Total} = \sum_{d=1}^{N} \sum_{t=1}^{T} \left\{x_{(d)}^t\, p_{RSVP}^t\right\} + \left\{x_{(d)}^{\max}\, p_{RST}^t\right\} \tag{5.5}$$

Here, $x_{(d)}^{\max}$ denotes the maximum demand (kWh) in a day $d \in N$. While in the Eqn. (5.4) and (5.5) p_{CPP}^t and p_{RST}^t are respectively CPP and RST prices for the time interval t in which peak demand occurred.

5.2.2 Operational Constraints

$$x_\ell^t(d) = 0 \quad t \notin T_\ell \tag{5.6}$$

Energy consumption of appliances other than their operational time T_ℓ will be zero (Shakouri 2017).

$$x_\ell^{min} \leq x_\ell^t(d) \leq x_\ell^{max} \quad t \in T_\ell \tag{5.7}$$

The power deferrable loads consumes energy within a certain power limit (Ahmad et al. 2018).

$$x_\ell^t(d) \in \begin{Bmatrix} 0, & \xi_\ell^t = 0 \\ P_\ell, & \xi_\ell^t = 1 \end{Bmatrix} \quad t \in T_\ell \tag{5.8}$$

Only ON–OFF control is allowed for those loads that consume a fixed power P_ℓ.

$$\sum_{t=1}^{24} x_\ell^t(d) = DR_\ell \tag{5.9}$$

The sum of energy consumption after rescheduling of all appliances should be equal to the requirement of energy for a day (DR_ℓ) (Mellouk 2018).

5.3 SOLUTION METHODS

In this research work objective functions of the total cost of energy consumption and peak-to-average ratio are optimized by CS, and ACS algorithms. The optimal results of both algorithms are also compared with Hybrid GA-PSO.

5.3.1 Cuckoo Search (CS) Method

Cuckoo search is one of the meta-heuristic type stochastic algorithms developed in 2009 (Yang & Deb 2009). This algorithm is inspired by the obligate brood parasitism of cuckoo species. These birds have a different kind of brooding behavior, they lay their eggs in the nest of other birds. The algorithm is named after the sweet sound made by these birds. Brooding behavior of Cuckoo birds is represented in Figure 5.1 (Goyal & Mehta 2015).

Figure 5.1 Brooding behavior of cuckoo birds (Yang & Deb 2009).

5.3.2 Adaptive Cuckoo Search (ACS) Method

The performance of CS method can be improved by adding new equations for adaptive adjustments of inertia weight (w_i), skewness (λ_i), and step size (α_i) as given by Eqn. (5.10), Eqn. (5.11), and Eqn. (5.12), respectively (Cheng et al. 2019).

$$w = 1 - e^{-\frac{1}{t}} \tag{5.10}$$

$$\lambda_i(t) = 0.5 + 0.1 \left| \frac{f_{best}^t - f_i^t}{f_{best} - f_{worst} + \varepsilon} \right|^t \tag{5.11}$$

$$\alpha_i(t) = 0.5 + 1.5 \left(\frac{1}{\sqrt{t}} \right) \left| \frac{f_{best}^t - f_i^t}{f_{best}^t - f_{worst}^t + \varepsilon} \right| \tag{5.12}$$

Here, w = inertia weight; t = number of iteration; f_{best}^t is best fitness value function f in iteration count t; f_{worst}^t is worst fitness value of function f in iteration count t; f_{best} and f_{worst} are global best and global worst fitness values of function f, respectively. ε is the smallest constant used to avoid error by zero value in the denominator.

5.3.3 Hybrid GA-PSO Algorithm

This algorithm is the amalgamation of Genetic algorithm (GA) and particle swarm optimization (PSO). In this algorithm, best features of GA like mutation and crossover are applied to improve the performance of PSO. Figure 5.2 gives the optimization process of this algorithm (Singhal & Goyal 2018).

5.4 RESULTS AND DISCUSSION

The proposed model is applied to seven residential smart homes. All seven households have different set of appliances and their preferences for uses.

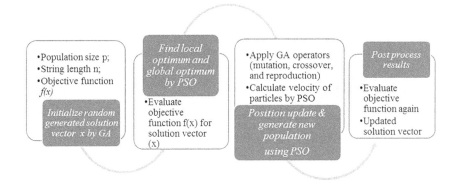

Figure 5.2 Process of hybrid GA-PSO algorithm (Singhal & Goyal 2018).

Detail of appliances and monthly power consumption by all the households is given in Table 5.1 (Goyal & Vadhera 2021). In this research work, real data of pricing schemes available in Waterloo North Hydro Inc. and Gulf Power's Company are considered to verify the performance of the proposed model. The pricing options available for retail consumers in the case of Waterloo North Hydro Inc. are flat-rate tariff, time-of-use (ToU) price, and critical peak price (CPP). In this case, pricing data is considered for December 2018 (Electricity prices in Canada 2019). While in the case of Gulf Power's Company pricing options are residential service (RS) price, residential select tariff (RST), and residential service variable pricing (RSVP). In this case, pricing data is considered for March 2000 (Samuel et al. 2018b).

5.4.1 Analysis of Results for Case Study I (Waterloo North Hydro Inc., Canada)

5.4.1.1 Scenario 1: Individual Smart Home Residents Reschedule His/ Her Power Consumption in Order to Minimize Electricity Bill Cost

The monthly cost of electricity bills calculated for seven households before minimization is given in Table 5.2. The electricity costs with ToU and CPP pricings given in the table are determined using standard and estimated scheduling of appliances. The estimated scheduling is based on the user's pattern of using appliances at various times of the day.

From Table 5.2, it can be observed that, estimated scheduling with a flat-rate tariff costs lesser than any other pricing scheme. But standard scheduling with ToU price reduced the monthly electricity bill by **7.48%** on average for all the households as compared to the estimated scheduling with ToU price. By the comparative analysis, it can be said that by the standard scheduling of deferrable appliances monthly cost of power consumption can be reduced.

Table 5.1 Energy consumption and appliance information of smart homes

S. No.	House hold no.	Range (kWh)	Monthly consumption (kWh)	Total appliance	Deferrable appliance
1	1	< 600	558.6	8	3
2	2	601–750	654.6	9	3
3	3	751–1000	947.4	14	6
4	4	1001–1250	1142.4	14	6
5	5	1251–1500	1312.5	12	7
6	6	1501–2000	1732.5	14	9
7	7	2001–2500	2392.5	15	10

Table 5.2 Monthly cost of power consumption before optimization

S. No.	House hold No.	Energy consumption (kWh)	Monthly electricity bill in ($) with				
			Flat rate tariff	Estimated scheduling		Standard scheduling	
				ToU price	CPP price	ToU price	CPP price
1	1	558.6	113.25	123.46	305.43	111.48	278.28
2	2	654.6	129.63	139.83	367.42	125.95	321.30
3	3	947.4	175.22	180.83	504.85	170.05	452.67
4	4	1142.4	201.30	214.27	591.90	199.43	540.23
5	5	1312.5	227.20	231.04	616.60	225.06	608.74
6	6	1732.5	291.15	311.36	866.89	288.30	805.75
7	7	2392.5	400.23	430.10	1393.76	387.75	1101.47

Table 5.3 gives the results of electricity cost minimized by all three optimization algorithms using Eqn. (5.2). The optimal scheduling of appliances resulted by CS, ACS, and Hybrid GA-PSO algorithms resulted in minimized electricity cost with ToU price for all the households by **6.83%**, **12.43%**, and **8.73%**, respectively, as compared to the estimated scheduling. Similarly, the optimal scheduling with CPP price resulted in minimized electricity cost by **9.97%**, **14.55%**, and **12.94%**, respectively, for all the households on average.

Reduction in cost of monthly bill of electricity by optimal scheduling with ToU price in comparison of flat rate tariff and standard scheduling with ToU price (minimum before optimization) is also given in Figure 5.3. The optimal scheduling resulted in reduced electricity bill by **7.15%** and **5.30%** compared to flat rate tariff and standard scheduling with ToU price, respectively.

Table 5.4 gives a comparison of the peak-to-average ratio (PAR) in estimated scheduling and optimal scheduling with ToU and CPP pricing schemes for all seven households. From the results given in Table 5.4, it can be observed that optimal scheduling with ToU and CPP prices resulted in

Table 5.3 Comparison for minimized electricity bill cost with different pricings

S. No.	House hold no.	With ToU price optimized using			With CPP price optimized using		
		CS	ACS	Hybrid GA-PSO	CS	ACS	Hybrid GA-PSO
1	1	113.05	110.38	112.40	258.79	242.64	250.2
2	2	127.54	120.05	125.90	321.22	295.4	300.52
3	3	171.60	165.66	168.81	460.84	438.58	455.13
4	4	200.14	184.90	195.25	543.12	530.9	540.31
5	5	223.90	200.41	220.50	587.71	571.09	580.09
6	6	289.96	268.96	274.61	805.15	782.03	790.25
7	7	391.65	372.93	385.77	1210.36	1098.65	1101.575

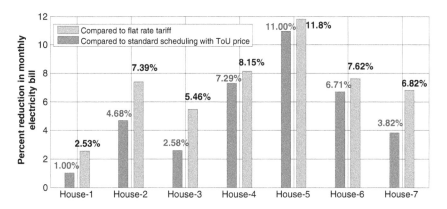

Figure 5.3 Reduction in monthly cost of electricity bill using optimal scheduling by ACS.

increased PAR for all the households by **44.89%** and **31.34%**, respectively. In this table, it can be noticed that rescheduling appliances with the aim to minimize the cost of electricity bill resulted in increased peak power demand.

5.4.1.2 Scenario 2: Individual Smart Home Residents Reschedule His/Her Power Consumption in Order to Minimize the Peak to Average Ratio (PAR)

Scenario 2 individual consumer schedules optimally his/her household appliances with the help of objective function given by Eqn. (5.3) in order to reduce the peak demand. Optimal values of peak-to-average ratios (PARs) and peak demand for all seven households given in Table 5.5 are results of ACS algorithm. From this table, it can be noticed that optimal scheduling of appliances in order to minimize the peak demand may result in raised

Table 5.4 PARs of optimized schedule with different pricings

S. No.	House hold no.	Estimated Scheduling		PAR with optimal scheduling		Resulted peak (kW) by optimal scheduling	
		PAR	Peak demand (kW)	ToU price	CPP price	ToU Price	CPP Price
1	1	2.990	2.33	4.937	3.389	3.830	2.629
2	2	3.203	2.92	4.443	4.212	4.039	3.829
3	3	2.689	3.35	2.725	2.683	3.586	3.530
4	4	2.325	3.68	2.912	2.870	4.620	4.554
5	5	2.184	3.98	2.715	2.468	4.948	4.499
6	6	2.450	5.88	4.207	3.687	10.123	8.872
7	7	1.983	6.59	3.724	3.724	12.374	12.374

electricity bill cost. Figure 5.4 gives the graphical representation of PARs for all seven households obtained by optimal scheduling with ToU and CPP prices and their comparison with PARs by estimated scheduling. From this graph, it can be observed that optimal scheduling with ToU price reduced the PAR and peak demand by **10.56%** and **9.94%** on average for all the households. The optimal scheduling with CPP price reduced the PAR and peak demand by **15.50%** and **19.51%** on average. From the results given in Table 5.5, it can be observed that optimal scheduling of appliances with ToU and CPP resulted in raised electricity cost for all the households by **8.86%** and **7.79%** on average.

5.4.1.3 Scenario 3: Individual Smart Home Residents Reschedule His/ Her Power Consumption in Order to Optimize the Electricity Bill Cost and Peak Demand Together

In scenario 3 individual consumer schedule optimally his/her household appliances in order to reduce the electricity bill cost with the help of the proposed objective function given by Eqn. (5.4). By the Eqn. (5.4) total cost of electricity is calculated with ToU price for the power consumption in 24 time slots. A component of CPP price corresponding to the time slot of peak demand is also added to the total cost. Optimal results for the cost of monthly bill of electricity, PAR, and peak demand are given in Table 5.6.

By analyzing optimal results given in Table 5.4 and Table 5.6, it is found that optimal scheduling in scenario 3 reduced the PARs for all the households by **21.09%** on average in comparison to estimated scheduling. Figure 5.5 shows the comparison of the cost of electricity bill before and after optimal scheduling in all three scenarios. Electricity cost before the optimization is calculated with flat rate tariff and ToU price. In scenario 3,

Table 5.5 Comparative results of minimized PAR by ACS algorithm

S. No.	House hold no.	Optimized PAR using ACS		Optimized peak demand using ACS in (kW)		Resulted monthly electricity cost in ($)	
		ToU price	CPP price	ToU price	CPP price	ToU price	CPP price
1	1	2.552	2.541	1.980	1.979	135.93	384.68
2	2	2.405	2.095	2.181	1.894	158.04	398.80
3	3	2.015	1.962	2.650	2.582	199.45	510.23
4	4	2.135	2.039	3.386	3.236	230.53	608.38
5	5	2.175	2.051	3.965	3.738	254.09	633.76
6	6	2.435	2.303	5.887	3.654	326.98	884.92
7	7	1.981	1.835	6.582	6.097	456.15	1551.83

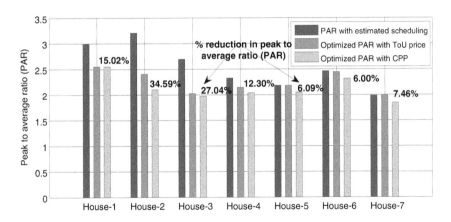

Figure 5.4 Comparison of PAR in scenario 2 of case I.

electricity cost and peak demand are reduced by **7.37%** and **16.67%** respectively on an average for all seven households.

5.4.2 Result Analysis for Case Study II (Gulf Power's Company, Northwest Florida)

5.4.2.1 Scenario 1: Individual Smart Home Residents Reschedule His/Her Power Consumption in Order to Minimize Electricity Bill Cost

In case II, cost of monthly bill of electricity before optimization (with estimated scheduling) given in Table 5.7 are calculated for seven households with RS price, RSVP, and RST pricing structures. While Table 5.8 is giving a comparison of bill cost obtained by all three optimization algorithms.

Table 5.6 Optimal results obtained for case-I

S. No.	House hold No.	Optimal monthly electricity cost in ($)	PAR with optimal scheduling	Peak (kW) with optimal scheduling
1	1	114.94	2.55	1.980
2	2	127.25	2.37	2.152
3	3	171.65	1.76	2.325
4	4	197.66	2.02	3.214
5	5	223.88	1.70	3.281
6	6	280.54	2.37	5.414
7	7	387.60	1.96	6.152

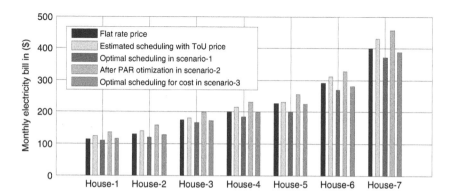

Figure 5.5 Monthly cost of electricity bill before and after optimal scheduling in all scenarios in case I.

Table 5.7 Cost of monthly bill of electricity ($) with estimated scheduling in case-II

S. No.	House hold No.	Monthly consumption (kWh)	RS price	RSVP	RST
1	1	558.6	40.14	42.83	50.08
2	2	654.6	48.28	50.19	57.95
3	3	947.4	64.92	70.21	77.87
4	4	1142.4	82.01	75.84	86.79
5	5	1312.5	91.86	89.42	98.5
6	6	1732.5	111.91	109.52	128.83
7	7	2392.5	149.47	147.01	158.23

Figure 5.6 shows the comparative analysis of the monthly cost of electricity bill before optimization (with RSVP and RS price) and after optimization (RSVP with optimal scheduling). In Figure 5.6 percentage reduction in the cost of monthly bill of electricity by optimal scheduling as compared to RS

Table 5.8 Comparison for minimized electricity bill cost with different pricings

S. No.	House hold No.	Optimized with RSVP using			Optimized with RST using		
		CS	Hybrid GA-PSO	ACS	CS	Hybrid GA-PSO	ACS
1	1	39.1	40.10	37.74	47.02	46.62	45.01
2	2	46.75	47.50	43.13	54.35	53.64	50.78
3	3	62.82	60.71	60.06	72.21	71.73	69.79
4	4	74.96	72.62	69.1	83.00	82.46	81.21
5	5	84.47	79.39	71.78	93.28	89.49	83.81
6	6	107.95	98.53	84.4	118.64	113.96	106.94
7	7	137.59	128.77	115.55	153.14	145.37	127.24

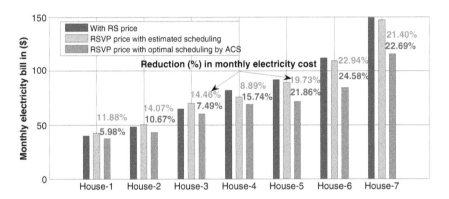

Figure 5.6 Monthly cost of electricity bill before and after optimization for case II.

price is given in blue color and a comparison with estimated scheduling is given in red color. It is also observed that optimal scheduling obtained by ACS algorithm minimized the electricity cost by **15.57%** and **16.19%** on average respectively in comparison of RS price (fixed price) and RSVP with estimated scheduling.

Table 5.9 gives PARs obtained by optimal scheduling by ACS algorithm and their comparison with estimated scheduling in case II. From the results given in Table 5.9, it can be observed that optimal scheduling with RSVP and RST pricing schemes in order to minimize the cost resulted in increased PAR for all the households by **49.10%** and **32.22%**, respectively.

5.4.2.2 Scenario 2: Individual Smart Home Residents Reschedule His/ Her Power Consumption in Order to Minimize the Peak to Average Ratio (PAR)

Similar to case I, in this case, study individual smart home consumer schedules his/her appliances in order to reduce the peak demand in scenario 2.

Table 5.9 PARs by optimized schedule with different pricings

S. No.	House hold no.	Estimated Scheduling		PAR with optimal scheduling		Resulted peak (kW) by optimal scheduling	
		PAR	Peak demand (kW)	RSVP	RST	RSVP	RST
1	1	2.990	2.33	4.936	3.389	3.83	2.63
2	2	3.203	2.92	4.443	4.441	4.04	3.98
3	3	2.689	3.35	2.729	2.725	3.59	3.58
4	4	2.325	3.68	3.857	2.712	6.12	4.30
5	5	2.184	3.98	2.468	2.468	4.50	4.50
6	6	2.450	5.88	4.208	3.792	10.12	9.12
7	7	1.983	6.59	3.724	3.724	12.37	12.37

Table 5.10 Comparative results of minimized PAR by ACS algorithm

S. No.	House hold no.	Optimized PAR using ACS		Optimized peak demand using ACS in (kW)		Resulted monthly electricity cost in ($)	
		RSVP	RST	RSVP	RST	RSVP	RST
1	1	2.552	2.551	1.98	1.98	47.75	53.37
2	2	2.626	2.439	2.39	2.22	52.03	59.51
3	3	1.983	1.847	2.82	2.30	71.52	78.94
4	4	2.215	2.057	3.51	3.26	79.88	86.23
5	5	2.054	2.065	3.76	3.74	98.51	99.45
6	6	2.233	2.201	5.85	4.07	110.92	130.29
7	7	1.980	2.123	5.19	7.05	153.99	145.21

Optimal values of PARs and peak demand obtained by ACS algorithm for all seven households are given in Table 5.10. By analyzing the results given in Table 5.9 and Table 5.10, it is observed that optimal scheduling in scenario 2 with RSVP and RST reduced the PAR by **11.23%** and **12.85%** respectively on an average for all the households. Figure 5.7 gives the graphical representation of the percent rise in monthly bill cost obtained by optimal scheduling with RSVP. From this graph, it is observed that optimal scheduling with RSVP resulted in the rise of electricity cost by **6.24%** and **5.51%** respectively in comparison to RS price and RSVP with estimated scheduling.

5.4.2.3 Scenario 3: Individual Smart Home Residents Reschedule His/ Her Power Consumption in Order to Optimize the Electricity Bill Cost and Peak Demand Together

Similar to case I in this case also in scenario 3 individual smart home consumer schedules optimally his/her household appliances in order to

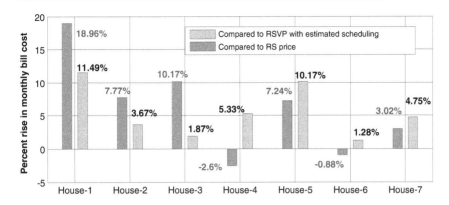

Figure 5.7 Rise in cost of electricity bill by optimum scheduling with RSVP in scenario 2 for case-II.

reduce the electricity bill cost with the help of the proposed objective function which is given by Eqn. (5.5). Optimal cost of monthly bill of electricity, resulting PAR and peak power demand are given in Table 5.11. By analyzing optimal results given in Table 5.9 and Table 5.11, it is found that optimal scheduling in scenario 3 reduced the electricity cost and PARs respectively by **4.96%** and **9.03%** on average for all the households in comparison to estimated scheduling.

Figure 5.8, Figure 5.9, and Figure 5.10 show the power consumption pattern and peak load demand for household 1, household 2, and household 3, respectively in all three scenarios in case study I. Figure 5.11 and Figure 5.12 show the power consumption patterns and peak load obtained by optimal scheduling in order to minimize the electricity bill cost under scenario 1 and scenario 3 for household 4 and household 5 in case study II. Data tips given on scheduling curves show the peak power consumption. Here, X shows the time slot and Y represents the value of

Table 5.11 Optimal results obtained for case-II

S. No.	House hold no.	Optimal monthly electricity cost in ($)	PAR with optimal scheduling	Peak (kW) with optimal scheduling
1	1	40.24	2.552	1.98
2	2	47.20	2.873	2.61
3	3	65.06	2.224	2.93
4	4	75.65	2.176	3.46
5	5	84.35	1.963	3.58
6	6	101.94	2.373	5.70
7	7	137.34	1.957	6.51

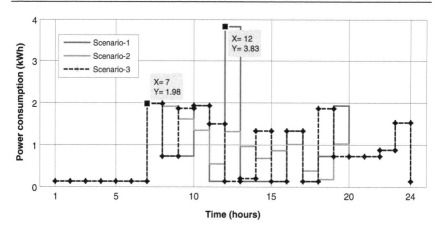

Figure 5.8 Power consumption curve with optimal scheduling for house-1.

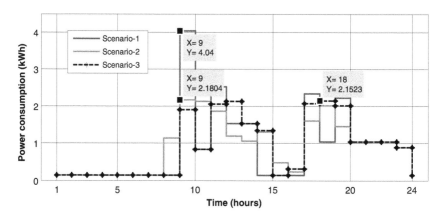

Figure 5.9 Power consumption curve with optimal scheduling for house 2.

peak demand that can be verified with the results given in Table 5.4, Table 5.5, and Table 5.6 in case study I and Table 5.9, Table 5.10, and Table 5.11 in case study II.

By the analysis of the results presented in all three scenarios of both the case studies, in a nutshell, it can be said that optimal scheduling with the proposed cost functions in **scenario 3**, PAR is reduced by **41.35%** as compared to the optimal results of scenario 1 and electricity cost is reduced by **14.89%** in comparison of the optimal results of scenario 2 in case study I. While optimal results in case II perceive that in scenario 3, PAR is reduced by **36.75%** as compared to the optimal results of scenario 1, and electricity cost is reduced by **10.37%** in comparison to the optimal results of scenario 2.

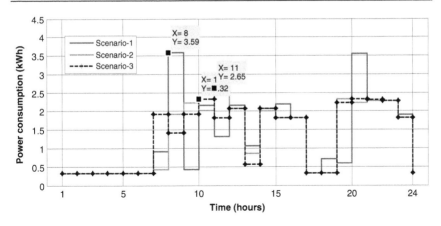

Figure 5.10 Power consumption curve with optimal scheduling for house 3.

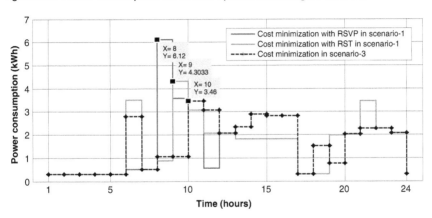

Figure 5.11 Power consumption curve with optimal scheduling for house 4.

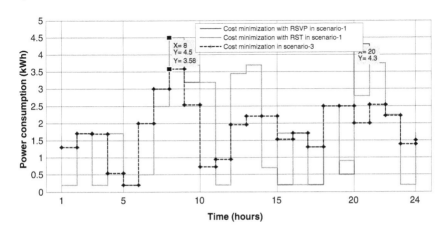

Figure 5.12 Power consumption curve with optimal scheduling for house-5.

5.5 CONCLUSION AND FUTURE SCOPE

The core objective of this research work is to minimize the cost of electricity bill and peak power demand simultaneously. Due to the conflicting behavior of these two objectives, this study has been divided into three scenarios. The first two scenarios deal with individual minimization of electricity cost and peak-to-average ratio. Also, their effects on each other have been studied. In the third scenario, both objectives have been achieved by minimizing the cost function proposed for both utilities. Optimal scheduling of smart home appliances is obtained for all three scenarios as per consumer preferences with the help of CS, Hybrid GA–PSO, and ACS as core algorithms of optimization. From the results of simulations for both of the case studies, it is observed that optimal scheduling in scenario 1 minimized the cost of electricity bill but also resulted in raised PAR. On the other hand in scenario 2 PAR is minimized but also resulted in raised electricity bill cost in comparison of before scheduling. But optimal scheduling with the proposed cost functions in scenario 3 using ACS algorithm resulted in the minimization of both objectives simultaneously. Comparative analysis of results demonstrated the competence of the proposed model to achieve both objectives. Future research can be carried out with the implementation of real-time pricing schemes available in other utilities in the optimization of different objective functions using ACS algorithm or any other technique.

REFERENCES

S. Ahmad, A. Ahmad, M. Naeem, W. Ejaz, and H. S. Kim, "A compendium of performance metrics, pricing schemes, optimization objectives, and solution methodologies of demand side management for the smart grid," *Energies*, vol. 11, no. 10, pp. 2801, 2018.

S. Ahmad, N. Muhammad, and A. Ayaz, "Unified optimization model for energy management in sustainable smart power systems," *International Transactions on Electrical Energy Systems*, vol. 30, no. 4, 2020.

S. Ahmad, M. M. Alhaisoni, M. Naeem, A. Ahmad, and M. Altaf, "Joint energy management and energy trading in residential microgrid system," *IEEE Access*, vol. 8, pp. 123334–123346, 2020.

A. Anees, T. Dillon, S. Wallis, and Y. P. Chen, "Optimization of day-ahead and real-time prices for smart home community," *International Journal of Electrical Power & Energy Systems*, vol. 124, no. 106403, 2021.

S. Bedi, Md. W. Ahmad, S. Swapnil, K. Rajawat, and S. Anand, "Online algorithms for storage utilization under real-time pricing in smart grid," *International Journal of Electrical Power & Energy Systems*, vol. 101, pp. 50–59, 2018.

Z. Cheng, J. Wang, M. Zhang, H. Song, T. Chang, Y. Bi, and K. Sun, "Improvement and application of adaptive hybrid cuckoo search algorithm," *IEEE Access*, vol. 7, pp. 145489–145515, 2019.

Electricity prices in Canada, 2019, https://www.energyhub.org/electricity-prices/. (Accessed: 09/01/2019).

G. R. Goyal, and H. D. Mehta, "Multi-objective optimal active power dispatch using swarm optimization techniques," In *Proc. 5th Nirma University International Conference on Engineering (NUiCONE)*, IEEE, pp. 1–6, 2015.

G. R. Goyal, and S. Vadhera, "Solution of combined economic emission dispatch with demand side management using meta-heuristic algorithms," *Journal Européen des Systemes Automatisés*, vol. 52, no. 2, pp. 143–148, 2019.

G. R. Goyal, and S. Vadhera, "Challenges of implementing demand side management in developing countries," *Journal of Power Technologies*, vol. 100, no. 1, pp. 43, 2020.

G. R. Goyal, and S. Vadhera, "Multi-interval programming based scheduling of appliances with user preferences and dynamic pricing in residential area," *Sustainable Energy, Grids and Networks*, vol. 27, pp. 100511, 2021.

H. M. Hussain, N. Javaid, S. Iqbal, H. Qadeer, A. Khursheed, and M. Alhussein, "An efficient demand side management system with a new optimized home energy management controller in smart grid," *Energies*, no. 11, pp. 190, 2018.

L. Mellouk, M. Boulmalf, A. Aaroud, K. Zine-Dine, and D. Benhaddou, "Genetic algorithm to solve demand side management and economic dispatch problem," In *Proc. 9th International Conference on Ambient Systems, Networks and Technologies (ICASNT), IEEE*, vol. 130, pp. 611–618, 2018.

E. Nezhad, R. Abolfazl, H. J. Nardelli, S. A. Gadsden, S. Sahoo, and F. Ghanavati, "A shrinking horizon model predictive controller for daily scheduling of home energy management systems," *IEEE Access*, no. 10, pp. 29716–29730, 2022.

O. Samuel, S. Javaid, N. Javaid, S. H. Ahmed, M. K. Afzal, F. Ishmanov, "An efficient power scheduling in smart homes using Jaya based optimization with time-of-use and critical peak pricing schemes," *Energies*, vol. 11, pp. 3155, 2018.

O. Samuel, N. Javaid, M. Ashraf, F. Ishmanov, M. K. Afzal, Z. A. Khan, "Jaya based optimization method with high dispatchable distributed generation for residential microgrid," *Energies*, vol. 11, pp. 1513, 2018.

B. Saravanan, "DSM in an area consisting of residential, commercial and industrial load in smart grid," *Frontiers in Energy*, vol. 9, no. 2, pp. 211–216, 2015.

H. G. Shakouri and A. Kazemi, "Multi-objective cost-load optimization for demand side management of a residential area in smart grids," *Journal of Sustainable Cities and Society*, vol. 32, pp. 171–180, 2017.

A. K. Sharma and A. Saxena, "A demand side management control strategy using Whale optimization algorithm," *Journal of SN Applied Sciences*, vol. 1, no. 870, 2019.

K. Singhal and G. R. Goyal, "Comparative study of power consumption minimization in analog electronic circuit using AI techniques," *European Journal of Electrical Engineering–n*, vol. 20, no. 4, pp. 427–438, 2018.

Z. Yahia and A. Pradhan, "Multi-objective optimization of household appliance scheduling problem considering consumer preference and peak load reduction," *Sustainable Cities and Society*, vol. 55, p. 102058, 2020.

X. S. Yang and S. Deb, "Cuckoo search via Lévy flights," In *World Congress on Nature & Biologically Inspired Computing (NaBIC)*, IEEE, pp. 210–214, 2009.

Chapter 6

A Comparison of Metaheuristic Algorithms for Estimating Solar Cell Parameters Using a Single Diode Model

Abhishek Sharma, Abhinav Sharma, Vibhu Jately, Sumit Pundir, and Wei Hong Lim

CONTENTS

6.1 INTRODUCTION

It is widely known that photovoltaic (PV) technology is a source full of promise for the generation of electricity due to its wide range of benefits. The output from PV modules majorly depends upon the incident irradiance and cell temperature. Therefore, identifying the parameters of photovoltaic modules is a very important task in ensuring that maximum power can be extracted from them [1–5]. Parameters used in the model do not find any direct mention in the manufacturers' data sheets. These sheets merely state the voltage of the cell or the model when its output terminals remain open without any load (V_{oc}), the current when its output terminals are short-circuited (I_{sc}), voltage (V_{mpp}), and current at maximum power point (I_{mpp}) under STC. Here STC stands for standard test conditions (i.e., at an Irradiance of 1000 W/m^2, and at a temperature of 25°C). Moreover, this task of identifying the cell parameters becomes more challenging due to the variation in irradiance and uneven irradiance levels on modules leading to partial shading conditions [6].

DOI: 10.1201/9781003356639-6

The equivalent circuit using the single-diode and double-diode models during analysis and simulations of PV cells is the most convenient and, therefore, popular for parameter extraction. Among these, the single-diode model (SDM) has fairly good accuracy and is of low complexity. The problem of parameter extraction is majorly solved using analytical or optimization methods [7–10]. The analytical approaches are the most straightforward and produce results rapidly, but they lack precision when used in daytime conditions with changing insolation levels.

The Newton-Raphson, nonlinear least squares, Lambert W-functions [11], iterative curve fitting [12], conductivity method [13], and Levenberg-Marquardt [14] algorithms are deterministic methods for parameter extraction as an option. These deterministic methods have several constraints related to continuity, differentiability, and convexity of objective functions. The use of the aforementioned analytical techniques is further constrained by the boundary conditions since, when applied to multi-modal situations, they yield local minima. Analytical techniques are, therefore, rendered inappropriate for extracting the parameters.

As they don't need intricate mathematics, the bio-system-based algorithms are simple and turn out to be more precise and potent optimization techniques for simplifying nonlinear systems. Some commonly available metaheuristic methods are particle swarm optimization [15], chaos particle swarm optimization (CPSO) [16], harmony search (HS) [17], cuckoo search algorithm (CSA) [18], artificial bee colony (ABC) [19], cat swarm optimization (CSO) [20], hybrid PSO [21], GWO [22], pattern search [23], differential evolution [24] are all attractive alternatives for determining the parameters of the cell.

In this chapter, the authors have compared the performance of three avant-garde metaheuristic optimization algorithms, which include PSO, GWO, and ASO. The proposed study analyses the behavior and drawbacks of the compared algorithms which will benefit researchers working within this area.

6.2 PROBLEM FORMULATION

6.2.1 Single-Diode Model

Figure 6.1 depicts the analogous circuit of an SDM. The voltage and current at the output of the cell can be established from the equivalent circuit and the diode theory [1,2].

$$I_L = I_p - I_d - I_{sh} \tag{6.1}$$

where I_L stands for the load current of the output of the cell, I_p for its photo-current, I_{d1} signifies current flowing through diode, I_{sh} is the current in parallel resistance.

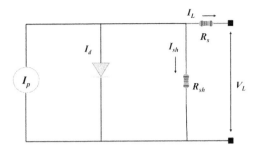

Figure 6.1 SDM and its equivalent circuit [1,2].

$$I_l = I_p - I_{SD}\left[exp\left(\frac{q(V_l + I_l R_s)}{a_1 k_B T}\right) - 1\right] - \frac{V_l + I_l R_s}{R_{sh}} \tag{6.2}$$

Five model parameters (I_p, I_{SD}, a_1, R_s, and R_{sh}) must be improved in the above equation employing observed I-V data from the experiments done on the PV cell. The SDM is thought to be a good working model that is simple to renew the I-V curve.

6.2.2 Objective Function

The primary goal of this chapter is to explain how to optimize the values of unknown parameters of the SDM and decrease the discrepancy between the empirical and estimated values of these parameters. The optimization problem in terms of error is explained as under:

$$RMSE = \sqrt{\frac{1}{k}\sum_{N=1}^{k} f(V_L, I_L, X)} \tag{6.3}$$

Here, V_l and I_l are experimentally observed for the module under consideration. Larger the number of these experimental values better the optimization. Parameter 'k' stands for this number. Vector X represents the best solution found by GWO.

We can write for SDM,

$$\begin{cases} f_{single}(V_L, I_L, X) = I_p - I_{SD}\left[exp\left(\frac{q(V_L + I_L R_s)}{a_1 k_B T}\right) - 1\right] - \frac{V_L + I_L R_s}{R_{sh}} - I_L \\ \left(X = I_p, I_{SD}, a_1, R_s, R_{sh}\right) \end{cases} \tag{6.4}$$

6.3 METAHEURISTIC ALGORITHMS

Metaheuristic is a Greek word that combines from two words meta which means high level and heuristic which means search, thus this word means high level search. These high-level search algorithms are widely used in the field of science and engineering because they are built on simple concepts, don't get trapped in locally optimal solutions, don't need gradient information, and can be utilized to solve any constraint and unconstraint problem irrespective of their field of operation. These algorithms are grouped into different categories as swarm-based, evolutionary-based, and physics-based algorithms. Swarm intelligence [25] algorithms are nature-inspired algorithms, which follow the behavior patterns of a clan of biological beings called agents, which includes insects, animals, birds, fishes, etc.

6.3.1 Particle Swarm Optimization

In 1995 Eberhart and Kennedy suggested a nature-inspired PSO algorithm [26]. The algorithm is population-based and stochastic in nature and is motivated by the social relations of a group of birds. The individual elements of the algorithm are birds referred to as particles which communicate with each other and stochastically modify their position to find the optimal solution in multidimensional search space. All possible solutions defined the search space and particles first explore and later exploit the search space by adjusting the flying of all particles with respect to their flying and the flying of the best particle.

To start with, a population of particles is assigned some initial values in a random manner within the identified search domain with some small velocity. As the iterations proceed, the velocity of all the particles is updated with respect to equation (6.5) which leads to a change in the position of all the particles with respect to equation (6.6) towards the best solution. Various steps in the process of the flow of the PSO algorithm can be seen in Figure 6.2.

$$vel_j^d(t+1) = w * vel_j^d(t) + c_1 * r_1 * \left(pbest_j^d(t) - y_j^d(t) \right)$$

$$+ c_2 * r_2 * \left(gbest^d - y_j^d(t) \right) \tag{6.5}$$

$$y_j^d(t+1) = y_j^d(t) + vel_j^d(t+1) \tag{6.6}$$

where $vel_j^d(t+1)$ and $vel_j^d(t)$; $y_j^d(t+1)$ and $y_j^d(t)$ symbolize the velocity and location of jth particles in d^{th} dimension at t^{th} and $(t+1)^{th}$ iteration. Terms

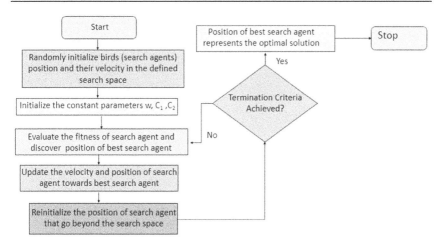

Figure 6.2 Flow-chart of PSO algorithm.

pbest and *gbest* symbolize the individual personal best location of particles and global best location of particle among all the particles. The cognitive coefficient is symbolized by term c_1, and the social coefficient by c_2. Here r_1 is a random number of range [0–1]; so is r_2. Finally, w represents an inertia weight that is defined differently by authors. This inertia weight tries to keep stability between exploration and exploitation over the course of iterations.

6.3.2 Gray Wolf Optimization

In 2014 Mirjalili et al. proposed a stochastic population-based GWO algorithm [27]. The algorithm is motivated by the manners and methods of how the gray wolves move to surround the prey and hunt in a pack, and how they follow their leader in their natural habitat. These carnivorous animals build communication among themselves through barking, howling, and different body gestures. Mathematically, the technique models how the wolves track potential prey, how they chase, how they harass, and finally attack their prey. Various blocks in Figure 6.3 show the sequential flow of the steps of the GWO algorithm. A population of gray wolves is initialized in the search space and the position corresponding to first three best gray wolves with respect to the prey represents alpha, beta, and delta wolves and the remaining wolves are the omega wolves. All these four classifications of wolves live in a group of five to fifteen so as to intelligently harass and attack the prey.

The location of all the gray wolves is improved depending on the location of alpha (Y_α), beta (Y_β) and delta (Y_δ) wolves based on equations (6.7)–(6.9).

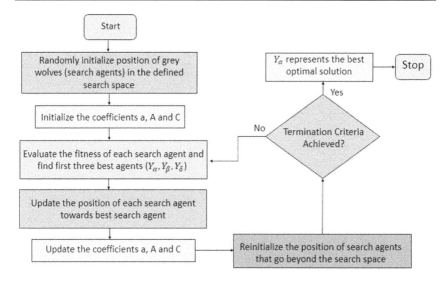

Figure 6.3 Flow-chart of GWO algorithm.

$$D_\alpha = |C_1 * Y_\alpha - Y|, \quad D_\beta = |C_2 * Y_\beta - Y|, \quad D_\delta = |C_3 * Y_\delta - Y| \qquad (6.7)$$

$$Y_1 = Y_\alpha - A_1 * (D_\alpha), \quad Y_2 = Y_\beta - A_2 * (D_\beta), \quad Y_3 = Y_\delta - A_3 * (D_\delta) \quad (6.8)$$

$$Y(k + 1) = \frac{Y_1 + Y_2 + Y_3}{3} \qquad (6.9)$$

where A_1, A_2, A_3 and C_1, C_2, C_3 symbolize the coefficients of α, β, δ wolves and k symbolizes the present iteration. These coefficients are represented based on the following equations:

$$A = 2 * a * r_1 - a \qquad (6.10)$$

$$C = 2 * r_2 \qquad (6.11)$$

The value of A decreases gradually over the course of iterations as outlined in equation (6.10), because initially the wolves chase the prey and once the prey stops moving then they attack the prey. This basically presents the exploitation phase of the algorithm. In the initial phase wolves explore the search space as A has a larger value but over the iterations value of A decreases and the algorithm exploits the search space and moves closer to the optimal solution.

6.3.3 Atom Search Optimization

In 2019 Zhao et al. proposed physics inspired stochastic population-based ASO algorithm [28]. The smallest component of a chemical compound is molecules which contain atoms that are bounded together through covalent bonds and are in a state of constant motion. All atoms have a certain mass and volume and are held together through some constraint and non-constraint forces. The algorithm mathematically models the natural atomic motion of atoms that occurs because of these forces. The Lennard-Jones (L-J) potential defines the attraction and repulsion forces (non-constraint) as defined in equation (6.12) while bond-length potential as defined in equation (6.13) defines constraint forces over a certain range of separation among the atoms. The process of the flow of the ASO algorithm can be seen in Figure 6.4.

A parameter K which decreases over the course of iterations checks that initially atoms interact with larger space of atoms and later interact with fewer atoms so as to maintain a balance between exploration and exploitation.

$$Force_{ij}(t) = \frac{24\beta(t)}{\alpha(t)} \left[2 \left(\frac{\alpha(t)}{c_{ij}(t)} \right)^{13} - \left(\frac{\alpha(t)}{c_{ij}(t)} \right)^{7} \right] \frac{c_{ij}(t)}{c_{ij}^{d}(t)} \qquad (6.12)$$

where α signifies the collision diameter, β represents the magnitude of the interactive force. $c_{ij}(t)$ is the distance between j^{th} and i^{th} atom at time t. The constraint force is defined as:

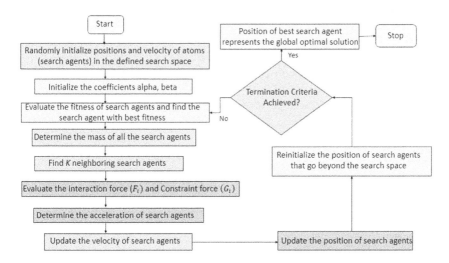

Figure 6.4 Flowchart of atom search optimization algorithm.

$$S_i^d(t) = \lambda(t)\left(y_{best}^d(t) - y_i^d(t)\right)$$
(6.13)

where $\lambda(t)$ represents the Lagrangian multiplier, $y_{best}(t)$ represents the position of the best atom, $y_i(t)$ is the location of ith atom at t^{th} iteration. Based on equation (6.12)–(6.13) and mass $m_i^d(t)$ of the atom's acceleration and velocity of all the atoms are updated and atoms try to move closer to the best atom.

$$acc_i^d(t) = \frac{F_i^d(t)}{m_i^d(t)} + \frac{G_i^d(t)}{m_i^d(t)}$$
(6.14)

$$vel_i^d(t + 1) = rand_i^d vel_i^d(t) + acc_i^d(t)$$
(6.15)

where $vel_i^d(t + 1)$ and $vel_i^d(t)$ is the velocity of ith atom in the dth dimension at $(t+1)^{th}$ and t^{th} time.

6.4 RESULTS AND DISCUSSION

In this sub-section, the efficacy of three metaheuristic techniques, namely PSO, GWO, and ASO, was investigated and assessed primarily utilizing a single solar cell known as an R.T.C France solar cell. The parameters obtained for each device type in the PV cell and module were analyzed and employed to simulate I-V data. Table 6.1 tabulates the upper and lower limits for individual parameters. These are identical to those employed by investigators in [3,4]. All the approaches are implemented on MATLAB 2018a platform with Intel ® core ™ i7-HQ CPU, 2.4 GHz, 16 GB RAM Laptop.

To carry out the simulations, the size of the sample is set at 30, and the anticipated number of objective function assessments is set at 50,000. In this case, RMSE is used as a performance metric to assess the efficacy of all

Table 6.1 Lower and upper limits of parameters for SDM

Parameter	SDM	
	Lower Bound	Upper Bound
$I_p(A)$	0	1
$I_{sd}(\mu A)$	0.01	0.5
$R_s(\Omega)$	0.001	0.5
$R_{sh}(\Omega)$	0	100
a_1	1	2

Table 6.2 Optimal values of the parameters using three algorithms for SDM of solar cell

Algorithms	I_p (A)	R_s (Ω)	R_{sh} (Ω)	I_{sd} (μA)	a	RMSE
GWO	0.7592	0.0385	74.9312	0.2501	1.45	7.1090×10^{-04}
PSO	0.0686	0.0322	44.9312	0.2501	1.65	8.4208×10^{-03}
ASO	0.0717	0.0399	25.5045	0.1427	1.44	6.9590×10^{-01}

comparable methods. Table 6.2 shows the optimal values for the five parameters for the selected solar cell. This table further shows that the GWO approach produces the lowest error (RMSE 7.1090×10^{-04}). While PSO produces the second-best RMSE value of 8.4208×10^{-03}, ASO produces the worst RMSE value of 6.9590×10^{-01} here.

Figure 6.5 depicts the redesigned I-V-voltage characteristics curve for the selected solar cell. This I-V characteristics curve is retraced by utilizing the optimized values of the parameters obtained in the experiment. The five parameters used are I_p, I_{sd}, a, R_s, and R_{sh}.

Furthermore, in terms of convergence rate, the efficiency of all strategies is examined with one another (i.e., the least value of RMSE). The convergence curve for all compared techniques is depicted in Figure 6.6. This figure clearly establishes that the GWO technique outperforms the other evaluated techniques. Here, the performance of ASO is very worst because of its tendency to get stuck in local minima.

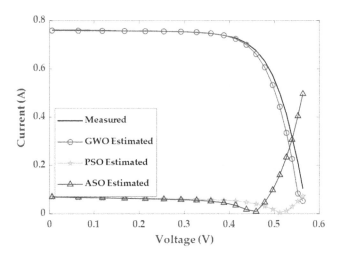

Figure 6.5 Comparison of measured and estimated values of current produced by PSO, GWO, and ASO for SDM of solar cell.

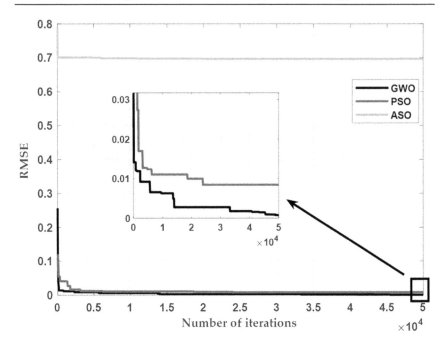

Figure 6.6 Convergence curve of all compared algorithms for SDM of solar cell.

6.5 CONCLUSION

Single diode model (SDM) being the most convenient and sufficiently accurate for all practical purposes has been used in this book chapter that does a brief comparison of metaheuristic strategies for estimating solar cell parameters. The performance of three modern metaheuristics techniques: GWO, PSO, and ASO are compared on the basis of error (RMSE) and speed (convergence rate). From this comparison, the following primary observations are made:

- The GWO technique provides a much superior value of RMSE than those of PSO and ASO.
- The best performance of the GWO can be attributed to its ability to keep a good balance between the exploration phase of the algorithm and its exploitation phase.
- The convergence curves show that the GWO approach generates the best-optimized value of all five parameters, and the lowest value of RMSE, 7.1090×10^{-04}.

REFERENCES

[1] V. Jately and S. Arora, "An efficient hill-climbing technique for peak power tracking of photovoltaic systems," 2016 IEEE 7th Power India International Conference (PIICON), Bikaner, India, 2016, pp. 1–5, doi: 10.1109/POWERI.2016.8077327.

[2] V. Jately and S. Arora, "Performance investigation of hill-climbing MPPT techniques for PV systems under rapidly changing environment," In: Singh, R., Choudhury, S., Gehlot, A. (eds) Intelligent Communication, Control and Devices. Advances in Intelligent Systems and Computing, vol 624. Singapore: Springer. 10.1007/978-981-10-5903-2_120

[3] V. Jately, S. Bhattacharya, B. Azzopardi, A. Montgareuil, J. Joshi, and S. Arora, "Voltage and current reference based MPPT under rapidly changing irradiance and load resistance," IEEE Trans. Energy Convers., vol. 36, no. 3, pp. 2297–2309, Sept. 2021, doi: 10.1109/TEC.2021.3058454.

[4] V. Jately, B. Azzopardi, J. Joshi, B. Venkateswaran V, A. Sharma, and S. Arora, "Comprehensive review of hill-climbing MPPT algorithms under low irradiance levels," Renewable Sustainable Energy Rev., vol. 150, October 2021. (IF: 14.982) doi: 10.1016/j.rser.2021.111467

[5] V. Jately and S. Arora, "Development of a dual-tracking technique for extracting maximum power from PV systems under rapidly changing environmental conditions," Energy, vol. 133, pp. 557–571, August 2017. (IF: 6.082) doi: 10.1016/j.energy.2017.05.049

[6] A. Sharma, A. Sharma, V. Jately, M. Averbukh, S. Rajput, and B. Azzopardi, "A novel TSA-PSO based hybrid algorithm for GMPP tracking under partial shading conditions," Energies, vol. 15, no. 9, p. 3164, Apr. 2022, doi: 10.3390/en15093164.

[7] A. Sharma, A. Sharma, M. Averbukh, V. Jately, and B. Azzopardi, "An effective method for parameter estimation of a solar cell," Electronics, vol. 10, no. 3, p. 312, Jan. 2021, doi: 10.3390/electronics10030312.

[8] A. Sharma, A. Dasgotra, S. K. Tiwari, A. Sharma, V. Jately, and B. Azzopardi, "Parameter extraction of photovoltaic module using tunicate swarm algorithm," Electronics, vol. 10, no. 8, p. 878, Apr. 2021, doi: 10.3390/electronics10080878.

[9] A. Sharma et al., "Opposition-based tunicate swarm algorithm for parameter optimization of solar cells," IEEE Access, vol. 9, pp. 125590–125602, 2021, doi: 10.1109/ACCESS.2021.3110849.

[10] A. Sharma, A. Sharma, M. Averbukh, S. Rajput, V. Jately, S. Choudhury, and B. Azzopardi, "Improved moth flame optimization algorithm based on opposition-based learning and Lévy flight distribution for parameter estimation of solar module," Energy Rep., vol. 8, May 2022. (IF: 6.87). doi: 10.1016/j.egyr.2022.05.011

[11] X. Gao, Y. Cui, J. Hu, G. Xu, and Y. Yu, "Lambert W-function based exact representation for double diode model of solar cells: Comparison on fitness and parameter extraction," Energy Convers. Manag., vol. 127, pp. 443–460, 2016.

[12] M. G. Villalva, J. R. Gazoli, and E. Ruppert Filho, "Comprehensive approach to modeling and simulation of photovoltaic arrays," IEEE Trans. Power Electron, vol. 24, pp. 1198–1208, 2009.

[13] M. Chegaar, Z. Ouennoughi, and A. Hoffmann, "A new method for evaluating illuminated solar cell parameters," Solid-State Electron, vol. 45, pp. 293–296, 2001.

[14] R. Abdallah, E. Natsheh, A. Juaidi, S. Samara, and F. Manzano-Agugliaro, "A multi-level world comprehensive neural network model for maximum annual solar irradiation on a flat surface," Energies, vol. 13, p. 6422, 2020.

[15] M. A. Mughal, Q. Ma, and C. Xiao, "Photovoltaic cell parameter estimation using hybrid particle swarm optimization and simulated annealing," Energies, vol. 10, no. 8, pp. 1213, Aug. 2017.

[16] A. T. Kiani, M. Faisal Nadeem, A. Ahmed, I. A. Sajjad, A. Raza, and I. A. Khan, "Chaotic inertia weight particle swarm optimization (CIWPSO): An efficient technique for solar cell parameter estimation", Proc. 3rd Int. Conf. Comput. Math. Eng. Technol. (iCoMET), pp. 1–6, Jan. 2020.

[17] M. Derick, C. Rani, M. Rajesh, M. E. Farrag, Y. Wang, and K. Busawon, "An improved optimization technique for estimation of solar photovoltaic parameters", Sol. Energy, vol. 157, pp. 116–124, Nov. 2017.

[18] J. Ma, T. O. Ting, K. L. Man, N. Zhang, S.-U. Guan, and P. W. H. Wong, "Parameter estimation of photovoltaic models via cuckoo search", J. Appl. Math., vol. 2013, pp. 1–8, Jun. 2013.

[19] M. Ketkar and A. M. Chopde, "Efficient parameter extraction of solar cell using modified ABC", Int. J. Comput. Appl., vol. 102, no. 1, pp. 1–6, Sep. 2014.

[20] L. Guo, Z. Meng, Y. Sun, and L. Wang, "Parameter identification and sensitivity analysis of solar cell models with cat swarm optimization algorithm", Energy Convers. Manage., vol. 108, pp. 520–528, Jan. 2016.

[21] A. Singh, A. Sharma, S. Rajput, A. Bose, and X. Hu, "An investigation on hybrid particle swarm optimization algorithms for parameter optimization of PV cells," Electronics, vol. 11 (6), p. 909, 2022.

[22] A. Sharma, A. Sharma, A. Moshe, N. Raj, and R. K. Pachauri, "An effective method for parameter estimation of solar PV cell using Grey-wolf optimization technique. International Journal of Mathematical," Eng. Manage. Sci., vol. 6 (3), p. 911, 2021.

[23] M. F. AlHajri, K. M. El-Naggar, M. R. AlRashidi, and A. K. Al-Othman, "Optimal extraction of solar cell parameters using pattern search," Renewable energy, vol. 44, pp. 238–245, 2012.

[24] W. Gong and Z. Cai, "Parameter extraction of solar cell models using repaired adaptive differential evolution," Solar Energy, vol. 94, pp. 209–220, 2013.

[25] A. Sharma, A. Sharma, J. K. Pandey, and M. Ram, Swarm intelligence: foundation, principles, and engineering applications. CRC Press, 2022.

[26] J. Kennedy and R. Eberhart, "Particle swarm optimization," In Proceedings of ICNN'95-International Conference on Neural Networks (Vol. 4, pp. 1942–1948). IEEE, 1995.

[27] S. Mirjalili, S. M. Mirjalili, and A. Lewis, "Grey wolf optimizer," Adv. Eng. Software, vol. 69, pp. 46–61, 2014.

[28] W. Zhao, L. Wang, and Z. Zhang, "Atom search optimization and its application to solve a hydrogeologic parameter estimation problem," Knowledge-Based Syst., vol. 163, pp. 283–304, 2019.

Chapter 7

Review on Controlling of BLDC Motor via Optimization Techniques for Renewable Energy Applications

Abhay Chhetri, Nafees Ahamad, and Mayank Saklani

CONTENTS

7.1 INTRODUCTION

For the development of an electrical motor, mechanical structure, materials, electronic sensors, and other control methods are required. During the industrial revolution, electric motors were available. These motors were divided into AC and DC categories. AC motors were further subdivided into numerous types [1]. DC motors were favored in applications such as elevators, steel mills, and locomotives due to their simple speed control and high torque availability. The addition of a commutator to DC motors increased their size, cost, and maintenance requirements. To solve this issue, brushless DC (BLDC) motors with an electronic controller instead of a standard mechanical commutator circuit were developed. The electronic controller comprises a speed control circuit and sensors. This controller made BLDC motors smaller and lighter while maintaining the same high torque and efficiency as DC motors. A BLDC motor requires a solid-state inverter, permanent magnets, polyphase stator windings, and hall sensors. The position of the rotor is detected by Hall sensors, which then provide a signal to the controller, which adjusts the commutation logic of the solid-state devices in the inverter based on the position of the rotor.

DOI: 10.1201/9781003356639-7

BLDC motor control consists of two loops. The inner and outer loops of a motor are responsible for controlling the motor's current and speed, respectively. For controller design, there are a variety of classical methodologies and, more recently, many optimization algorithms, including Salp Swarm Optimization [2,3] and Antlion Optimization [4]. Numerous controllers, including Fuzzy controller [5,6], H-infinity controller [7], PID controller employing genetic algorithm [8], and root locus approach [9], have been created. Various methods of regulating the BLDC motor have been proposed by various writers. Three separate controllers are used to regulate the motor's speed, and the mathematical model is generated using state space [10]. Artificial Neural Network (ANN), Proportional Integral (PI), and ANN-PI. Alternately, the speed of the BLDC motor can be controlled using sliding mode control [11]. Although there are a variety of methods for regulating the BLDC motor, there is a dearth of in-depth analyses of how particular algorithms function.

In this paper, PID and PD controllers are used to control the speed of a BLDC motor. The controller parameters (K_p, K_i, and K_d) are tuned or optimized utilizing various optimization approaches, such as SCA, MFO, PSO, GWO, WOA, and COOT, with varying Lower and Upper limits. Various limits are employed to determine whether the strategy works better within a specific range. In PID and PD controllers, the values acquired from various optimization strategies are incorporated. The performance of the controller is evaluated by analyzing the step response of the BLDC motor coupled in series with the PID and PD controllers. The time-domain requirements acquired from the step response of the BLDC motor, including rise time (t_r), settling time (t_s), and maximum overshoot ($M_p\%$), are compared with the time-domain specifications of existing controllers.

This paper is broken into the sections listed below. The first section is an introduction. The second section describes the mathematical modeling of BLDC motors. Section 7.3 demonstrates the various optimization strategies utilized for BLDC motor control. Section 7.4 presents the implementation methods for various optimization techniques with PID and PD controllers. Section 7.5 depicts the step response of all optimal values derived using various optimization methods. The conclusion of Section 7.6 identifies the optimal controller for the control of the BLDC motor.

7.2 MATHEMATICAL MODEL OF BLDC

The BLDC mathematical model is derived using the following procedure. The two supplied equations help us determine the mathematical model of the BLDC motor [9].

$$\frac{di_a(t)}{d(t)} = \frac{R_a}{L_a}(t) - \frac{K_a}{L_a}w_m(t) + \frac{1}{L_a}V_s(t) \tag{7.1}$$

$$\frac{dw_m(t)}{d(t)} = \frac{K_t}{L_a}i_a(t) - \frac{K_f}{J_m}w_m(t) + \frac{1}{J_m}T_L(t) \tag{7.2}$$

$i_a(t) \rightarrow$ Armature current $R_a \rightarrow$ Armature resistance
$L_a \rightarrow$ Armature inductance $W_m \rightarrow$ Angular velocity
$J_m \rightarrow$ Rotor Inertia $K_e \rightarrow$ Back EMF
$V_s(t) \rightarrow$ Voltage applied $T_L \rightarrow$ Load torque
$K_f \rightarrow$ Frictional constant $K_t \rightarrow$ Torque constant
$K_a \rightarrow$ Armature constant

By combining eq (7.1) and eq (7.2), we can get the transfer function of the BLDC motor [12].

$$G(s) = \frac{1/k_e}{(\tau_m\tau_e)s^2 + \tau_m s + 1} \tag{7.3}$$

Here, τ_m represents the mechanical constant and τ_e represents the electrical constant, both of which are defined below.

$$\tau_m = \frac{3RJ}{K_e K_t} \tag{7.4}$$

$$\tau_e = \frac{L}{3R} \tag{7.5}$$

The parameters' values are obtained from reference [9]. The closed-loop transfer function with unity feedback is represented by the transfer function $G_p(s)$.

$$G_p(s) = \frac{9.306}{(5.997e^{-8})s^2 + 0.0019s + 10.306} \tag{7.6}$$

7.3 PID AND PD CONTROLLER

In several industrial applications, PID and PD controllers are used to regulate temperature, pressure, speed, and other processes. By adjusting the PID and PD parameters, we may regulate both the transient and steady-state response of the system's output [13].

The following describes the standard form of PID and PD controllers: -

$$U(t) = K_p e(t) + K_i \int_0^t e(t)\,dt + K_d \frac{d}{dt} e(t) \tag{7.7}$$

Standard form of PD Controller: -

$$U(t) = K_p e(t) + K_d \frac{d}{dt} e(t) \tag{7.8}$$

where $K_p \to$ Proportional Gain, $K_i \to$ Integral Gain, $K_d \to$ Derivative Gain

The parameters of a controller can be tuned using either the traditional or intelligent tuning method. Classical tuning techniques include the Ziegler Nichols method, the Ziegler Nichols Frequency Response method, the Relay tuning technique, and the Cohen-coon technique. Historically, only first-order and second-order models could be tuned using classical methods, which was one of the disadvantages of the classical tuning method [14]. Intelligent tuning approaches include techniques for pole positioning, optimization techniques such as Particle Swarm Optimization (PSO) and Grey Wolf Optimization (GWO), the use of an ANFIS controller, and Fuzzy Logic. Using optimization approaches, the values of controller parameters (K_p, K_i, and K_d) are optimized in this research.

Tuning controller parameters with optimization is straightforward and user-friendly. Some of these optimizations are inspired by nature, while others are based on mathematical concepts. The two guiding concepts of optimization are exploration and exploitation. Exploration is the process of discovering new regions to discover optimal values, whereas exploitation focuses primarily on changing values to improve existing ones. Prior to optimizing the issues, these methods require some predetermined values. These parameters are the number of variables to be optimized, as well as the Upper bound (UB) and Lower Bound (LB) values for each parameter. The objective function determines the results of the optimization. The objective function is the mathematical problem for which the function value must be maximized or minimized. Using objective function-based optimization approaches, the values are determined iteratively until the optimal values are attained. Integral Time Squared Error is the objective function that must be minimized in this article (ITSE). The formula for calculating the ITSE is as follows: -

$$ITSE = \int_0^\infty t\,[e(t)]^2\,dt \tag{7.9}$$

After getting the optimum values:

The pseudo-code for the fitness function used while tuning controller parameters: -

Create function name and output variable
Declare transfer function of BLDC motors
Allot output variable values to K_p, K_i, and K_d
Create controller transfer function
Combine transfer function of BLDC and Controller with unity feedback
Calculate different types of error with respect to time

End

7.4 OPTIMIZATION TECHNIQUES

Today, optimization techniques are employed virtually everywhere, from the engineering industry to the financial markets to the fashion industry to domestic applications. In our daily lives, we face a variety of difficulties. The human mind employs numerous optimization techniques to solve these difficulties. The objective is to maximize profit or minimize expense. Nonetheless, if the nature of the problem changes, the previously employed technique may or may not be able to locate the optimal solution. Consequently, dependent on the nature of the problem, numerous optimization approaches such as Particle Swarm Optimization (PSO), Grey Wolf Optimization (GWO), Whale Optimization Algorithm (WOA), Sine Cos algorithm (SCA), and Moth Flame Optimization (MFO) have been created (MFO).

The primary drawback of the optimization method is that it can become mired in local optima. In order to circumvent this issue, the strategies presented in this work are constrained by distinct range values for K_p, K_i, and K_d. Appendices A and B display the code for PID and PD controllers that are utilized in various optimization strategies.

7.4.1 Different Optimization Techniques

7.4.1.1 Particles Swarm Optimization

J. Kennedy and R. Eberhart created the Particle Swarm Optimization (PSO) method in 1995 for tackling non-linear problems. This algorithm is simpler than other algorithms since it just requires a few objective function definitions and solution-related parameters.

PSO is a stochastic and self-adaptive approach to optimization. It generates random particles and assigns initial velocities to them. It calculates the goal function at each of the particle's positions. It determines the optimal location and value of the function. It selects new velocities based on the existing velocity, the optimal placement of particles, and their neighbors. PSO iteratively updates the position, velocity, and neighbors of a particle. This loop continues until this algorithm meets a termination requirement [15].

7.4.1.2 Grey Wolf Optimization

Grey Wolf Optimization (GWO) is a sophisticated algorithm inspired by the leadership qualities and hunting abilities of grey wolves. They typically hunt in packs, and each pack has a hierarchy that reflects the wolf's dominance and power. The most powerful wolf in a pack is the alpha, which leads the pack while hunting, feeding, and wandering from region to region.

The second level of the grey wolf social hierarchy is beta. Betas are subordinate wolves who aid the alpha in decision-making and other pack duties. The beta wolf is either male or female, and if one of the alpha wolves dies or ages, he/she is the most likely contender to become the alpha.

If the alpha wolf becomes ill or dies, the strongest beta wolf assumes leadership of the pack. Power-wise, the presence of delta and omega is less than that of alphas and betas [16].

7.4.1.3 Whale Optimization Algorithm

In engineering, algorithms inspired by nature are gaining popularity since they are based on simple notions and can circumvent the issue of local optima. Whale Optimization Algorithm is one of the naturalistic algorithms (WOA).

The challenge is solved via an algorithm inspired by nature that imitates physical processes. Whales are regarded as the largest creatures on earth. They can reach lengths of 30 meters and weights of 180 tons. They are regarded as predatory. Whales do not sleep since they must constantly breathe at the ocean's surface. Consequently, half of the brain only sleeps and is deemed brilliant and emotionally complex.

WOA requires fewer control settings, as the whale population searches for food in multidimensional space. The distance between a whale and its food is proportional to its objective cost. As in multidimensional space, the optimal site cannot be selected. Assumedly, the best answer is the intended prey. Whales exert effort to locate their prey and update their position when they are close to it [17].

7.4.1.4 COOT Algorithm

COOTs are water birds belonging to the Rallidae family. They have shields and other ornamentation on their forehead. Their eyes are red to dark red in color; however, many have a white area under their tail. On the water, coots exhibit distinctive behavior and movement. The behavior of the coot swarm can be categorized into three groups. A disorganized movement of an activity, a synchronized movement, or chain movement on the water's surface, with the coots moving following the lead coot.

Although these coots exhibit a variety of activities, the group of coots is intent on achieving their objective (food). Front coots steer the group towards their intended objective. These geese are regarded as leaders [18].

7.4.1.5 Sine Cos Algorithm

The Sine Cosine Algorithm (SCA) is a metaheuristic optimization method created in 2016 by Seyedali Mirjalili. Using a mathematical model based on the sine and cosine functions, SCA provides random solutions that diverge or converge toward the optimal answer.

This algorithm integrates random variables to enhance the exploration and exploitation of the search space. The SCA is intended to solve only functions with a single aim [19].

7.4.1.6 Moth Flame Optimization

Moth Flame Optimization (MFO) was created by Seyedali Mirjalili in 2016. Moths are little insects belonging to the same family as butterflies. Their size and shape resemble that of butterflies. This approach is inspired by the moths' transverse orientation navigational system. In this strategy, the moth flies by maintaining a constant angle with respect to the moon, which is extremely distant. They appear to be flying in a straight path.

As the moon is so far away, these moths are susceptible to artificial lighting. When moths encounter artificial light produced by humans, they attempt to maintain a stable angle with the light source, resulting in a spiraling flight path [20].

7.4.2 Common Optimization Steps

The generalized steps involved in different optimizations methods are given below: -

Step 1. Initialize parameters (PSO & GWO)
　　Randomly set all the whale population (WOA)
　　Random movement from side to side (COOT)
　　Initialize location of search agents (SCA)
　　Define parameters of algorithm (MFO)

Step 2. Initialize population (PSO)
　　Evaluate Fitness function for search agents (GWO)
　　Evaluate objective function (WOA)
　　Chain movement (COOT)
　　Evaluate the search agents by using objective function (SCA)
　　Generate initial moths randomly (MFO)

Step 3. Evaluate fitness value of fitness function (PSO)
   If the max iteration is not reached repeat 1 and 2 steps (GWO)
   Update the position (WOA)
   Adjusting the position of Coots based on the group leader (COOT)
   Update the location of the obtained best solution (SCA)
   Calculate fitness function and tag the best solution by flames (MFO)

Step 4. Find the best particle (PSO)
   Update search agent location (GWO)
   Change the component of each whale (WOA)
   Leaders' movement towards the optimal area (COOT)
   Update the parameter (SCA)
   Update the flame number (MFO)

Step 5. Find global best (PSO)
   Update the values (GWO)
   If criteria not fulfilled repeat from 2 to 5 again (WOA)
   Update the position of search agent (SCA)
   Update the corresponding moth (MFO)

Step 6. Update velocity (PSO)
   Again, evaluate fitness value (GWO)
   Report the best solution found out by the algorithm (WOA)
   If best solution is obtained, end else repeat steps 2 to 5 again (SCA)
   If the criteria are met, report the best position of moth (MFO)

Step 7. Update Position (PSO)
   Store the best solution (GWO)
   END (SCA)
   END (MFO)

Step 8. Evaluate (PSO)

Step 9. Repeat steps 4 to 8 until criteria are met (PSO)

7.5 SIMULATION AND RESULTS

In this section, the controller parameter values (K_p, K_i, and K_d) are derived from various optimization techniques and implemented in the PID & PD to control the speed of the BLDC motor. The time-domain specifications derived from their step response are contrasted with the root locus technique (RLT) [8] and other control methods. Table. I demonstrate the time response analysis of BLDC motors with PID & PD controllers for all ranges, RLT, Ziegler-Nichols (ZN), Genetic Algorithm (GA), Ant Colony Optimization (ACO), and Existing PSO [8]. Closed loop step response describes the step response of a BLDC motor with unity feedback (CLSR).

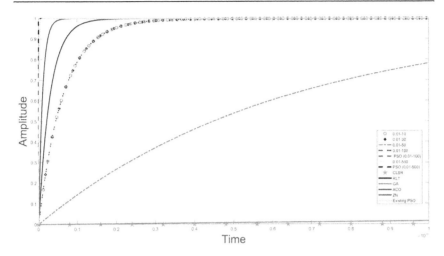

Figure 7.1 Step response of BLDC motor with optimized PID controller (All range).

Within the interval [0.01–10], all optimizations have obtained identical controller parameter values. The optimized PID with BLDC motor has longer rise and settle times than the new design technique. ITSE, the objective function for the optimized PID, is greater than RLT's error. In terms of rise time and settling time, the optimized PID controller with the BLDC performs better than the ZN, ACO, GA, and current PSO. However, the ITSE is still lower using these alternative ways.

For the range [0.01–30], it is noticed that the rise time and settling time improve very marginally but are still greater than the RLT response. The ITSE improves dramatically and approaches the value determined by RLT. All optimization methods continue to produce identical results, indicating that the values determined for this range are optimal. The ITSE obtained inside this range is greater than all other approaches except for the ZN method. Figure 7.1 depicts the step response of a BLDC motor with a PID controller that has been optimized using all available algorithms and methodologies, including RLT, GA, ACO, ZN, and the existing PSO.

All optimizations perform identically, obtaining the same controller values for the [0.01–50] interval. The time-domain specification improves imprecisely, whilst the objective function lowers little but remains greater than the RLT. Table 7.1 demonstrate the time response analysis of BLDC motors with PID & PD controllers for all ranges, RLT, Ziegler-Nichols (ZN), Genetic Algorithm (GA), Ant Colony Optimization (ACO), and Existing PSO [8]. Closed loop step response describes the step response of a BLDC motor with unity feedback (CLSR).

In the larger ranges, [0.01–100] and [0.01–500], all optimization strategies, with the exception of PSO, perform identically to those in the lower range. The system outperforms the RLT with respect to rising time, settling

Table 7.1 Time domain specification of BLDC motor with optimized PID and PD controller

Optimization Techniques	LB & UB Limits	Controller Parameters			Rise Time (T_r)	Settling Time (T_s)	Overshoot $(M_P\%)$	ITSE
		K_p	K_i	K_d				
SCA, MFO, PSO, WOA, COOT, GWO	0.01–10	10	10	0.01	$1.51 * 10^{-6}$	$4.63 * 10^{-6}$	0	$2.61 * 10^{-5}$
SCA, MFO, PSO, WOA, COOT, GWO	0.01–30	30	30	0.01	$1.50 * 10^{-6}$	$3.93 * 10^{-6}$	0	$2.90 * 10^{-6}$
SCA, MFO, PSO, WOA, COOT, GWO	0.01–50	50	50	0.01	$1.50 * 10^{-6}$	$3.62 * 10^{-6}$		$1.04 * 10^{-6}$
SCA, MFO, WOA, COOT, GWO	0.01–100	100	100	0.01	$1.48 * 10^{-6}$	$3.20 * 10^{-6}$		$1.05 * 10^{-8}$
PSO	0.01–100	100	100	100	$1.42 * 10^{-10}$	$2.52 * 10^{-10}$		$2.61 * 10^{-7}$
SCA, MFO, WOA, COOT, GWO	0.01–500	500	500	0.01	$1.37 * 10^{-6}$	$2.27 * 10^{-6}$	0.909	$1.05 * 10^{-8}$
PSO	0.01–500	500	500	500	$2.83 * 10^{-11}$	$5.04 * 10^{-11}$		$2.21 * 10^{-8}$
SCA, MFO, PSO, WOA, COOT, GWO	0.01–10	10	0	10	$1.36 * 10^{-9}$	$2.25 * 10^{-9}$	0.9667	$1.19 * 10^{-4}$
SCA, MFO, PSO, WOA, COOT, GWO	0.01–30	30	0	30	$4.65 * 10^{-10}$	$8.06 * 10^{-10}$	0.2524	$1.33 * 10^{-5}$
SCA, MFO, PSO, WOA, COOT, GWO	0.01–50	50	0	50	$2.81 * 10^{-10}$	$4.91 * 10^{-10}$	0.1096	$4.79 * 10^{-6}$
SCA, MFO, PSO, WOA, COOT, GWO	0.01–100	100	0	100	$1.41 * 10^{-10}$	$2.49 * 10^{-10}$	0.0024	$1.20 * 10^{-6}$
SCA, MFO, PSO, WOA, COOT, GWO	0.01–500	500	0	500	$2.83 * 10^{-11}$	$5.03 * 10^{-11}$	0.0188	$4.80 * 10^{-8}$
RLT [8]		20	100	5	$2.83 * 10^{-9}$	$5.04 * 10^{-9}$	0	$9.95 * 10^{-7}$

ACO [8]	10	200	0.21	$1.76 * 10^{-5}$	$2.16 * 10^{-5}$	0	$1.26 * 10^{-7}$
ZN [8]	9.3883	36.417	0.6051	$6.35 * 10^{-5}$	$7.77 * 10^{-5}$	0	$3.21 * 10^{-6}$
GA [8]	3	90	0.0001	$2.43 * 10^{-4}$	∞	0	$3.20 * 10^{-7}$
Existing PSO [8]	1.5	500	0.02	$1.07 * 10^{-5}$	∞	0	$9.60 * 10^{-8}$
CLSR				$3.37 * 10^{-4}$	$6.11 * 10^{-4}$	0	0.1883

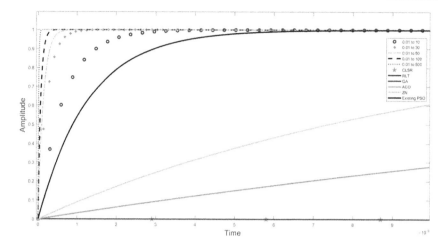

Figure 7.2 Step response of BLDC motor with optimized PD controller (All range).

time, and ITSE. In the larger ranges, [0.01–100] and [0.01–500], all optimization strategies, apart from PSO, perform identically to those in the lower range. The system outperforms the RLT with respect to rising time, settling time, and ITSE.

In the instance of the PD controller, all optimization strategies achieve the same values for both the lower and higher ranges. In terms of rise time and settling time, the system performs better than the RLT for the lower frequency range. Nonetheless, the target ITSE is significantly less than the value attained by RLT, GA, ACO, ZN, and Existing PSO. However, over the [0.01–500] range, ITSE improves, and the total system performance is superior in every way to RLT, ZN, ACO, GA, and the present PSO. As the range of the PD controller expands, the system's performance continues to improve. Figure 7.2 depicts the step response of the BLDC motor with PD controller that has been tuned using various algorithms and controlling approaches.

For the lower range, it is noticed that all optimization techniques produce greater values for K_p and K_i, while K_d approaches its minimum. Figure 7.3 shows the convergence graph of all the algorithms, it is observed that the GWO algorithm approaches very fast to the optimum value.

7.6 CONCLUSION

In this study, PID and PD controllers are used for regulating the speed of BLDC motors used in a variety of renewable energy applications, including solar-powered irrigation and the propulsion of electric vehicles. The controller's parameters were fine-tuned using different optimization methods, for various ranges which were evaluated to determine the ideal range. It was

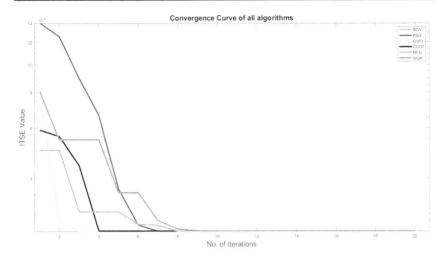

Figure 7.3 Convergence graph of all algorithms.

found that the performance of both PID and PD controllers improves as the range increase, but the performance of PD controller is better than the PID controller in the lower range. Both PID and PD controllers, when optimized, outperformed the existing controllers in terms of time domain specifications.

The BLDC motor, with its high reliability, will be in high demand in hospitals and other medical facilities in the future. This will make BLDC testing and development easy on the wallet. While the BLDC motor is now expensive, its potential applications are expanding rapidly as the world moves toward cleaner energy sources and equipment. As a result, the regulatory outcomes can improve with the introduction of newly developing algorithms, as they will be more advanced and durable against the local optimal difficulties in optimization techniques.

REFERENCES

[1] Mahmud, M., Motakabber, S. M. A., Alam, A. Z., & Nordin, A. N. (2020, December). Utilizing of flower pollination algorithm for brushless DC motor speed controller. In *2020 Emerging Technology in Computing, Communication and Electronics (ETCCE)* (pp. 1–5). IEEE.

[2] Ahamad, N., Sikander, A., & Singh, G. (2022). Order diminution and its application in controller design using salp swarm optimization technique. *International Journal of System Assurance Engineering and Management*, 13(2), 933–943.

[3] Sharma, A., Sharma, A., Pandey, J. K., & Ram, M. (2022). *Swarm intelligence: foundation, principles, and engineering applications.* CRC Press.

[4] Ahamad, N., Sikander, A., & Singh, G. (2022). A novel reduction approach for linear system approximation. *Circuits, Systems, and Signal Processing*, 41(2), 700–724.

[5] Veni, K. K., Kumar, N. S., & Gnanavadivel, J. (2017, September). Low cost fuzzy logic based speed control of BLDC motor drives. In *2017 International Conference on Advances in Electrical Technology for Green Energy (ICAETGT)* (pp. 7–12). IEEE.

[6] Walekar, V. R., & Murkute, S. V. (2018, August). Speed control of BLDC motor using PI & fuzzy approach: A comparative study. In *2018 International Conference on Information, Communication, Engineering and Technology (ICICET)* (pp. 1–4). IEEE.

[7] Ahamad, N., Singh, G., Khan, S., & Sikander, A. (2017, March). Design and performance analysis of optimal reduced order H-infinity controller: L1 norm based genetic algorithm technique. In *2017 International Conference on Power and Embedded Drive Control (ICPEDC)* (pp. 8–13). IEEE.

[8] Kamal, M. M., Mathew, L., & Chatterji, S. (2014, May). Speed control of brushless DC motor using intelligent controllers. In *2014 Students Conference on Engineering and Systems* (pp. 1–5). IEEE.

[9] Uniyal, S., & Sikander, A. (2018). A novel design technique for brushless DC motor in wireless medical applications. *Wireless Personal Communications*, 102(1), 369–381.

[10] Wongkhead, S. (2021, May). State space model for speed control BLDC motor tuning by combination of PI-artificial neural network controller. In *2021 18th International Conference on Electrical Engineering/Electronics, Computer, Telecommunications and Information Technology (ECTI-CON)* (pp. 874–877). IEEE.

[11] Shah, P., Ubare, P., Ingole, D., & Sonawane, D. (2021, September). Performance improvement of BLDC motor speed control using sliding mode control and observer. In *2021 International Symposium of Asian Control Association on Intelligent Robotics and Industrial Automation (IRIA)* (pp. 247–252). IEEE.

[12] Santhosh, P., & Vijayakumar, P. (2017). Performance study of BLDC motor used in wireless medical applications. *Wireless Personal Communications*, 94(4), 2451–2458.

[13] Ahamad, N., Uniyal, S., Sikander, A., & Singh, G. (2019). A comparative study of PID controller tuning techniques for time delay processes. *UPB Scientific Bulletin, Series C: Electrical Engineering Computer Science*, 81(3), 129–142.

[14] Borase, R. P., Maghade, D. K., Sondkar, S. Y., & Pawar, S. N. (2021). A review of PID control, tuning methods and applications. *International Journal of Dynamics and Control*, 9(2), 818–827.

[15] Jain, N. K., Nangia, U., & Jain, J. (2018). A review of particle swarm optimization. *Journal of The Institution of Engineers (India): Series B*, 99(4), 407–411.

[16] Faris, A., Faris H., Aljarah I., Al-Betar M. A., & Mirjalili S. (2018). Grey wolf optimizer: A review of recent variants and applications. *Neural Computing and Applications*, 30(2), 413–435.

[17] Kirkpatrick, S. (1983). Dg jr., and mp vecchi. *Optimization by Simulated Annealing Science*, 220(4598), 671–680.
[18] Naruei, I., & Keynia, F. (2021). A new optimization method based on COOT bird natural life model. *Expert Systems with Applications*, 183, 115352.
[19] Rizk-Allah, R. M. (2018). Hybridizing sine cosine algorithm with multi-orthogonal search strategy for engineering design problems. *Journal of Computational Design and Engineering*, 5(2), 249–273.
[20] Mirjalili, S. (2015). Moth-flame optimization algorithm: A novel nature-inspired heuristic paradigm. *Knowledge-Based Systems*, 89, 228–249.

Chapter 8

Energy-Efficient Task Offloading in Edge Computing with Energy Harvesting

Sonali Deshpande and Nilima Kulkarni

CONTENTS

8.1 INTRODUCTION

Due to the rapid advancement of mobile communication technology and the broad deployment of the Internet of Things (IoT), terminal equipment and data are expanding quickly. Intelligent linked vehicles and driving without human intervention, virtual reality, industrial IoT, smart homes, and smart cities are just a few of the IoT industries that are quickly growing. To meet their own needs, these growing businesses will require a significant quantity of computing resources. Mobile devices, sensors, and other mobile edge computing service objects are the key service objects. These gadgets are primarily powered by batteries, and when the device is used for a large number of computer operations, the battery will quickly be depleted. Miniaturized gadgets, in particular, have little battery life and transmit data over an unlicensed frequency. Devices' data transmission coexists with other networks using the unlicensed frequency range even

DOI: 10.1201/9781003356639-8

145

with sufficient energy, leading to a shortage of spectrum. In the prototype for spectrum sensing and energy harvesting, researchers have concentrated on resource allocation. The system's overall communication quality can be ensured by properly allocating time for energy harvesting, energy transfer, and job dumping. The complexity of the solution, however, also rises with the number of optimization parameters. The solution to this issue is to provide a differential evolution-based optimization technique for energy harvesting and job computing, taking into consideration the constrained energy and processing power of sensor nodes in wireless communication networks [1,2]. As a result of the growing energy consumption in many edge computing applications, IoT devices with power limitations or edge cloud sides with limited power sources could experience problems. Because of the vast number of edge devices present there, the edge computing eco-system has a massive overall energy consumption that is comparable to that of cloud data centers. For instance, power-constrained edge nodes or battery-powered devices can last longer thanks to energy-conscious edge computing, which can also boost system throughput. Edge computing applies energy awareness across all operations carried out during the data life cycle, including data production, transport, assemblage, archiving, and processing. This is in contrast to server systems and cloud data centers.

8.1.1 An Overview of the Energy-Harvesting Capabilities of the IoT

The process of turning readily available environmental energy into usable electrical energy is known as energy harvesting, commonly referred to as scavenging. This is a practical method for supplying continuous power to a variety of loads. Numerous environmental resources, both natural and man-made, can be used to generate energy. These resources include a wide range of others as well as motion, light, heat, and electromagnetic influence. The energy-harvesting procedure is broken down into four stages, as shown in Figure 8.1.

Energy resources: The availability of energy resources is the first phase [3]. In the deployed system's setting, it's critical to select an acceptable and energy source that is widely accessible.

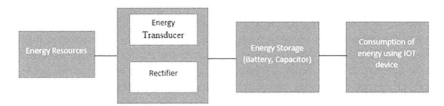

Figure 8.1 An energy-harvesting system block diagram.

Energy conversion: The second step entails systems for energy conversion. The energy is detected and converted using the harvester or transducer. A converter circuit further provides rectification during this phase.

Energy storage: During the third step, energy is stored using supercapacitors or batteries. This phase also includes the power management and control unit.

Energy consumption: The equipment most suited for the job uses the energy that has been captured during the last step of energy consumption.

Devices installed at the network's edge are referred to as edge devices. Network edge devices with additional processing power and capability are called edge servers. They are located nearer to the network edge and farther from cloud data centers. Edge gadgets frequently have limited computing power and battery life. In some circumstances, programs that require a lot of power and a lot of knowledge processing can't be run on edge devices.

On many edge devices, there are restrictions on computing power, storage capacity, and network connectivity. The power-restricted with limited power sources, IoT devices, or edge cloud-side apps may suffer as a result of increased energy demand. Energy-conscious edge computing can extend the life of battery-operated devices or edge nodes with limited power by ensuring service quality and increasing system throughput within a set power budget.

Computation offloading is usually utilized in edge computing to scale back latency and ensure Quality of Service. Energy efficiency is currently a major problem for both mobile devices and cloud servers. Energy efficiency in edge computing has largely been unexplored because of the intricate connections between edge devices, edge servers, and cloud data centers. Energy efficiency has become one of the most important challenges for both cloud servers and mobile devices.

To deal with this issue associated with power and computational capability different techniques are overviewed [4–6]. Every mobile device has a computation task that can be performed either locally on the device or remotely at the offloading locations using a wireless connection and the energy that was harvested. Because of the energy and space constraints of a mobile device's processing processor, it should be unable to execute a major computation task. It required pushing a dynamic offloading decision mode supported by the communication link condition and job requirements of every mobile device, therefore, each mobile device has the option to select the PRN for calculation and communication services.

The industrial workplace, the smart home, smart cities, automobiles, and data and communication infrastructures are just a few of the places where edge devices are used. On the other hand, these edge devices have limited resources, either because of a lack of power or because they have less potent processing and storage capabilities for computing-intensive jobs. Therefore, the fundamental design objective for edge hardware, such as processors, sensors, edge servers, switches, and routers, should be energy efficiency.

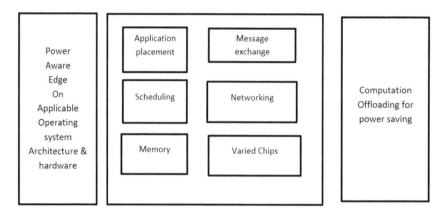

Figure 8.2 Comprehensive view of edge computing's energy awareness.

When using edge devices in planet contexts, energy awareness at the hardware level can dramatically minimize energy consumption.

The majority of the time, edge devices have low computing capability and are power-constrained. Therefore, it's crucial to use alternative power supply equipment that is lighter, more powerful, and has a longer lifespan shown in Figure 8.2. In today's mobile device sectors, lithium-ion batteries (LIBs) are highly prevalent, with energy densities increasing by 7%–10% per year. However, research has revealed that the LIB's capability is approaching theoretical limits. The use of Si-containing graphite composites, which have excellent capacity retention and can reduce electrode expansion, is one option for the LIB power supply. Chemical vapor deposition (CVD) in a scalable furnace is used to create graphite/carbon hybrids with integrated Si nanolayers (SGC).

Edge computing requires energy-conscious architecture design even though modern edge devices contain components that save energy at the hardware level. A variety of levels of energy-conscious strategies may be addressed and integrated into the architecture design, as well as features and capabilities for the development and use of energy-aware programming interfaces.

8.1.2 Energy Efficient IoT Protocols

MQTT, CoAP, XMPP, and AMQP are the most widely used IoT application protocols. MQTT (message queue telemetry transit) and CoAP (constrained application protocol) were created with resource-constrained devices in mind, such as IoT end nodes and gateways [7,8].

MQTT is a low-bandwidth publishing-subscription messaging protocol. The protocol for transfer is TCP (transmission control protocol. It was developed for use in gadgets with little memory and processing capacity. Because it can function on networks with little bandwidth, low memory, and low power, MQTT is regarded as the finest messaging protocol for M2M and IoT applications [7].

The CoAP protocol can function as a publish-subscribe protocol even though it is a request-response protocol by default. CoAP transports information using UDP (user datagram protocol), although it can also use TCP. CoAP includes a lot of support for limited devices [8].

Two additional well-liked protocols are XMPP (extensible messaging and presence protocol) and AMQP (advanced message queuing protocol), however, they use more resources and are not advised for devices with basic capabilities.

8.2 THE REASONS FOR ENERGY OPTIMIZATION

People can access network services anytime and wherever they choose via wireless devices like smartphones, tablets, and IoT devices. However, while appreciating the enormous convenience that these devices provide, consumers are becoming increasingly concerned about their energy consumption. The MCC and MEC provide new information for increasing device capabilities and battery life by delegating computation-intensive parts of an application to nearby edge/fog servers or distant servers. In order to reduce the energy consumption of your device, you must carefully analyze the complete strategy to offload functions under intermittent wireless channels.

We address the issues of energy optimization for mobile devices from the perspectives of device hardware and software, computation offloading methodologies, wireless transmission strategies, and cloud execution mechanisms.

8.2.1 Hardware and Software for Mobile Devices

In order to provide services, devices with mobile hardware and software connect to the Internet through Bluetooth, cellular networks, or WiFi. Processors, memory, battery, display, and sensors are all common components of mobile devices. Mobile software consists of mobile operating systems (OSs) as well as apps and services that run on those OSs. Managing device energy consumption is critical, but it can be difficult due to the following factors. To begin, it's critical to manage device resources in an energy-efficient manner for application utilization. Mobile devices require an energy-conscious OS to monitor and govern the utilization of resources by apps efficiently. Second, certain components, such as processors, sensors, and displays, utilize more energy than others. The thermal coupling effects between CPUs must be taken into account when it comes to energy optimization. Third, these applications require energy-efficient techniques because they are becoming increasingly complicated, and deep neural networks are demanding, resource-constrained systems that are challenging to implement.

8.2.2 Offloading Strategies for Computation

There are different granularity levels at which a mobile application can be divided. The mobile application's partitioned components are offloaded to powerful computing resources for execution. The energy efficiency of computation offloading for mobile devices must be evaluated, taking a variety of scenarios into account, such as intermittent wireless network connections. Considering the following elements is necessary, in order to fully realize the potential energy-saving advantages of computing offloading on mobile devices. First, decide if computation offloading is an effective way to increase battery longevity. Due to the incurred expenses associated with transmission energy, offloading for distant execution can occasionally be useless in comparison to local execution. After offloading selections have been made, think about which application component should be moved to the clouds. Finally, contemplate how to judiciously choose whether to transfer computational workloads from an application to the clouds in a variable wireless network environment (i.e., using static or dynamic offloading). The non-offloadable sections will be carried out locally, while the offloadable portions will be carried out on powerful servers (such as remote clouds or edge clouds). Preparation carries out the steps required for offloadable sections to be successfully offloaded and executed, such as selecting remote servers, transmitting code, and so on. The offloading decision is the last step before sending offloadable components to remote cloud or edge servers. Offloading can be classified as either data offloading or computational offloading, depending on the offloading object. The costs associated with processing the tasks that have been offloaded to the edge-cloud servers should be compensated by the MDs [9]. Each MD (Mobile device) purchases task-processing resources from appropriate edge-cloud servers which can be seen as a "market" in this context. In this MDs will be considered as buyers and edge cloud will be considered as a seller.

8.2.3 Offload Computation from Devices

The main energy constraints placed on mobile devices by their short battery lives include limited computing and storage capability. Offloading is a useful technique for improving the computing and storage capabilities of devices by moving computational jobs to capable servers for execution. The majority of offloading research emphasizes two things: enhanced functionality and energy savings. We'll concentrate on offloading solutions for mobile devices in this section. Offloading normally entails three key steps: application split, preparation, and offloading choice. [10]. The offloadable and non-offloadable elements of an application are separated by application partition. Partial offloading and complete offloading are the two types of offloading strategies available. Application is separated and only some part of it is offloaded in partial offloading, transmitting as little data as feasible, whereas complete offloading strategies typically relocate the complete application to a cloud server to relieve application programmers of the burden. Once computation offloading is identified, the application off-loading decision should be made carefully before sending the offloaded sections to the clouds.

8.2.4 Energy Aware Computing Offloading

A potential method for extending the capabilities of edge devices while maintaining battery life is to offload computing to the cloud. [11]. However, offloading applications to the cloud is not always energy efficient. More energy could be wasted through ineffective offloading, increasing electricity costs and carbon footprints [12]. Mao et al.'s [13] proposal of a MEC system with energy harvesting (EH) reduces execution energy consumption by providing an efficient dynamic computation offloading mechanism. Bi et al. [14–18] investigated the binary technique and deployed a binary strategy in a wireless MEC network with a server and several UEs to boost the weighted sum calculation rate. Previously published research has focused on either increasing total throughput or reducing total energy use. However, in order to make the best offloading option possible, the following concerns must be addressed:

1. Is it possible to outsource a task for processing to the cloud?
2. Whose duties can be shifted to the cloud if multiple individuals wish to have their respective responsibilities offloaded?
3. When should offloading calculations be performed?

Computation can be transported from the cloud to the edge in addition to being offloaded from the edge. To speed up execution, complex jobs can be divided and given to edge nodes in cloud data centers. With computation offloading from clouds to edge nodes, it is possible to make use of the resources of edge devices while also lowering overall latency and energy usage. Figure 8.3 shows the entire compute offloading architecture. Table 8.1 lists the terminologies used in Figure 8.3.

Because both edge and cloud computing systems contain a range of workloads, distinct tasks should be transferred to various servers. For instance, it is best to offload energy-intensive work to cloud servers, computing-intensive operations to edge servers, and data-intensive duties to servers close to the data source. Taking into account this paradigm for three-tier hierarchical offloading. For efficient workload placement in the hybrid cloud and edge computing architecture for energy savings, a thorough understanding of server energy proportionality is necessary.

Considering latency and task type, Figure 8.4 depicts workload type aware computing offloading. The best devices should only be used when a task is moved from the cloud to the edge.

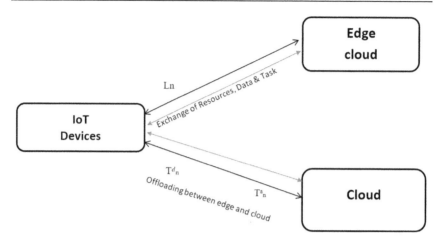

Figure 8.3 Computing offloading architecture.

Table 8.1 Terms and notation

Terms	Explanation
Computing offloading	The computational task is moved from edge to edge cloud, centre cloud, or cloud to edge devices.
Computing task	The task moved from the edge to the cloud.
Ln	Device m must accomplish a calculation task with a latency of Ln milliseconds.
T^a_n	The data-arrival time instant.
T^d_n	The computation deadline.

8.2.5 Offloading over Device to Device

As a replacement for the powerful but far-off clouds, cooperative computing has been proposed [19]. It enables pervasive services and applications to be accessed by mobile users, allowing them to benefit from nearby, fast, and low-latency wireless connectivity. In a standard offloading situation, the mobile device transmits data to the helper to be processed, where the desired tasks are completed and the results are then transmitted back to the mobile device. So the mobile device required resources for computation which required high-speed connection. A promising method is data offloading over Device-to-Device (D2D) networks, where mobile users compete for access to computational resources on neighboring devices based on their requests for task offloading. The device makes use of a peer device's computing capabilities for device-to-device offloading. In the context of device-to-device communications, several incentive strategies have been suggested to encourage data offloading.

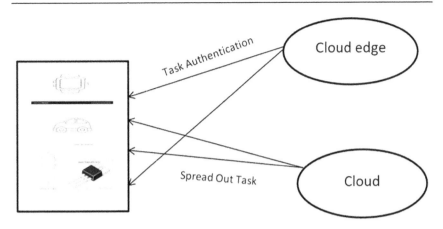

Figure 8.4 Where to offload from the cloud.

8.3 TASK OFFLOADING SCHEME

We assume that a client can establish connections via a variety of means to several edge clouds and a single central cloud. The edge clouds will collect data from the mobile device and then transfer it back to the mobile device, including information about the job such as input data amount, task type, and the greatest delay the device can support [20]. The mobile device analyses the best edge cloud for a job when it offloads it based on the knowledge of the edge clouds. We will compare local task execution to the best edge cloud execution after selecting the best edge cloud to determine whether the job should be offloaded to the edge cloud. The local device will connect to the central cloud if there isn't an edge cloud available to do the task and it's preferred (cheaper) to offload the work there. Figure 8.5 shows our task offloading approach.

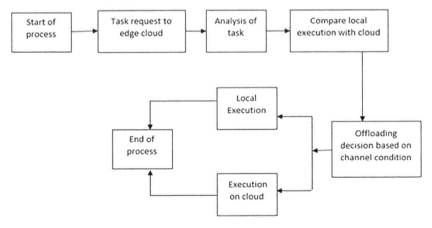

Figure 8.5 Execution of task offloading scheme.

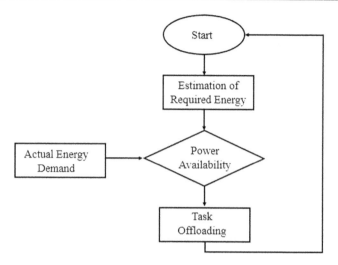

Figure 8.6 Flow of execution.

8.4 OFFLOADING ALGORITHM

The goal of offloading algorithms is to determine which processor, given a particular limitation, is most suited to carry out a task. Offloading in wearables can occur in two stages: from wearables to edge devices or from edge devices to cloud devices [21]. The offloading mechanism continuously assesses the estimated available power and contrasts it with the power requirements of the forest. When the power demands are more than the power supply and the communication unit's energy consumption is lower than the task processing's energy consumption, the offloading algorithms are activated as shown in Figure 8.6.

8.5 CONCLUSION

This study investigated the total energy consumption reduction problem for EH-enabled MEC networks by concurrently optimizing the task offloading ratio and resource allocation. The state-of-the-art in edge computing for energy-aware computing various areas of energy awareness are discussed. Middleware, service quality control, improved low-power hardware design, and architectural feature-based energy consumption optimization are all included in this. A thorough survey is been done for recent research on joint task offloading and energy-harvesting methods for the IoTs. The majority of the present research, despite the various aspects and application fields of energy-aware edge computing, focuses on a single objective, such as low latency, data privacy, power savings, or energy efficiency. The future work will focus on performance metrics such as task completion rate, task completion delay, and total energy consumption for device-to-device task offloading as well as on the effective hardware implementation of joint energy harvesting and reinforcement learning-based task offloading for wearable devices.

REFERENCES

[1] J. Fu, J. Hua, J. Wen, H. Chen, W. Lu, J. Li, "Optimization of energy consumption in the MEC-assisted multi-user FD-SWIPT system," *IEEE Access* 8, pp. 21 345–21 354, 2020.

[2] D. Ma, G. Lan, M. Hassan, W. Hu, S. K. Das, "Sensing, computing, and communications for energy harvesting IoTs: A survey," *IEEE Communications Surveys Tutorials* 22(2), pp. 1222–1250, 2020.

[3] S. Zeadally, F. K. Shaikh, A. Talpur, Q. Z. Sheng, "Design architectures for energy harvesting in the Internet of Things", Renewable and Sustainable Energy Reviews 128, p. 109901, 2020.

[4] M. Wang, L. Zhu, L. T. Yang, M. Lin, X. Deng, L. Yi, "Offloading assisted energy-balanced IoT edge node relocation for confident information coverage," *IEEE Internet of Things Journal* 6(3), pp. 4482–4490, 2019.

[5] J. Haimour, O. Abu-Sharkh, "Energy efficient sleep/wake-up techniques for IoT: A survey," in *2019 IEEE Jordan International Joint Conference on Electrical Engineering and Information Technology (JEEIT)*, pp. 478–484, 2019.

[6] O. Vaananen, T. Hamalainen, "Requirements for Energy Efficient Edge Computing: A Survey", *In Internet of Things, Smart Spaces, and Next Generation Networks and Systems: 18th International Conference, NEW2AN 2018, and 11th Conference, ruSMART 2018*, St. Petersburg, Russia, August 27–29, 2018 Proceedings, 18, pp. 3–15, 2018.

[7] M. B. Yassein, M. Q. Shatnawi, S. Aljwarneh, R. Al-Hatmi, "Internet of Things: Survey and open issues of MQTT protocol," In: *2017 International Conference on Engineering and MIS (ICEMIS), Monastir*, pp. 1–6, 2017.

[8] S. Bandyopadhyay, A. Bhattacharyya, "Lightweight Internet protocols for web enablement of sensors using constrained gateway devices". In: 2013 International Conference on Computing, Networking and Communications (ICNC), San Diego, CA, pp. 334–340, 2013.

[9] S. Xia, Z. Yao, Y. Li, S. Mao, "Online distributed offloading and computing resource management with energy harvesting for heterogeneous MEC-Enabled IoT," *IEEE Transactions on Wireless Communications* 20(10), October 2021.

[10] Akherfi, M. Gerndt, H. Harroud. 2018. "Mobile cloud computing for computation offloading: Issues and challenges," *Applied Computing and Informatics* 14, pp. 1–16, 2018.

[11] C. Jiang, X. Cheng, H. Gao, X. Zhou, J. Wan, "Toward computation offloading in edge computing: A survey", *IEEE Access* 7, pp 131543–131558, 2019.

[12] C. Jiang, Y. Wang, D. Ou, B. Luo, W. Shi, "Energy proportional servers: Where are we in 2016", In: *IEEE 37th International Conference on*

Distributed Computing Systems (ICDCS) IEEE, 2017, pp. 1649–1660, 2017.

[13] [216] Y. Mao, J. Zhang, K. B. Letaief, "Dynamic computation offloading for mobile-edge computing with energy harvesting devices", *IEEE Journal on Selected Areas in Communications* 34 (12) pp. 3590–3605, 2016.

[14] S. Bi, Y. Zhang, "Computation rate maximization for wireless powered mobile-edge computing with binary computation offloading", *IEEE Transactions on Wireless Communications* 17 (6) pp. 4177–4190, 2018.

[15] C. Jiang, T. Fan, H. Gao, W. Shi, L. Liu, C. Cérin, J. Wan, "Energy aware edge computing: A survey", *Computer Communications*, 151, pp. 556–580, 2020.

[16] U. M. Malik, M. A. Javed, S. Zeadally, S. ul Islam, "Energy efficient fog computing for 6G enabled massive IoT: Recent trends and future opportunities", *IEEE JIOT*, pp. 2327–4662, 2021.

[17] S. Zeadally, F. K. Shaikh, A. Talpur, Q. Z. Sheng, "Design architectures for energy harvesting in the internet of things," *Renewable and Sustainable Energy Reviews* 128, 2020.

[18] Y. Wu, Y. Wang, Y. Wei, S. Leng, "Intelligent deployment of dedicated servers: Rebalancing the computing resource in IoT," In: *2020 IEEE Wireless Communications and Networking Conference Workshops (WCNCW)*, pp. 1–6, 2020.

[19] M. Hamdi, A. B. Hamed, D. Yuan, M. Zaied, "Energy-efficient joint task assignment and power control in energy-harvesting D2D offloading communications," *IEEE Internet of Things Journal* 9(8), April 15, 2022.

[20] Q. Wang, S. Guo, J. Liu, Y. Yanga, Chongqing, "Energy-efficient computation offloading and resource allocation fordelay-sensitive mobile edge computing," *Elsevier, Sustainable Computing: Informatics and Systems* 21, pp. 154–164, 2019.

[21] M. B. Ammar, I. B. Dhaou, D. El Houssaini, S. Sahnoun, A. Fakhfakh, O. Kanoun, "Requirements for energy-harvesting-driven edge devices using task-offloading approaches," *MDPI Electronics* 11, p. 383, 2022.

Chapter 9

Blockchain Application in Sustainable Energy Solution

Akanksha Rai, Vikas Thapa, Amit Kumar Mondal, and Surajit Mondal

CONTENTS

DOI: 10.1201/9781003356639-9

9.1 INTRODUCTION

Energy Internet (EI), symbolized by "New Energy + Internet," has emerged as the next frontier of technological innovation in the international energy academic community and business. It maintains the energy industry's smart grid development [1]. EI's growing player count and diversity of energy sources make it difficult to monitor and govern scattered sustainable energy sources. At this point, EI research is conceptual and design-based. EI is rare. Deploying the EI requires new technologies [2–4].

Nakamoto Sang's 2008 work was titled "Bitcoin: A Peer-to-Peer Electronic Cash System." According to the paper, a digital payment system that depends on cryptographic evidence rather than trust and may be used by any two parties to send and receive payments is needed. In January 2009, he created the "Genesis Block" for the blockchain. Nobody thought of a blockchain then. Users chose Blockchain despite the Bitcoin network being insecure for years [5]. The Economist claimed in a cover story titled "The promise of the blockchain: the trust machine" [6] that blockchain technology can dramatically alter business and human-to-human contact norms. Figure 9.1 depicts how this article has helped the public comprehend blockchains and how they function. Baidu's blockchain index has exploded since 2017. Internet, mobile/social networks, mainframes, PCs, and blockchain are paradigm-shifting computing technologies. This is the fourth major turning point in the history of consumer credit [7]. The banking industry is spearheading blockchain research, but other businesses are embracing it. The EI may be developed using consensus procedures, a blockchain technology. Blockchain technologies include encryption techniques, distributed ledgers, and smart contracts. EI includes microgrids and decentralized renewable energy. These two parts represent the producer and the customer. They need independent commercial, industrial, and consumer monitoring procedures. Since energy and information systems are interconnected, data security and transparency are major considerations for intelligent transactions [8]. If Energy of Internet takes a conventional strategy and creates a single organization as the trusted centre, all transactions will be channelled to that company. A central authority couldn't manage or influence this situation [9]. The Internet's easy access to energy sources has some worried about the institution's reputation. EI uses blockchain technology. If the blockchain were used to implement EI, a decentralized, consensus-based energy trading platform might be established. Contrasts ensure profitable, automated trading. The platform's transparency is ensured by blockchain transaction queries. Distributed data storage and encryption safeguard system data. The EI may benefit from blockchain technology [10].

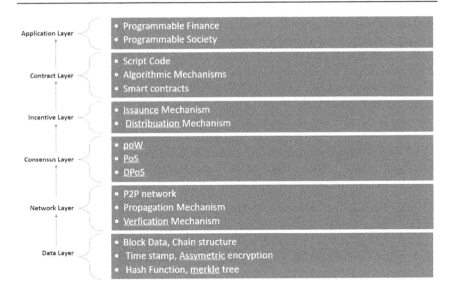

Figure 9.1 Blockchain technology architecture.

9.2 BLOCKCHAIN

9.2.1 Blockchain Term Definition

"Blockchain" has been greatly discussed, but no official definition exists. All investigative fronts are advancing quickly. Melanie Swan discusses this in "Blockchain: blueprint for a future economy" [11] and says Blockchain is a decentralized, public database. Harald [12,13] suggests that blockchain might be utilized to maintain a trustworthy database communally. In its 2016 white paper, China's Ministry of Industry and Information Technology defines blockchain both narrowly and broadly. The blockchain is a chained data structure with chronologically linked data blocks and encryption to secure non-defective modification and unforgeability. It mixes point-to-point transmission, distributed data storage, consensus procedures, and encryption technologies. Yan et al. [7] and Yuan and Wang [14] define it as follows: Blockchain is a novel distributed ledger system. To add and alter data, the system relies on consensus procedures reached by a network of nodes, cryptographic techniques, and smart contracts written in a programming language designed to execute automatically [7]. A "block and chain" data structure with a chronological log of events is also used. With this clarification, blockchain's operation and similarly varied utility become more comprehensible.

9.2.2 The Making of a Blockchain

Blockchains are data structures made of blocks. Data with accompanying records and metadata makes up a blockchain block. A blockchain consists mostly of a block body and block header [15,16]. Block headers carry most of the hash value from the previous block to preserve blockchains. Body is where most of the block's material is (such as transaction information). Data, the previous block's hash value, and a random integer are used to calculate the current block's hash value. In Bitcoin, each block holds system-wide transaction data broadcast by nodes within a given time period. Transaction data includes sender and receiver identities, the amount exchanged, date and time, and more. In addition to transaction data, each data block has a block ID and date. Connecting the blocks creates a chain that maintains network transaction history. These data packets go instantly over the communal network. When authenticated and added to the chain, they become irrefutable and tamper-proof, maintaining the integrity and authenticity of the entire database [17].

9.2.3 The Blockchain Technology Architecture

Several levels of a blockchain's architecture, including the data layer, incentive layer, consensus layer, contract layer, network layer, and application layer, are shown in Figure [14]. Transaction logs, information records, data blocks, timestamps, and other blockchain-related meta-data are all kept at this layer.

Network technologies, propagation methods, and verification processes make up the network layer (Figure 9.1). The consensus layer uses a peer-to-peer (P2P) consensus technique to allow nodes to agree on block data validity in a decentralized system with distributed decision-making. The incentive layer mixes economic variables with the blockchain via issuing tokens. Incentivized computer donations. Contract layer includes algorithmic algorithms, script codes, and intelligent contracts with auditable specs.

9.2.4 The Grouping of Blockchain

The investigation [18] was out by Lei and Gang distinguished between consortium blockchains, public blockchains, and private blockchains. In this particular version, Bitcoin, Ethereum, Blockchain Alliance R3, and Hyperledger, as well as Coin Science and Eris Industries, are utilized. These two companies are at the forefront of competition within the blockchain sector [19,20].

The characteristics of the public, consortium, and private blockchains are contrasted in Table 9.1 [12,21–23]. These characteristics include read/write access, transaction speed, anonymity, and decentralization.

9.2.5 Blockchain's Core Technologies

Instead of being a singular method, blockchain technology is a broad technological system that incorporates many different areas of study. The

Table 9.1 Comparison of compatibility between Blockchain and Energy Internet

Characteristics	Blockchains	Energy Internet
Decentralization	There is no control center for operation. Each node saves all the information of blockchains, and the peers have equal rights and obligations. The operation of system is decentralized, and equal decision making is made by each node.	Include more distributed energy and microgrids which can be either consumers or producers. The operation of the system will change the trust center decision model of traditional energy networks. The participants in the network can independently merge their own consumption and transactions.
Interconnected Economy	The high degree of interconnection between nodes ensures that each node can read, write, and verify blocks at any time. The blockchains system has no control center and operator is maintained by all of nodes in network.	Each system module can realize the full interconnection of energy and information. It emphasizes the automatic scheduling and ecological operation of the system, with high security and economy.
Openness	It provides network interference in a wide range. Each body can participate in the maintenance and operation of the independent system and a component become decentralized database. And it can establish a fair and open market mechanism by using blockchain technology.	The structured network is open for all types of entities, thus providing a platform for physical information exchange for the energy industry and other industries. It also conductive to the establishment of a market-oriented mechanism.
Intelligence	Automatic execution of contract through smart contracts or 'Programmable currency'	Automated transaction of participating parties is everywhere, and transaction are intelligent.

main components of this system are shown in Figure 9.4: distributed data storage, a consensus process, encryption techniques, and smart contracts [12,21,24–27]. The use of smart contracts is also crucial.

9.3 SPECIFICATION OF BLOCKCHAIN

From Figure 9.2, a basic knowledge of five properties of the blockchain can be explained.

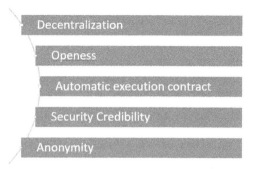

Figure 9.2 Five properties of the blockchain.

9.3.1 Decentralization

Due to P2P networking, the blockchain system is decentralized. All network nodes are given the same amount of attention by the system. Each component of the system is responsible for updating its copy of the created data blocks. Each node has its own copy of the transaction log, which greatly increases the database's durability.

9.3.2 Accessibility

Through the application of trustworthy mathematical methods, the blockchain system regulates the conduct of transactions. It is not required for the nodes in the system to trust one another in order to communicate information. As far as I can tell, the operational procedures are very clear. The technique both makes the node's private data visible to the public while simultaneously encrypting it. The data on the blockchain is accessible to anybody with the hash value of the block header, and it is stored in many locations for redundancy. The system's information is entirely visible since nodes cannot mislead one another because mutual authentication between them is required for any changes to be made.

9.3.3 An Automatic Execution Agreement

On the blockchain, one may create "smart contracts" that detail the responsibilities of each participant and the conditions under which those responsibilities must be met. Blockchain technology performs the automated evaluation of contract execution conditions. Once the conditions for making a decision have been met, the blockchain-based contract will be automatically enforced. This has had two positive effects: first, it has boosted the speed with which contracts are completed; second, it has successfully assured that the contract would be carried out even in the absence of a powerful third party to monitor its execution [28].

9.3.4 Credibility, Security, Data Integrity, and Traceability

For a transaction to be traceable, it must be recorded on the blockchain and the relevant trader's details must be attached to that record. As the whole transfer path of the transaction's object can be recorded and traced, transaction monitoring is simplified [22]. Data on a blockchain is encrypted using asymmetric cryptographic principles, and the powerful algorithm used in the consensus method protects against hacking, ensures that changes to the blockchain are immutable, and prevents forgeries.

Consider the Bitcoin blockchain as an illustration of where data modification is impossible without the control of 51% of the network's computer power [29]. Due to the high cost of tampering with the blockchain's ledger, it's highly improbable that all participants will try to change the data despite its high security.

9.3.5 Anonymity

Neither side needs to reveal their identities since a blockchain system uses a specified protocol for data transfer between nodes. Instead, the blockchain's established protocols are used to build trust among participants.

9.4 BLOCKCHAIN TECHNOLOGY: DEVELOPMENT AND APPLICATIONS

There may be three stages of blockchain development. Bitcoin is the first implementation of blockchain technology that underpins the digital currency system known as Blockchain 1.0. Blockchain 2.0's primary use case is the financial sector. With the introduction of smart contracts in blockchain 2.0, a wider variety of assets might be converted, taking blockchain beyond the realm of only digital currencies. A key feature of Blockchain 3.0 is the programmable society. The blockchain is finding more widespread applications in a variety of sectors, including research, education, culture, and others [12,27,30,31]. This is done in addition to the existing network, which may include the Internet and mobile communications.

Processing payments, documentation, and exchanges, as well as other efforts to enhance operational efficiency, are all part of the supplier's business. The British government published a research report on blockchain technology in January 2016 called "Blockchain: Distributed Ledger Technology." It was the first study of its kind on a national scale, and it included not only an in-depth investigation of blockchain's potential uses but also directions for further study. The paper backed the use of blockchain technology in a variety of industries, including banking and energy, and said that it should be incorporated into the United Kingdom's national plan. As early as February of 2016, the European Commission pegged the cryptocurrency sector as a key area for future expansion. Because of this, several institutions have begun investigating digital currency regulation. For example, in May 2016, Japan enacted the first version of the Digital Money Monitoring Act, which defines digital currency as property. Blockchain Cooperation Alliance, Japan's first business group, was founded there (BCCC). The US Department of Homeland Security invested in six blockchain application development firms in June 2016. In December 2016, the Chinese State Council issued "The 13th Five-Year Plan for National Informatization" [32]. Blockchain technology is included in this scheme. In April 2017, China held its first-ever Global Blockchain Finance (Hangzhou) Summit, marking the first time a government-level organization in China has organized the submission of blockchain technology. There was a presentation during the conference on the first blockchain industrial park in the country, located in Hangzhou. Businesses that relocate there would be eligible for tax breaks and recognition for their contributions to science and technology.

Countries are looking at the potential business uses of blockchain technology in areas including digital currency, securities trading, cross-border payments, identity, academic accreditation, and even love donations. Only Bitcoin, however, has witnessed the birth of really mature blockchain applications on a global scale. Currently, China is at the same level as the rest of the world. The US Nasdaq's debut of the blockchain-based equities trading platform Linq [33,34] in December 2015 was a watershed moment in the movement toward decentralization in the financial and securities industry. The firm R3 CEV is committed to the widespread use of blockchain technology, and it has already signed cooperation agreements with more than 40 major institutions, including Goldman Sachs, HSBC, and Citibank.

9.5 EI INTRODUCTION AND DEFINITION

Understanding the technology behind the Internet of Energy might be difficult, so it's important to start with the basics. The term "Internet of Energy" (IoE) describes the integration of IoT technology into existing energy infrastructures. The "Internet of Things" refers to the notion of connecting everyday objects to the web. Everything from stereos and refrigerators to headphones and autos falls under this category.

Inefficiencies in the present energy infrastructure may be reduced if manufacturers and producers increase power generation, transportation, and utilization. By enhancing electric infrastructures, we can increase the efficiency of energy production and use, and cut down on unnecessary energy waste. Without the necessary upgrades, they can't transfer it efficiently, thus a lot of the power is wasted in transit. The lines just can't handle the whole quantity of power being sent.

Given the severe environmental constraints and the limited availability of traditional fossil fuels, it is difficult to maintain the expansion of an energy system based on them. Substituting renewable energy sources for dirtier fuels is gaining popularity. Some progress has been made in the study of renewable energy sources, but even well-established technologies like wind and solar power have their share of problems. These include geographical dispersion, inefficient administration and use, and expensive energy conversion prices. Therefore, there are significant limitations on the commercialization and use of novel forms of energy at the present time [35]. The National Science Foundation's [36] "Future Renewable Power Energy Transmission and Management System" project in 2008 brought the idea of the EI into the limelight. The EI is an entirely new kind of power grid structure, and this theoretical framework explains how distributed energy storage devices, renewable energy generation, and the current Internet all function together. Furthermore, it asserts that research into the energy industry will centre on the EI as a method of fixing the problems that now exist. Rifkin [37] predicted that humans will transition to a system that combines new energy and communication technologies called the EI when the world's present resources ran out and the environment continued to worsen. The Japan Digital Grid Alliance has suggested a "power router"-based EI, and there is a strong emphasis on this topic in Japan's academic community. Dong et al. [38] characterize the EI as a closed-loop, complicated, multi-network flow system that relies mostly on distributed renewable energy. It's also linked to things like natural gas distribution and transportation networks. The electrical grid serves as its backbone, with the Internet and other cutting-edge IT systems providing necessary support. The EI concept put out by Ma et al. [37] is more in-depth; it revolves around the electrical system, with the smart grid as its backbone, and is connected to the Internet, big data, the cloud, and other state-of-the-art ICTs.

Modern power electronics and intelligent management technologies are heavily incorporated into the next-generation energy system, allowing for the coordinated integration of energy and information across a wide variety of horizontal, multi-source, complementary, vertical sources, net, and storage. There is a commercial element directed toward the end user, making it resemble a flat platform. By incorporating a wider variety of energy forms and participants and shifting the interactive mode of information, the EI paves the way for the development of a new type of energy supply system that makes use of multiple complementary energy sources and a high degree of energy and information integration [39]. Research on EI is still in the early stages of idea development and analysis. The EI is rarely used in practice.

9.5.1 Features of the EI

Accurate measurement, widespread multi-source collaboration, intelligent control, and open trade are some of the aspects of the EI [37,40,41] (Figure 9.3).

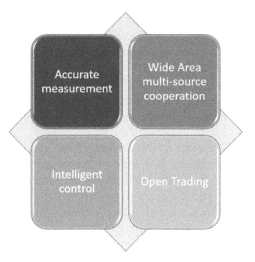

Figure 9.3 Features of EI.

9.5.1.1 Accurate Calculation

To regulate the operation of diverse energy systems and the delivery of energy data, measurement is the backbone. The EI has the challenge of addressing the issue of consensual confidence among many participants in the measurement data, in addition to the challenge of accurate measurement.

9.5.1.2 Regional Multi-source Collaboration

The EI is characterized by its large size, breadth of coverage, and reliability. Multi-source cooperation includes activities such as coordinating the operation of large-scale energy production bases, working together on energy transmission, and sharing the end usage of generated energy. Concluding a mutually beneficial agreement between the parties involved is the key to achieving the goal of maximizing earnings.

9.5.1.3 Intelligent Command

Big data analysis and machine learning are two examples of intelligent techniques that will be of great technological assistance in managing the EI's utilization of a vast number of distributed energy sources. By using intelligent control technology from the point of energy production all the way through to the point of consumption, the system is able to convert power more effectively and adapt to changing conditions, as well as optimize the energy transmission channel, increasing both its efficiency and its reliability.

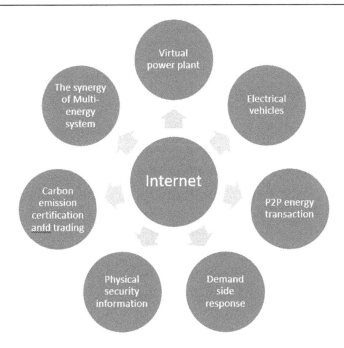

Figure 9.4 Seven different ways that blockchain used in the EI.

9.5.1.4 Open Trading

The EI is the backbone of modern society. It comprises both large, centralized grids and smaller, decentralized microgrids. Everyone, without exception, has unrestricted access to the Internet. There is a dramatic growth in the potential for energy consumers to also play a role in the energy production process. The EI provides on-demand access to a variety of energy services such as demand response, auxiliary services, and power purchase and sales. Bringing the EI's peaks and valleys down will improve its operating efficiency.

9.5.1.5 EI and Blockchain Technology Compatibility

Blockchain technology and the EI need to be compatible with one another for the two to function together; compatibility comparisons between the two are offered in [12,28,39]. Blockchain technology and the EI share a commitment to decentralization, networked autonomy, openness, and intelligence (Table 9.1). Some of the stumbling blocks to expanding the EI can be removed with the use of blockchain technology. For instance, due to the large number of nodes involved in the EI, the trust problem inherent in decentralized decision-making poses serious challenges. However, blockchain technology solves the trust issue that comes with decentralized organizations. Among the EI's essential technologies is the energy router. Through the data flow, it might learn about the current energy flow status, facilitating tasks like scheduling and control. Blockchain technology may be used in the manufacturing of the energy router. For this reason, EI networks may adopt blockchain technology.

9.5.2 Blockchain in the EI: Application Scenarios and Use Cases

9.5.2.1 Blockchain in the EI: Application Scenarios

This section (Figure 9.4) explains the seven different ways that blockchain might be used in the EI.

9.5.2.2 P2P Energy Transaction

The conventional energy market is regulated by a single body. As more people gain access to the EI, its complexity grows. Centralized organizations have problems including high operating costs and weak data protection. Distrust in the commercial entity is inevitable in the absence of a unified management structure. Integrating blockchain technology into the energy trading sector is the key to resolving these difficulties. The EI may benefit from the efficiency, low cost, transparency, and dependability of the P2P energy trading model based on blockchain.

Aitzhan and Svetinovic [42] propose using multi-signature technology, blockchain, and anonymous information flow to secure distributed energy transactions in a smart grid when third parties cannot be trusted. Based on their research and conjecture, Burger and Kuhlmann [43,44] propose that Enercoin, a cryptocurrency comparable to Bitcoin, should serve as the Euro in the energy trading business. There was also a qualitative assessment of how shifts in distributed power and load influenced the demand for Enercoin, as well as ramifications of the ECB's currency adjustment strategy.

The unique characteristics of energy have been disregarded in favour of a more generic approach in all of these research. Because energy trading cannot work without some type of regulation, the results of this study are insufficient to provide guidance on how to carry it out in practice. In their study of the safety of grid transactions, Mannaro et al. investigated the use of blockchain technology to record all information about power trade in the form of automated payment transfers and smart contracts, as well as a strategy for weakly centralized administration of energy trading. In addition, a centralized authority with restricted powers is required to deal with blocks on finalized transactions and to carry out security checks. Problems that need to be addressed in order to realize energy commerce on the EI were analysed by Sabounchi and Wei [45]. Then, using blockchain technology, they developed a tiered structure for the sale and purchase of power (extension layer, transaction layer, and blockchain layer). Because of the issues brought on by decentralization, they resorted to a feeble attempt at centralization in order to control the organization. The participants in trade operations, energy transfers, etc., are regulated by the weak central institution, which may be thought of as a specialized node in the blockchain network, to ensure the smooth flow of transactions.

9.5.2.3 The Electric Vehicles

When it comes to promoting green mobility and energy savings, the broad adoption of electric vehicles will be one of the most effective means of addressing environmental problems. However, charging may be a problem for drivers of electric vehicles. The absence of charging stations is the greatest hurdle to the widespread adoption of electric vehicles. Despite the availability of a variety of charging station providers and payment systems for electric vehicles now, customers must contend with vexing variances in charging standards. Since a unified bottom payment platform has been built, the general public is more receptive to blockchain technology. The issue can be addressed for a limited number of charging piles by the timely leasing of private charging piles using distributed general ledger technology and smart contracts [46]. Power battery cascading cannot ensure battery quality, and the location where electric cars connect to the electric grid lacks V2G incentives. Energy Blockchain Labs suggested a blockchain-based system based on a virtual currency incentive mechanism in order to automate the V2G (vehicle to grid) response, blockchain storage, and certification of battery cell lifespan data in electric automobiles (EVs).

The California company eMotorWerks provided a market-driven Internet of Things platform called JuiceNet [47,48]. The owners of charging stations may utilize JuiceNet, a blockchain network, to rent out their stations to people driving electric vehicles. Simply said, this is the same as installing extra plugs for charging devices. It's possible that the owners of charging piles will receive a comparable financial incentive. Through the utilization of blockchain technology for the storage and processing of data in real time, JuiceNet enables its users to connect and share charging services in a safe and practical manner. Additionally, the JuiceNet app allows any EV driver to view a map of charging stations, search for one in close proximity, and make a charging station reservation.

9.5.2.4 Physical Information Security

Vital is the security of the electrical information system. Accurate information will benefit the system in making intelligent judgments. After the system has been compromised or damaged, erroneous data may have devastating repercussions. The construction of specialized communication connections to segregate internal and external networks is currently the primary form of security protection utilized by power grid businesses. If information-gathering equipment data were utilized in a dedicated line transmission system, system building costs would increase, however, if power line carriers or open networks were used for information exchange, the system would be more susceptible to assaults and interference. In 2010, the control system detected the first cases of the Stuxnet virus, which was meant to attack industrial computers. Using infected USB devices, might infiltrate the organization's internal network and steal confidential data. In 2015, hackers got access to Ukraine's electrical information system, causing a catastrophic blackout [49]. To defend against cyber-attacks, the energy infrastructure must be fortified.

The blockchain is the foundation of the EI's data infrastructure. Due to the blockchain's decentralized structure, high redundancy storage, high security, and privacy protection, some of the security concerns that affect both physical and digital systems can be resolved. However, there is a paucity of research on the use of blockchain technology to tackle EI security issues at this moment. Ding et al. [12] and the Internet investigate the security challenges associated with blockchains in the energy industry from the perspectives of private key loss, privacy leakage, and protocol attacks. It also provides a security defence paradigm that takes into consideration structural, ontological, and managerial security measures for energy blockchains. The future energy blockchain will only be able to achieve its development objectives if its information system is safeguarded against attacks during its full life cycle.

9.5.2.5 Carbon Emissions Trading and Certification

The rapid increase in greenhouse gas concentration has led to a worsening of the global climate. In order to fulfil the aim of reducing emissions, the United Nations adopted the Kyoto Protocol [48], which allows for the certification and trade of carbon dioxide emission rights. That's being done to push for worldwide energy efficiency and pollution cuts. Per the industry's carbon output, China issues a certain number of permits to polluters. Businesses that exceed their pollution restrictions must purchase additional emission rights from other companies that have not yet used up their allocation. If a company has more emission rights than it needs, it can sell the extras to other companies at a profit. Recently, the carbon emissions market has been plagued by problems, such as a difficulty in tracking down transaction data and a high cost for certifying emission limits. The blockchain technology has the potential to serve as a streamlined administration hub for the authentication and exchange of carbon emission permits. By allowing for the tracking of each and every carbon tonne and transaction, this system helps to eliminate fraud and information asymmetry. Tokenized carbon credits, also known as China Certified Emission Reductions (CCER), will be traded. Time stamps, unique identifiers, and blockchain storage are all features of each carbon ticket. Carbon trading will be automated with the use of smart contracts.

There is a lengthy process involved in establishing carbon assets, one that includes enterprises, government bodies, carbon asset exchanges, third-party verification and certification organizations, etc. Due to the lengthy development time, each node will be subject to numerous file transfers, many of which will be prone to mistakes. Blockchain technology can potentially be used to tackle this problem. IBM and China's Energy Blockchain Labs will develop the first blockchain-based "green asset management platform" to facilitate low-carbon emission technology. The platform will reduce the time and money needed to generate carbon dioxide assets by 20–30% [50].

9.5.2.6 Virtual Power Plant

The EI virtual power plant is an essential component of the network (VPP). The EI's energy demands are fulfilled by a variety of decentralized, ecologically friendly energy sources. Their instability, volatility, and intermittent production differentiate green energy sources. Using a virtual control centre for centralized administration and standard scheduling, VPP may connect DERs and DESs to build a structure comparable to that of conventional power plants [51]. It is necessary for both the organization of decentralized power sources and the growth of virtual power resource transactions.

Similar to the spatial distribution and scheduling of virtual power plants, blockchain technology is decentralized and mutually complementary. However, transaction costs between customers and virtual power plants are significantly higher. Each VPP also has a closed profit-sharing plan. As a result of dispersed energy and VPP's inability to make a two-way choice of information symmetry, credit costs are increased throughout a transaction (Table 9.2). Due to the blockchain's positive properties in transaction applications, it can support a trustworthy, cost-effective, and equitable

Table 9.2 Comparison between a VPP based on energy blockchain and a conventional virtual power plant (VPP)

	Conventional VPP	VPP Based on Energy Blockchain
Information transparency	Low	High
System information security	Low	High
Transaction cost	Low	High
Demand-side information	Non – Real Time	Real Time
Coal consumption	Low	High
Greenhouse gas emissions	Low	High

trading platform for virtual power plants [52]. Therefore, the usage of blockchain for VPP makes it logical [53].

To fix the problems with the original concept, Wei and Yue [54] modified the VPP operation and scheduling framework and included blockchain technology in VPP. When compared to the conventional VPP operating models, this approach has advantages in coal use, GHG emissions, and overall economic expenses. In addition, it takes advantage of the blockchain's cryptographic capabilities to make the virtual power plant's data more secure.

9.5.2.7 The Multiple Energy System's Synergy

The EI allows for the flexible flow of energy in a variety of physical systems, the flexible storage and cascading utilization of energy, and the major improvement of energy conversion and utilization efficiency through energy conversion equipment [55]. Because different energy sources have different physical properties, it is difficult to establish a centralized dispatching organization for the management and operation of the EI.

To settle over many complementary energy networks, Mihaylov et al. [56] propose using blockchain technology. Zhang Ning, Wang Yi, and others have proposed using blockchain to create a decentralized platform for a variety of energy systems [28]. Manufacturing data and costs for various energy systems are stored in blockchains in real time. When a trans-energy market is in place, it is possible to keep tabs on the buying and selling of energy from different sources and the associated prices. It is on this basis that marginal pricing for various forms of energy across different regions may be calculated in real time (e.g., node electricity price, node gas price, node thermal price). Various energy systems may function more effectively if they use the marginal price data recorded on the blockchain. Smart contracts may also be used to settle energy expenses and automatically schedule jobs based on marginal price data. Ming and Jun [39] proposed a mechanism architecture that makes use of blockchain technology to enable decentralized decision-making and cooperative autonomous operation of EI systems.

9.5.2.8 Customer Demand Response

Recent research [57–59] on the supply side of ancillary services has yielded some intriguing findings. There is a growing body of evidence [60] that suggests demand response services are one of the most cost-effective technological options to backing up real-time regional power networks. Also, they may offer emergency assistance with a quick reaction time. Energy trading firms are expected to multiply in China as the country liberalizes its power-selling sector. Current market mechanisms still have regulatory problems when it comes to monitoring, accounting, etc. during the actual operation and execution of demand response services. Centralized administration and control mechanisms make it difficult to obtain low-cost, widespread user involvement during the large-scale adoption of demand response systems [61]. The distributed general ledger system lies at the heart of blockchain technology. It might be implemented to address the issue of erroneous and incorrect accounting in ADRS, as well as to construct a full suite of traceability systems.

Demand-side resources were discussed in research that was done jointly by the University of Michigan and the Zurich Federal Institute of Science and Technology as a means to both up-reserve and down-reserve. It exerts direct command over its involvement in the administration of the auxiliary services market [62]. Using game theory, Mohsenian-Rad et al. [63] designed a decentralized, algorithmic approach to demand-side management for the purpose of user anonymity preservation. Automatic demand response (ADR) was proposed by Yang and Zhang [64] for a blockchain-based energy local network (ELN) energy storage system. After evaluating the current state of automatic demand response systems, Bin and Chao [65] developed a blockchain-based application architecture. It also analysed the most pressing problems associated with blockchains, including how they affect autonomous demand response, workload proofing methods, smart contracts, interconnection consensus, and data security. Fortum, a Finnish energy firm, plans to introduce a smart load demand-side response system based on the blockchain. By leveraging blockchain technology and real-time data from the electrical generation market, smart appliances may be mobilized to dynamically engage in the load-side reaction and solve issues like plan determination, load assessment, and income distribution [66].

9.6 PRACTICAL APPLICATIONS

In the Gowanus and Park Slope neighbourhoods of Brooklyn, the US energy business LO3 Energy and the blockchain company ConsenSys launched the TransActive Grid initiative. The digital grid branch of Siemens eventually became involved. This micropower trading network is built on blockchain technology and is comprised of ten separate households. All of the rooftop solar panels in the neighbourhood contribute to a ten-node distributed ledger. Depending on the choices of the individual, each dwelling may either be a consumer or a producer. Each node is able to circumvent electricity suppliers by selling excess power to other nodes [64]. The EU Synergy project also seeks to develop a small-scale user green power trading system using the NRG-X-Change protocol and the TransActive Grid. The initial purpose of the trading system was to settle transactions utilizing NRG currencies after monitoring user output and consumption every fifteen minutes [67]. The German energy provider RWE and the blockchain business Slock have worked on electric car charging programmes [68].

Using blockchain smart contracts, they developed the Block Charge payment mechanism for electric vehicle charging. Then, instead of executing contracts with firms or individuals, customers will use Ethereum smart contracts to do so. Once the smart contract is accepted, the user can engage in trade with the charging station. To round out the whole automated management of certification, billing, and transaction in this use case, they developed a system called Share and Charge.

The most up-to-date prototype of this product allowed individual users to advertise both their own charging stations and those of their RWE charging station partners using a mobile app (APP). The widespread adoption of EVs will benefit financially and practically from these two projects. Blockchain and IoT technologies are being used by the U.S. Embassy in Australia's Filament to update the transmission infrastructure of the traditional grid. A number of "taps," Internet of Things detection devices, are mounted on the utility pole, which has been converted into a network node. These nodes have a communication method for their detecting equipment that is based on blockchain technology. Ascertaining the grid node's operational status, the detection tool then broadcasts this information to the network as a whole through blockchain in a decentralized, peer-to-peer fashion.

This information is accessible to the government, the press, power grid repair businesses, and users to guarantee the safe management of energy and its equipment [69]. As a further illustration, Filament and the IDEO Colab in the United States collaborated on the development of a solar panel gadget that employs blockchain technology. It may have direct bidirectional contact with the Nasdaq platform using the Filament interface in order to create renewable energy in real time. Renewable energy certificates (RECs) that may be used for solar power generation, new energy subsidies, and electricity payments can be provided in real time while monitoring electricity output.

9.7 EI-RELATED BLOCKCHAIN TECHNOLOGY CHALLENGES

9.7.1 Some Barriers in Blockchain Technology Still Exist

As the number of nodes in the access blockchain increases, the efficiency of the consensus process and the response time will decrease. Storage solutions that can keep up with the synchronized accumulation of blockchain transaction records and associated data are a must for all participants (hardware and software). In addition, a lot of energy is consumed by the activities of all the nodes in the blockchain that are contributing to the accounting process. When looking at Bitcoin specifically, 2017 saw around

30 million Bitcoin transactions throughout the world. According to Diginominist's research, verifying those 30 million transactions required the expenditure of 30 billion kWh of power or 0.13% of global consumption. As a result of the excessive drain on the city's power grid, Plattsburgh, New York, has banned the mining of commercial cryptocurrencies for the next 18 months.

9.7.2 Applying Blockchain Technology to the Complicated EI is Insufficient in Terms of Dependability and Security

The intricate physical nature of energy makes studying it difficult. There must be a thorough analysis of the physical principles governing the energy system while using blockchain technology. Today, value transfer is the cornerstone of blockchain applications. Value is transferred alongside energy transmission on the EI blockchain, while energy is transmitted via a different channel. Physical networks are used to transmit energy from one area to another. Examples of such networks are the power grid, which transmits electricity, and pipelines, which carry natural gas. Energy is lost as it is transformed from one form to another or when it is transmitted, both of which are tied to the question of how closely the real and virtual worlds are mapped to one another. A large portion of the population relies on a small number of energy providers. In all likelihood, one special interest group has access to more than 51% of the EI's processing power. At this time, there is a serious threat to the integrity of blockchain-stored data. In its infancy, the EI's implementation of blockchain technology makes it hard to predict whether or not it will encounter any snags.

9.7.3 Blockchain Technology's Standards and Oversight Systems Require Improvement

The development of the essential rules and standards for Blockchain-based applications, with the exception of Bitcoin, is still in its infancy. Energy is not like any other commodity, hence it must be used and traded in ways that are strictly regulated. As of yet, however, no appropriate laws or regulations have been enacted. The use of blockchain technology in the EI is not only tied to government policy but is also technically secure and reliable.

9.7.4 The Blockchain Industry is Lacking in Skill

Despite having been under development for around 10 years, blockchain technology has only lately attracted broad interest. Just recently have academics begun to take an interest in blockchain's progress. According to the Boss Direct Employment Research Institute, the demand for blockchain specialists grew rapidly in the second half of 2017. As of February 2018, blockchain-related posts accounted for 0.41% of all business-related content published online. However, there is a serious shortage of blockchain professionals, with just 0.15 of them available for everyone who needs them. Neither the demand for blockchain professionals nor their education can be pushed off any longer.

9.8 CONCLUSIONS

This paper provides a foundation for future research on blockchain technology's potential use in regenerative energy applications and other Internet-based uses of sustainable energy solutions. Based on the findings and major insights from the literature review, the following are the most important contributions of this study.

We looked at the potential applications of blockchain technology in the energy sector, particularly the distributed renewable energy market (e.g., distributed energy market management, P2P energy trading, EV charging scheme, carbon emission trading, and green certificate management). By analysing these services, we were able to learn how features of blockchain like decentralization, anonymity, transparency, and tamper resistance may be used in the next generation of distributed energy solutions. We were discussing the privacy benefits of these systems while they were in use. We also found some new and continuing problems that could direct future research.

The reasons behind blockchain's meteoric rise in popularity may be deduced. As the value transfer mechanism gains trust amongst nodes in the network, it may eventually stop depending on a single hub. To add to or change existing network data, a distributed node consensus technique is used. Using encryption technologies also guarantees data security. The use of blockchain technology facilitates cheaper, more transparent, and more efficient trade of goods and services. The EI has expanded both in terms of energy kind and the number of participants. It's an innovative approach to supplying energy that integrates a wide variety of energy sources in a cohesive manner. Furthermore, it provides a possible answer for the broad deployment of a wide range of renewable energy sources with variable requirements.

Together, blockchain technology and the EI can do great things. By addressing issues like the coordination of dispersed renewable energy resources, blockchain technology presents a promising new avenue for the growth of the EI. Several problems and incidents in the author's life are recounted in this study.

In comparison to previous literature analysis, this work's key additions include research on the EI's compatibility with blockchain technology and an introduction to the use cases and blockchain application possibilities for the EI. The difficulty of integrating blockchain technology into the EI system was then brought up. This research aims to modernize the EI research ecosystem so that other scientists may get started on their own investigations and further the EI's advantageous blockchain integration. Although studies are still in their infancy, blockchain technology might have several applications in the energy sector. Despite the fact that academics and businesses have taken some tiny steps in the right direction, there are still a number of problems with the applications, including high power consumption and the absence of regulatory frameworks. Future research that aims to identify answers to the issues revealed by reality might use the results of this study as a road map.

REFERENCES

[1] K. Zhou, S. Yang, and Z. Shao, "Energy internet: The business perspective," *Appl Energy*, vol. 178, pp. 212–222, 2016.

[2] G. Bedi, G. K. Venayagamoorthy, R. Singh, R. R. Brooks, and K.-C. Wang, "Review of Internet of Things (IoT) in electric power and energy systems," *IEEE Internet Things J*, vol. 5, no. 2, pp. 847–870, 2018.

[3] J. Zhu, P. Xie, P. Xuan, J. Zou, and P. Yu, "Renewable energy consumption technology under energy internet environment," in *2017 IEEE Conference on Energy Internet and Energy System Integration (EI2)*, 2017, pp. 1–5.

[4] L. Cheng, N. Qi, F. Zhang, H. Kong, and X. Huang, "Energy Internet: Concept and practice exploration," in *2017 IEEE Conference on Energy Internet and Energy System Integration (EI2)*, 2017, pp. 1–5.

[5] L. W. Park, S. Lee, and H. Chang, "A sustainable home energy prosumer-chain methodology with energy tags over the blockchain," *Sustainability*, vol. 10, no. 3, p. 658, 2018.

[6] Y. Yan, J. Zhao, F. Wen, and X. Y. Chen, "Blockchain in energy systems: Concept, application and prospect," *Electric Power Construction*, vol. 38, no. 2, pp. 12–20, 2017.

[7] K. Wang *et al.*, "A survey on energy internet: Architecture, approach, and emerging technologies," *IEEE Syst J*, vol. 12, no. 3, pp. 2403–2416, 2017.

[8] C. Dou, D. Yue, Q.-L. Han, and J. M. Guerrero, "Multi-agent system-based event-triggered hybrid control scheme for energy Internet," *IEEE Access*, vol. 5, pp. 3263–3272, 2017.

[9] P. Giungato, R. Rana, A. Tarabella, and C. Tricase, "Current trends in sustainability of bitcoins and related blockchain technology," *Sustainability*, vol. 9, no. 12, p. 2214, 2017.

[10] M. Swan, *Blockchain: Blueprint for a new economy*. O'Reilly Media, Inc., 2015.

[11] H. Vranken, "Sustainability of bitcoin and blockchains," *Curr Opin Environ Sustain*, vol. 28, pp. 1–9, 2017.

[12] J. Wu and N. K. Tran, "Application of blockchain technology in sustainable energy systems: An overview," *Sustainability*, vol. 10, no. 9, p. 3067, 2018.

[13] N. Zhang, Y. Wang, C. Kang, J. Cheng, and D. He, "Blockchain technique in the energy internet: preliminary research framework and typical applications," in *Zhongguo Dianji Gongcheng Xuebao/Proceedings of the Chinese Society of Electrical Engineering*, 2016.

[14] M. B. Mollah *et al.*, "Blockchain for the internet of vehicles towards intelligent transportation systems: A survey," *IEEE Internet Things J*, vol. 8, no. 6, pp. 4157–4185, 2020.

[15] K. Yu, L. Tan, M. Aloqaily, H. Yang, and Y. Jararweh, "Blockchain-enhanced data sharing with traceable and direct revocation in IIoT," *IEEE Trans Industr Inform*, vol. 17, no. 11, pp. 7669–7678, 2021.

[16] H. Sun, H. Mao, X. Bai, Z. Chen, K. Hu, and W. Yu, "Multi-blockchain model for central bank digital currency," in *2017 18th International Conference on Parallel and Distributed Computing, Applications and Technologies (PDCAT)*, 2017, pp. 360–367.

[17] Z. Zheng, S. Xie, and H. Dai, "X, Chen, H. Wang, 'An overview of blockchain technology: Architecture, consensus, and future trends," in *IEEE International Congress on Big Data*, 2017, pp. 557–564.

[18] D. Yang, X. Zhao, Z. Xu, Y. Li, and Q. Li, "Developing status and prospect analysis of blockchain in energy Internet," *Proceedings of the CSEE*, vol. 37, no. 13, pp. 3664–3671, 2017.

[19] R. Wang, "Research on development method of application system based on blockchain," *International Journal of New Developments in Engineering and Society*, vol. 3, no. 1, 2019.

[20] X. OuYang, X. Zhu, L. Ye, and J. Yao, "Preliminary applications of blockchain technique in large consumers direct power trading," *Proc. CSEE*, vol. 37, no. 13, pp. 3672–3681, 2017.

[21] W. Ding, G. C. Wang, A. D. Xu, H. J. Chen, and C. Hong, "Research on key technologies and information security issues of energy blockchain," *Proc. CSEE*, vol. 38, pp. 1026–1034, 2018.

[22] K. J. O'Dwyer and D. Malone, "Bitcoin mining and its energy footprint," 2014.

[23] G. W. Peters and E. Panayi, "Understanding modern banking ledgers through blockchain technologies: Future of transaction processing and smart contracts on the internet of money," in *Banking beyond banks and money*, Springer, 2016, pp. 239–278.

[24] M. Swan, "Blockchain thinking: The brain as a decentralized autonomous corporation [commentary]," *IEEE Technology and Society Magazine*, vol. 34, no. 4, pp. 41–52, 2015.

[25] A. Q. Huang, M. L. Crow, G. T. Heydt, J. P. Zheng, and S. J. Dale, "The future renewable electric energy delivery and management (FREEDM) system: the energy internet," *Proceedings of the IEEE*, vol. 99, no. 1, pp. 133–148, 2010.

[26] J. Rifkin, *The third industrial revolution: how lateral power is transforming energy, the economy, and the world*. Macmillan, 2011.

[27] Z. Dong, J. Zhao, F. Wen, and Y. Xue, "From smart grid to energy internet: Basic concept and research framework," *Automation of Electric Power Systems*, vol. 38, no. 15, pp. 1–11, 2014.

[28] T. Yang *et al.*, "Applying blockchain technology to decentralized operation in future energy internet," in *2017 IEEE Conference on Energy Internet and Energy System Integration (EI2)*, 2017, pp. 1–5.

[29] Z. Ma, X. Zhou, Y. Shang, and W. X. Sheng, "Exploring the concept, key technologies and development model of energy internet," *Power System Technology*, vol. 39, no. 11, pp. 3014–3022, 2015.

[30] Z. Ming and C. Jun, "Research in multi-modularized cooperative self-managed Energy Internet in structure of blockchain," *Proc. CSEE*, vol. 37, pp. 3672–3681, 2017.

[31] N. Z. Aitzhan and D. Svetinovic, "Security and privacy in decentralized energy trading through multi-signatures, blockchain and anonymous messaging streams," *IEEE Trans Dependable Secure Comput*, vol. 15, no. 5, pp. 840–852, 2016.

[32] C. Burger, A. Kuhlmann, P. Richard, and J. Weinmann, "Blockchain in the energy transition. A survey among decision-makers in the German energy industry," *DENA German Energy Agency*, vol. 60, pp. 1–44, 2016.

[33] K. Mannaro, A. Pinna, and M. Marchesi, "Crypto-trading: Blockchain-oriented energy market," in *2017 AEIT International Annual Conference*, 2017, pp. 1–5.

[34] M. Sabounchi and J. Wei, "Towards resilient networked microgrids: Blockchain-enabled peer-to-peer electricity trading mechanism," in *2017 IEEE Conference on Energy Internet and Energy System Integration (EI2)*, 2017, pp. 1–5.

[35] Y. Hou et al., "A resolution of sharing private charging piles based on smart contract," in *2017 13Th International Conference on Natural Computation, Fuzzy Systems and Knowledge Discovery (Icnc-Fskd)*, 2017, pp. 3004–3008.

[36] S. Pazouki and M.-R. Haghifam, "The impacts of virtual power plants on multiple carrier energy networks," in *2014 5th Conference on thermal power plants (CTPP)*, 2014, pp. 51–55.

[37] H. Watanabe, S. Fujimura, A. Nakadaira, Y. Miyazaki, A. Akutsu, and J. Kishigami, "Blockchain contract: Securing a blockchain applied to smart contracts," in *2016 IEEE International Conference on Consumer Electronics (ICCE)*, 2016, pp. 467–468.

[38] S. Wei and H. Yue, "Operation and dispatch model for virtual power plant based on power blockchain network," *Proc. CSEE*, vol. 37, pp. 3729–3736, 2017.

[39] W. Yi and Z. Ning, "Optimized design and operation to energy pivots in energy internet review," *Proc. CSEE*, vol. 35, pp. 5669–5681, 2015.

[40] M. Mihaylov, S. Jurado, N. Avellana, K. van Moffaert, I. M. de Abril, and A. Nowé, "NRGcoin: Virtual currency for trading of renewable energy in smart grids," in *11th International Conference on the European Energy Market (EEM14)*, 2014, pp. 1–6.

[41] G. S. Pavlak, G. P. Henze, and V. J. Cushing, "Optimizing commercial building participation in energy and ancillary service markets," *Energy Build*, vol. 81, pp. 115–126, 2014.

[42] O. Ma et al., "Demand response for ancillary services," *IEEE Trans Smart Grid*, vol. 4, no. 4, pp. 1988–1995, 2013.

[43] T. W. Haring, J. L. Mathieu, and G. Andersson, "Comparing centralized and decentralized contract design enabling direct load control for reserves," *IEEE Transactions on Power Systems*, vol. 31, no. 3, pp. 2044–2054, 2015.

[44] W. Zhe, Z. Zhang, Z. Xuefei, X. Jing, and C. Fujian, "Research on distribution network data fusion considering renewable energy," in *2017 2nd International Conference on Power and Renewable Energy (ICPRE)*, pp. 500–504, 2017.

[45] A.-H. Mohsenian-Rad, V. W. S. Wong, J. Jatskevich, R. Schober, and A. Leon-Garcia, "Autonomous demand-side management based on game-theoretic energy consumption scheduling for the future smart grid," *IEEE Trans Smart Grid*, vol. 1, no. 3, pp. 320–331, 2010.

[46] X. Yang, Y. Zhang, B. Zhao, F. Huang, Y. Chen, and S. Ren, "Optimal energy flow control strategy for a residential energy local network combined with demand-side management and real-time pricing," *Energy Build*, vol. 150, pp. 177–188, 2017.

[47] V. Paliwal, S. Chandra, and S. Sharma, "Blockchain technology for sustainable supply chain management: A systematic literature review and a classification framework," *Sustainability*, vol. 12, no. 18, p. 7638, 2020.

[48] J. J. Sikorski, J. Haughton, and M. Kraft, "Blockchain technology in the chemical industry: Machine-to-machine electricity market," *Appl Energy*, vol. 195, pp. 234–246, 2017.

[49] C. Prisco, "An energy blockchain for European prosumers," *(2016-05-02)*. https://bitcoinmag-azine.com/articles/an-energy-blockchain-for-european-prosumers-1462218142. 2016.

[50] D. Tapscott and A. Tapscott, "How blockchain technology can reinvent the power grid," *(2016-05-15)*. http://fortune.com/2016/05/15/blockchain-reinvents-power-grid. 2016.

[51] H. Hao, B. M. Sanandaji, K. Poolla, and T. L. Vincent, "A generalized battery model of a collection of thermostatically controlled loads for providing ancillary service," in *2013 51st Annual Allerton Conference on Communication, Control, and Computing (Allerton)*, 2013, pp. 551–558.

[52] S. P. Meyn, P. Barooah, A. Bušić, Y. Chen, and J. Ehren, "Ancillary service to the grid using intelligent deferrable loads," *IEEE Trans Automat Contr*, vol. 60, no. 11, pp. 2847–2862, 2015.

[53] T. Economist, "The promise of the blockchain: the trust machine," *The Economist*, vol. 31, p. 27, 2015.

[54] S. Zhu, M. Song, M. K. Lim, J. Wang, and J. Zhao, "The development of energy blockchain and its implications for China's energy sector," *Resources Policy*, vol. 66, p. 101595, 2020.

[55] J. Luu and E. J. Imwinkelried, "The challenge of Bitcoin pseudo-anonymity to computer forensics," *Crim Law Bull*, vol. 52, no. 1, 2016.

[56] R. Anderson, I. Shumailov, M. Ahmed, and A. Rietmann, "Bitcoin redux," 2019.

[57] A. A.-N. Patwary *et al.*, "Towards secure fog computing: A survey on trust management, privacy, authentication, threats and access control," *Electronics (Basel)*, vol. 10, no. 10, p. 1171, 2021.

[58] K. R. Özyilmaz, M. Doğan, and A. Yurdakul, "IDMoB: IoT data marketplace on blockchain," in *2018 Crypto Valley Conference on Blockchain Technology (CVCBT)*, 2018, pp. 11–19.

[59] K. B. Vikhyath, R. K. Sanjana, and N. V. Vismitha, "Intersection of AI and blockchain technology: Concerns and prospects," in *The International Conference on Deep Learning, Big Data and Blockchain*, pp. 53–66, 2022.

[60] M. Walport, "Distributed ledger technology: Beyond blockchain," *UK Government Office for Science*, vol. 1, pp. 1–88, 2016.

[61] Y. Pan *et al.*, "Application of blockchain in carbon trading," *Energy Procedia*, vol. 158, pp. 4286–4291, 2019.

[62] W. Song, "Bullish on Blockchain: Examining Delaware's approach to distributed ledger technology in corporate governance law and beyond," *Harv. Bus. L. Rev. Online*, vol. 8, p. 9, 2017.

[63] I. Faria, "Trust, reputation and ambiguous freedoms: financial institutions and subversive libertarians navigating blockchain, markets, and regulation," *J Cult Econ*, vol. 12, no. 2, pp. 119–132, 2019.

[64] M. Andoni *et al.*, "Blockchain technology in the energy sector: A systematic review of challenges and opportunities," *Renewable and sustainable energy reviews*, vol. 100, pp. 143–174, 2019.

[65] Z. Fu, P. Dong, and Y. Ju, "An intelligent electric vehicle charging system for new energy companies based on consortium blockchain," *J Clean Prod*, vol. 261, p. 121219, 2020.

[66] T. Alladi, V. Chamola, J. J. P. C. Rodrigues, and S. A. Kozlov, "Blockchain in smart grids: A review on different use cases," *Sensors*, vol. 19, no. 22, p. 4862, 2019.

[67] M. Schletz, L. A. Franke, and S. Salomo, "Blockchain application for the Paris agreement carbon market mechanism—A decision framework and architecture," *Sustainability*, vol. 12, no. 12, p. 5069, 2020.

[68] J. E. Sullivan and D. Kamensky, "How cyber-attacks in Ukraine show the vulnerability of the US power grid," *The Electricity Journal*, vol. 30, no. 3, pp. 30–35, 2017.

[69] M. Pournader, Y. Shi, S. Seuring, and S. C. L. Koh, "Blockchain applications in supply chains, transport and logistics: A systematic review of the literature," *Int J Prod Res*, vol. 58, no. 7, pp. 2063–2081, 2020.

Index

Milton Keynes UK
Ingram Content Group UK Ltd.
UKHW051657141024
449570UK00005B/36

9 781032 392752